I0868187

Dehexing Sex

Dehexing Sex

Russian Womanhood During and After Glasnost

Helena Goscilo

ANN ARBOR

THE UNIVERSITY OF MICHIGAN PRESS

To Nadia Azhgikhina

my champagne-sister—
for tenderness, raunch, generosity,
invaluable collaboration,
and the unique delights
of our Koktebel' caper

Published in the United States of America by
The University of Michigan Press
Manufactured in the United States of America
⊗ Printed on acid-free paper
1999 1998 1997 1996 4 3 2 1

A CIP catalog record for this book is available from the British Library.

Library of Congress Cataloging-in-Publication Data

Goscilo, Helena, 1945–
Dehexing sex : Russian womanhood during and after glasnost / Helena Goscilo.
p. cm.
Includes bibliographical references and index.
ISBN 0-472-09614-1 (hardcover : alk. paper).— ISBN 0-472-06614-5 (pbk. : alk. paper)
1. Russian literature—20th century—History and criticism. 2. Women in literature. 3. Russian literature—Woman authors—History and criticism. 4. Popular culture—Soviet Union. 5. Popular culture—Russia (Federation). 6. Glasnost. 7. Soviet Union—Politics and government—1985–1991. I. Title.
PG3026.W6G67 1996
891.709'352042—dc20 95-48855
CIP

Preface and Acknowledgments

Throughout I have relied on a nondiacritical version of the Library of Congress system for transliterating Russian. Exceptions include names of writers whose prolonged sojourn in the West has resulted in a Westernized spelling of their names, which I adopt in all instances except when documenting original Russian publications. Accordingly, Tatyana Tolstaya, Victor Erofeyev, Vasily Aksyonov, and Alexander Solzhenitsyn appear as such in the body of the text but as their doubles, Tat'iana Tolstaia, Viktor Erofeev, and so forth, in bibliographical material.

All passages from Russian sources are given in English translation (usually mine, unless indicated otherwise). When a point of style is critical to the argument, the original Russian appears first, transliterated, followed by English in parentheses.

Loving appreciation to Bożenna Goscilo, the family Petronius, in questions of writing style, who also served as an inestimable source of witty resistance to some of my more fanciful formulations. Likewise to Stephanie Sandler and Josephine Woll, generous and sharp-eyed readers of the unrevised manuscript, not all of whose astute recommendations I had the sense to follow—so my thanks are tinged with rueful apologies.

Gratitude galore to Beth Holmgren for an ongoing dialogue that invariably energizes and shifts my thoughts in directions that I value.

As with any project I've undertaken in the last five years, this volume would be a different beast were it not for Volodia Padunov's unparalleled largesse in sharing everything from information, articles, and Gitanes to outrageous observations in which I place more faith than he does.

Portions of the volume have benefited from a number of pleasurable exchanges with Susan Larsen; from invitations by colleagues and students to rehearse my ideas in the form of oral presentations; and from conferences in Moscow organized by Nadia Azhgikhina, Irina Iurna, and Natal'ia Kamenetskaia.

For entrusting their manuscripts to me and for producing those manuscripts in the first place, I thank Liudmila Ulitskaia, Galina Shcherbakova, Svetlana Vasilenko, Marina Palei, and Nina Sadur.

My friendship with Nadia Azhgikhina over the last four years has become inseparable from my study of Russian womanhood in its contemporary constructions and articulations, which is why I dedicate this volume to her, with love and admiration.

Several chapters or parts of them have been published previously in journals or collections: in slightly different guise chapter 1 appeared as "Domostroika or Perestroika?" in *Late Soviet Culture*, ed. Thomas Lahusen (Durham: Duke University Press, 1993); and chapter 2, "The Gendered Trinity of Russian Cultural Rhetoric Today," in *Soviet Hieroglyphics*, ed. Nancy Condee (Bloomington: Indiana University Press, 1995). The final section of chapter 3 served as the introduction to *Skirted Issues*, ed. Helena Goscilo (Armonk, N.Y.: M. E. Sharpe, 1992), while the middle section of chapter 4 was included in *Gender Restructuring in Russian Studies*, ed. Marianne Liljeström, Eila Mäntysaari, and Arja Rosenholm (Tampere: University of Tampere Press, 1993). Two earlier versions of the final chapter, "New Members and Organs," appeared in *The Carl Beck Papers*, no. 1007 (University of Pittsburgh, REES, 1993); and in *Genders* 22 (New York: New York University Press, 1995). I thank the publishers who hold copyright to the original incarnations of the pertinent chapters for granting permission to reprint.

Pittsburgh, December 1994

Contents

Introduction *1*

1 Perestroika or Domostroika? The Construction of Womanhood under Glasnost *5*

2 The Gendered Trinity of Russian Cultural Rhetoric *31*

3 Ona-ism Despecularized: The Grammar of Womanhood as Revisioned by the New Grammarians *57*

4 Inscribing the Female Body in Women's Fiction: Stigmata and Stimulation *87*

5 Women's Space and Women's Place *117*

6 New Members and Organs: The Politics of Porn *135*

Works Cited *171*

Index *181*

Introduction

This volume contains six separate but interrelated discussions of Russian womanhood as reconstructed and deconstructed in Russian culture during the last decade. Throughout I make no assertions regarding women's identity, place no equal signs followed by nouns and epithets after the words *woman* and *women,* and mount only those soapboxes that are *not* marked "authoritative." My intention is to offer my (inevitably subjective) reading of various cultural manifestations that I deem indicative of Russia's preoccupation with generating signs of womanhood and to assess the shifts and transformations in those signs over the last ten years.

Chapter 1 examines developments symptomatic of gender politics during glasnost, a period normally lauded for its liberalism and openness to democratic forces, yet one whose achievements barely impinged on gender disposition within the society and, indeed, in some respects intensified its misogynistic tendencies. Against this complex background the strongly individualized writings of Liudmila Petrushevskaia, Tatyana Tolstaya, and Valeriia Narbikova sounded the most provocatively transgressive note against a geriatric sociopolitical and cultural order. This chapter, written in 1990 and revised in 1992, represents the only narrowly historical perspective in the volume, in the sense that I purposely have refrained from refining or altering its basic argument in light of more recent developments. Accordingly, the chapter does not take into account the fact that Tolstaya has not authored any fiction in the last four years or that Narbikova's name is rarely mentioned in the press, despite her two nominations for the Booker Prize and her publication in 1994 of a volume of prose, *Shepot shuma* (The Rustling of Noise), which contains a novel. The chapter is intended to capture a particular moment during perestroika when the heady atmosphere of optimistic political expectation at large coincided with the promise of a vigorous female fiction.

Chapter 2 traces a prevailing paradigm in Russian culture—one that equates women with maternity and nationhood and, more recently, with the prostitute, while conceiving of culture and cultural production as purely masculine realms. On the basis of recent publications and films I identify the contemporary feminization of history as static in the context of the mythological revisionist undertaken by the intelligentsia during glasnost. With historical idols toppling, redoubled veneration of Pushkin as the national cultural sign has elevated him to the status of a transcendental signifier/d. Texts by Petrushevskaia and Galina Shcherbakova, as well as more "popular" publications and several films—for example, *Adam's Rib* and *Sideburns*—provide the materials that illustrate my argument.

Chapter 3 pinpoints and contextualizes the subversive potential of "new women's prose," specifically its authors' explosion of dominant male-empowering myths through reversals or revisions in subject/object relations and in role assignments within those myths. How Russian critics have responded to this writing and what their commentaries reveal about the current conventions and gender assumptions of "literary criticism" in Russia are addressed in the second half of the chapter.

Chapter 4 treats the productive, gender-bending heterodoxy of women writers who inscribe the female body in ways that resist automatic identification of femaleness with femininity, hence with sentiment (metaphorized as heart), passive body, and absence of subjectivity. In the introduction and three sections of the chapter, I analyze, respectively, the tradition of and possibilities for body inscriptions; the tendency in new women's prose to write across value-freighted polarized binarism; the interpolation of Christ's Passion into texts that favor physiological *realia;* and, finally, the articulation of female subjectivity through sexuality, as evidenced in the emergence of what I call the hormoned heroine.

Chapter 5 scrutinizes the relationship between gender and spatial categories. It explores the prevalence of the hospital chronotope in recent women's fiction at large before narrowing its purview to individual writers: carceral space in Petrushevskaia's prose, adventure-space as regendered by Tolstaya, and the hypothetically unbounded space of the outdoors as a locus of action frequently favored by new women's prose.

Chapter 6 surveys the nature, structure, and marketing of the pornography that overran Russia's two major cities in 1991–92, with the removal of externally imposed constraints on the production and circulation of printed matter. I close with a brief glance at the status of pornography and its diffusion throughout printed and visual genres in Moscow today.

1

Perestroika or Domostroika? The Construction of Womanhood under Glasnost

To see ourselves as others see us!

—Robert Burns, "To a Louse"

So many representations, so many appearances separate us from each other.

—Luce Irigaray, "When Our Lips Speak Together"

Messages from Russia:

> A woman should primarily love, care [for], and cherish her own family.[1]

> Women by nature are destined to be weaker. . . . Men are women's major game. . . . A woman without a family is without a master, like a stray animal.[2]

> Women in the West [who] always ask why so few women in our country hold government and other leading posts don't imagine how many women tyrants have made themselves comfortable in these posts and are tormenting both sexes. Female bureaucracy is more horrible than its male counterpart—a male bureaucrat can still be moved to pity by one's belonging to the fair sex [*sic*], whereas a female bureaucrat can't be moved by anything. I feel sorry for our embittered women, running wild and tortured by the burdens of life. But I pity the men just as much. In the West it is

> now fashionable to fight men to the death. Nothing has been heard about this yet in our country. Thank God. If women enter the lists, they will win. For they are more cunning, wily and tenacious. And I would very much resent living in a land of conquered men.[3]
>
> Western women feminists have teeth like sharks.[4]

Clearly, from Russia without love.

These opinionated pronouncements emanate not from men but, rather, from educated Russian women of the intelligentsia, whose reflex response to the very terms *woman writer* and *feminist* recalls Dracula recoiling from a cross. That seismic reaction symptomatizes the fundamental discrepancies in assumptions and orientation between Russian female authors and the majority of their Western readers. The two operate by different, often antithetical, codes. Witness the case of Natal'ia Baranskaia, whose story "Nedelia kak nedelia" (A Week Like Any Other, 1969) impressed Western feminists by its purported exposé of patriarchal oppression. Some have even dubbed this piece, which chronicles the dehumanizing effects of women's double duty on the professional and home fronts, the angriest feminist cry to emerge from the Soviet Union.[5] Yet during an interview with me in spring 1988 Baranskaia (not having read Roland Barthes and learned of the author's death) asserted that her story, far from exposing the heroine's husband as a chauvinistic exploiter, actually portrays the power of love. Although she intended to document the hardships endured by today's women in Russia, Baranskaia protested, she deemed it unjust to hold men responsible for conditions that she imputes exclusively if hazily to the "system." What Baranskaia *did* criticize was Western women's efforts to displace men from their "natural" position of superiority and the "unfeminine" tactics deployed in that campaign. Why, for instance, did the British publishing house adopt the name Virago—which Baranskaia understood only in its secondary meaning, as a termagant, a loud, overbearing woman, and not in its primary dictionary definition, as a woman of great stature, strength, and courage?[6] As Baranskaia's indignant bafflement evidences, a Western audience reads according to a set of presuppositions and assimilated imperatives that Russians manifestly do not embrace—indeed, even find alien and repugnant.

As a result of the radical self-assessment by the educated segment of society in the West during the last two decades, feminism has fundamentally transformed people's way of perceiving and thinking about women. That transformation in turn has influenced the norms guiding the production and consumption of culture. For the reconceived image of woman (womanhood "with a human face") has infiltrated not only the process of reading texts, watching films, viewing paintings, and decoding advertisements and commercials, but also the very environment that incubates these artistic and media forms. In the United States, Germany, France, and England, where awareness of gender problems inflects the sensibilities of readers, viewers, writers, and directors alike, a more or less shared set of cultural experiences allies authorial choices with audience expectations and reactions. Recent fiction and film in the United States and England, for example, draw on a cultural context informed by the issues, if not necessarily the values, of the twenty-year-old feminist movement. Examples range from Margaret Atwood's *The Handmaid's Tale* (1985), Erica Jong's series of unzipped novels, and Fay Weldon's mordant shockers to Alison Lurie's *The Truth About Lorin Jones,* David Lodge's best-seller *Nice Work* (1989), such films as *Working Girl, The Life and Loves of a She-Devil* (1989), and *Switch* (1991), and various media messages (e.g., the commercial for Virginia Slims claiming "You've come a long way, baby!") that subliminally or overtly promote a more self-conscious version of gender.

Recent Soviet films and prose authored by men *or* women lack a comparable context and, consequently, the fund of referents available to Western artists and their public. Since discourses and artistic codes and conventions partially derive from specific sociocultural circumstances, it is critical to contextualize contemporary Russian inscriptions of womanhood in order to grasp what underlies the failure at communication, let alone agreement. Accordingly, my discussion offers a selective commentary that falls into four unequal segments: (1) a summary of institutionalized concepts of gender in Soviet society, with a glance at the status of feminism within that structure; (2) an assessment of the impact glasnost has had on the Soviet concept of womanhood; (3) an examination of how orthodox Soviet views are reflected, challenged, or subverted in late Soviet women's writing in general; and (4) a necessarily brief, closer look at three women writers whose heterodox authorial practices discomfited Soviet readers in the late 1980s and provoked heated debate.[7]

Context

Formally, Russian women in the Soviet Union enjoyed rights that their Western counterparts might have envied. In the classic Marxist conviction that women's emancipation depends upon their integration into productive labor, the egalitarian Soviet Constitution guaranteed women not only full political and civil rights but also access to most trades and professions, in addition to fixed equal pay for equal work.[8] Because an ongoing need for an expanding labor force intensified the government's efforts to retain female workers, until de-Sovietization 90 percent of Russian women were employed (the highest percentage in the world)[9] in areas ranging from engineering and law to sanitation and construction. Women, in fact, accounted for 52 percent of the labor force.[10] Moreover, thanks to the legislation written in 1988 by the Soviet Women's Committee under Zoia Pukhova, the state vouchsafed women two years of maternity leave and job security for three years after parturition. It also provided free public child care facilities and legal abortion and divorce for a nominal fee.

As no less a figure than the once omniscient and now roundly discredited Lenin declared, however, "Equality before the law does not automatically guarantee equality in everyday life." The disjunction between the paper rights conferred upon women and the bleak reality of their empirical experience dimmed the glow of the pseudo-utopian picture implied by the Constitution. Ever since the Stalin period, when the official culture joined women's economic role to the glorification of maternity and the reaffirmation of women's traditional familial duties, the Soviet state and the society exhorted women to be both producers and *re*producers. As a consequence, they bore the double load of full-time work and all domestic responsibilities. One might say that Russian women were in labor wherever they turned. Men's unwillingness to assume any household or parental obligations left the woman alone to cope with rearing children and cleaning house, cooking, laundering, shopping, etc. Over a million women suffered the stress of single parenting while holding down regular jobs.[11] In a country in which perpetual shortages of goods, shoddy products, lack of appliances, poor medicine, deplorable services, and inefficiently run institutions made everyday life a trial, women with a family had insufficient time and energy for career advancement. Hence, in spheres considered suitable for women, they disproportionately clustered on the lowest rungs of the personnel hierarchy, even though employers readily acknowledged that female employees were more reliable and quick (not to mention sober) than their male counterparts. According to a free-lance journalist in Moscow, few women harbored ambitions to assume top positions, knowing that prestigious establishments, especially, strictly observed a quota system, based on the unofficial but widespread formula: "We already have one Jew, two non-Party members, and two women."[12] The writer Tatyana Tolstaya and others deploring the so-called recent feminization of Russian society pointed out that women account for over 80 percent of the country's doctors and teachers, but she overlooked the low prestige of these specializations in the USSR as well as their links with nurturing and child raising. Women constituted 90 percent of pediatricians but only 6 percent of surgeons; in the late 1970s the powerful USSR Academy of Sciences boasted 14 women among its 749 members (Lapidus 188); in 1986 men made up over 84 percent of the influential Soviet Writers' Union. Of the approximately 15 percent of women, none held key executive posts. Editorial boards typically consisted of 7 to 8 men, with one token woman, at best.

Under Soviet rule most Russian women concurred that they felt crushed by emancipation. They complained that the average woman underwent twelve abortions during her lifetime (abortion was the chief mode of contraception, and some women had as many as thirty);[13] that she received no help from her husband with the children or the housework yet was forced to work for economic reasons, often under hazardous physical conditions, and so lived in a state of unrelieved tension and exhaustion.[14] Although women writers and sundry commentators repeatedly lamented the arduousness of women's lives in the USSR, few appeared to make connections between official policy and women's situation. In that connection an article by the American journalist Robert Scheer entitled "Where Is She, the New Soviet Woman?" expressed outraged bemusement:

> Many of my Soviet male friends tended to be primitive oppressors as regards women, viewing them as a mixture of beast of burden and sexual toy. More depressing, they seemed to find some moral confirmation in the laws of nature for clearly supremist and exploitative views that would be abhorrent [to them] in any other

> arena of life. It seems never to have occurred to anyone here that if women had political power in the Soviet Union one result might have been the greater efficiency of shopping and a vast increase in the production of labor-saving devices for the household. Why has there been such scant improvement, after decades of socialist organization, in the objective conditions that women now find themselves in? The answer is that women in the Soviet Union lack political power even to the degree experienced in the capitalist West. The disenfranchisement of more than half of the population is no minor discrepancy in a society struggling with questions of freedom and representation.[15]

Gender disposition in the Soviet Union corroborated Simone de Beauvoir's aperçu that men have found more complicity in women than the oppressor usually finds in the oppressed. Russian women internalized official propaganda and the traditional male system of prerogatives so thoroughly that they themselves propagated the very inequities that marginalized them. Even among the tiny minority of self-proclaimed feminists, some believed that a woman completely realized her essence and her destiny only through motherhood; that domestic tasks were "unfitting for a man"; that nature endowed women with the traits of nurturing, softness, compliance, and patience.[16] In short, they essentialized, by mistaking social constructs (femininity) for biology (femaleness).[17]

In the springs of 1988 and 1990, while conducting interviews in Moscow and Leningrad with some thirty female authors encompassing the full spectrum of background, age, and worldview, I repeatedly (and often in unexpected contexts) encountered the refrain: "A woman shouldn't lose her femininity." When asked what constitutes femininity, most cited gentleness, sensitivity, maternal instincts, and the capacity to love. When I suggested that these were not necessarily inborn traits, virtually all of the women resisted the very concept of a constructed identity.[18] Ironically, in a country ruled by ideological impositions women did not grasp the politics of gender formation. In irrationally hoping that general improvements in living conditions would ease their lot, without agitating for a fundamental reassessment of entrenched female-male roles, Russian women unwittingly reinforced gender stereotypes. Whereas Western women sought a "room of their own," years of officially promoted self-sacrifice habituated Russian women to "burdens of their own"—which they seemed reluctant to jettison on the grounds (or, rather, quicksands) of a biologically ordained self.

Russian women frankly admitted that the majority of Russian men scorned domestic tasks as an inherently female province, proved often unsatisfying sexual partners (given to "premature congratulations"), and were conspicuously absent parents (*paternity* had virtually disappeared from the vocabulary); they likewise recognized that conditions of employment invariably favored men, even though they were less reliable workers. Yet, when exhorted to seek redress through political action on their own behalf, Russian women not only shied away from feminism but violently denounced it. As Nina Beliaeva, a feminist lawyer, observed, the very word "smacks of the indecent, the shameful," and for many was associated with masculinization or lesbianism (universally despised).[19] Feminism conjured up the specter of "bright, slovenly, raucous [women] with blunt gestures, bugging eyes, and cigarette smoke, [in] a small but vociferous procession of women declaring war on the opposite sex."[20] Indeed, even otherwise enlightened Russians conceived of feminists as vengeful, mustached hags or harridans thirsting for the wholesale metaphorical (if not literal) castration of men, intent on crushing or replacing them so as to gratify their lust for power, compensate for their self-doubts, or enact their lesbian inclinations.

In addition to equating feminism with the masculinization or perversion of women, Soviets also stigmatized it on two counts: for decades it had been discredited as springing from bourgeois values. Many Westerners puzzled by Soviets' uncompromising rejection of it failed to realize that Russians entertained a reduced and uninformed, or historically overmarked, concept of feminism.[21] Second, given its manifestly political nature, feminism during glasnost had little chance of taking root in a country that had suddenly lost faith in *any* political engagement as an activity. Many women, in fact, maintained that they preferred to leave the "dirty business" of politics to men, confining their energies to the more "authentic" spheres of family and intimate circles of friends, in a replay of Western Victorian scenarios.

Glasnost

Glasnost witnessed a growing receptivity on Soviets' part to Western tendencies and a readiness to assimilate what earlier would have been dismissed as quintessentially Western phenomena incompatible with Soviet principles. Indeed, one might reasonably attribute to Western influence the influx in the then USSR of what in the West could signal a burgeoning feminist awareness: (1) surveys of popular responses to questionnaires designed to highlight possible gender differences, such as the opinion polls reflecting attitudes to sexual practices, marriage, and divorce;[22] (2) articles in various publications devoted to women's issues and exhorting increased attention to them;[23] (3) the opening in 1990 of a Center for Gender Studies within the Academy of Sciences;[24] (4) the formation of a separate women's section within the Writers' Union, headed in Moscow by Larisa Vasil'eva;[25] (5) a sudden spate of publications of neglected women's literature from the past (Ekaterina Dashkova, Nadezhda Durova, Karolina Pavlova, Evdokiia Rostopchina) and various collections of contemporary women's prose that materialized in the late 1980s and early 1990s (*Zhenskaia logika, Chisten'kaia zhizn', Ne pomniashchaia zla, Novye Amazonki*);[26] (6) the emergence (and prominence in the media) of individuals who committed themselves, despite formidable odds, to the dissemination of feminist ideas, for example, the independent Leningrader Ol'ga Lipovskaia, editor of *Zhenskoe chtenie*, founded in 1988 and consisting of articles, original poetry and prose by women, and translations of texts pertinent to characteristic feminist concerns; and (7) the proliferation of women's organizations, including Preobrazhenie, LOTOS (an acronym for the League for Society's Liberation from Stereotypes), the club SAFO, a network of women's councils,[27] and an international women's press club called 33 Women and One Man, the man being the rotating elected "hero of the month," ironically dubbed the "Knight of Perestroika," whom the thirty-three women interviewed collectively in an effort to enhance mutual understanding between the sexes.

Parenthetically, it is worth noting that the reaction of a prominent male political analyst on Soviet TV to the formation of this club drove home the dire need for consciousness-raising in Soviet society. According to his "professional" judgment, women could be reporters and good interviewers, "especially if they are young and attractive, but never political commentators or serious analysts because the latter are at variance not only with tradition, but with the very makeup of women, their physiology [*sic*] and way of thinking."[28] In a similar vein a lawyer deploring the morals of prostitutes branched out into the following startling generalization:

> I respect the emancipation of women, but one perhaps ought to think of restoring the old rule banning women from restaurants in the evening unless accompanied by men. The woman who hangs outside a restaurant waiting to be let in, who sits at a table without a man, a glass of cognac in her hand, does not give others any reason to have a flattering opinion of her.[29]

Items appearing in such publications as *Moscow News* in the late 1980s testified to a strong division of opinion among Soviets regarding woman's "proper niche" in life. That such issues were being debated at all awakened moderate optimism among some Soviets.[30]

These, however, were miniature pockets of revolutionary change, more cosmetic than systemic. Isolated developments on a modest scale, they virtually drowned in countercurrents, some new and imported from the West, others of immemorial domestic origins. After years of essentially denying that sex and the body exist, the Soviets discovered both—as a source of pleasure and economic gain. Especially the exploitation of women's bodies as marketable commodities and objects of displaced male violence, which Western feminists (notably Andrea Dworkin, Catharine MacKinnon, and Susan Brownmiller)[31] have combatted, suddenly found unsavory expression in diverse aspects of late Soviet culture: (1) the highly publicized beauty contests that secured the then sixteen-year-old Mariia Kalinina (Miss Moscow 1988) and seventeen-year-old Iuliia Sukhanova (Miss USSR 1989) dubious fame; (2) a relentless barrage of films onanistically relying on female nudity, explicit sexual acts, and prolonged or repeated rape as a means of attracting viewers so as to amass profits (e.g., Kh. Kaiziev's *Shakaly* [Jackals, 1990], A. Eidamdzhan's *Za prekrasnykh dam!* [To Beautiful Ladies, 1990]); (3) a wave of video parlors (*videosalony* and *videokluby*) trafficking principally in sadomasochism and pornography—artistic milestones with such subtle titles as *Devushki, Jazdevaites'!* (Take It Off, Girls!), *Obnazhennaia sredi kannibalov* (Naked Among the Cannibals), *Ty ne oboidesh'sia bez nebol'shogo rasputstva* (You Can't Do Without a Little Sluttishness), and *Biust i taz—vot chto samoe glavnoe* (The Bust and Pelvis Are What's Most Important);[32] (4) heavy metal concerts during which female performers bared all (apart from musical talent); (5) display of female bodies au naturel on covers of any and all publications, ranging from fashion magazines to scholarly economic journals (e.g., *Eko*), on dashboards of taxis, on posters peddled in subway stations, and so forth; (6) the Soviet issue of *Playboy* photographed by Sasha Borodanin, which raised hopes of a profitable career abroad in many a pneumatic Soviet breast; and (7) a dramatic increase in, and a cynical respect for, prostitution as a ticket to material well-being and social prestige. In a 1990 survey, Soviet women ranked prostitution eighth in a list of twenty top professions; over one-third of high school girls freely admitted that they would exchange sex for hard currency (Koppel).

The significance of these novelties in the Soviet Union could not be compared to that in the West, given the primitive level of knowledge among Russians then about anything pertaining to sex. Virtually no sex education existed in the USSR; condoms were in disastrously short supply, and 70 percent of high school students who engaged in sexual intercourse did not use contraceptives the first time; owing to Russians' fundamental ignorance of biology, some women reached the fifth month of pregnancy before realizing their condition; and, finally, every fourth abortion that occurred in the world was performed in the USSR (Koppel). These were not ideal circumstances for the radical sexual revolution of the type that took place under glasnost.[33] After decades of puritanism Russian males flocked in thousands to inspect, and to parade their appreciation for, what the society had denied them for so long. Within one social category, at least, the politics of erogenous commitment ousted earlier political idols: truck drivers quickly replaced the portraits of Stalin decorated with medals, which they used to display routinely on their windshields, with coyly pouting pinups free of any and all decoration.

One might argue that such regressive sexist innovations pervaded only popular culture, and a minority within it, without impinging on "high culture," the intelligentsia's arena of significant activity. Such arguments, however, do not withstand close scrutiny. While pornography may be purchased by the proletariat, it is produced by writers—not necessarily talented ones but members of the intelligentsia, nonetheless. Surveys canvassing opinions regarding sexual, marital, and familial issues during the late 1980s unambiguously confirmed that *both* sexes across a broad social spectrum upheld the double standard.[34] Women's organizations, while affording members platforms for self-expression, not only failed to be taken seriously by those empowered to change women's lot but also lacked the political weight to effect improvements in women's social and political status. And scholarly feminist publications sparked enthusiasm in the West but left the educated Russian public largely skeptical and indifferent.[35]

If beauty contests and pornographic videos propagated a degrading and reductionist image of womanhood, the titles of recent prose collections, such as those mentioned, likewise enforced hoary gender stereotypes through their code-affirming implications: for example, *Zhenskaia logika* (Female Logic, 1989) relied on the tiresome and tireless fantasy of women as irrational, unpredictable creatures ruled by emotion and whim; *Chisten'kaia zhizn'* (A Clean/Pure Life, 1990) evoked the hackneyed pseudo-ideal of woman as virgin or sterile/sterilized housekeeper, and so forth. Editors continued not only to exclude or drastically underrepresent women in anthologies of prose and poetry but also to withhold their birthdates while supplying that information for all the male contributors, on the understanding that women, unlike men, wish to hide their age (according to the cliché that women grow old, while men become distinguished).[36] To the perceptive reader the markedly different treatment of these authors, who, moreover, served as isolated representatives of their gender, set them apart—outside the "malestream"—and betrayed the deep-rooted gender bias that for decades prevailed in all spheres of Soviet cultural life and continued to do so during glasnost. Yet the majority of Russians, including those trained in deciphering the values and political allegiances attaching to ostensibly innocuous discourse, seemed impervious to sexist language or strategies. Though sensitized to the encoded sociopolitical connotations of literary and journalistic statement, they could not detect the articulation of gender politics in verbal formulations that any educated Westerner would find crudely chauvinistic.

Women Writers

How do women born and raised in such a culture perceive and inscribe themselves in their texts? The answer is—problematically. Russian women's reluctance to explore the liberating political and psychological potential of feminism[37] paralleled Soviet female authors' categorical disavowal of themselves as specifically women writers, even though they and their society at every turn underscored their Otherness. Whenever gender issues were raised, irreconcilable self-contradictions riddled the impassioned reactions of both. Asked by an American scholar how she felt as a *woman* writer, Viktoriia Tokareva replied:

> It is no disadvantage that I am a woman. I am different because I write with humor. Humor is rare, even [*sic*] with male writers. I prefer male prose, though often women's prose is overloaded with attention to detail. If the woman is talented this is delightful. But I like terse literature, not *babskaya* [broads' or typical women's] literature. (McLaughlin 75)

Liudmila Petrushevskaia claimed to write in a "male mode," focusing on the essentials of plot and character, as opposed to wallowing in the ornateness that she, like many others, associated with women's style.[38] For Tatyana Tolstaya, women's writing was synonymous with superficiality and a philistine outlook, with a saccharine air and a mercantile psychology. But her revealing comment that men also write such "women's prose" left unanswered the question why hack work of this sort merits a gendered label.[39]

Although the highly successful critic-journalist Natal'ia Ivanova doubted the validity and usefulness of a gendered literary category, she nonetheless proceeded to define "women's prose"—in purely derogatory terms. For her it denoted a parochial outlook, an exclusive preoccupation with women's emotional life and a concomitant glut of weddings, infidelities, and divorces; its stylistic earmarks were triviality, coquettishness, and empty decoration.[40] Her contentious model recalled an earlier article (1963) by the writer Natal'ia Il'ina, who summed up what she ironically dubbed "ladies' literature" as a stultifying succession of narcissistic self-contemplations in mirrors, breathless declarations of improbable desires and aspirations, littered with pretentious references to pseudolegitimating sources from Heraclitus to Kant, and unintentionally hilarious stereotypes of incarnated masculine and feminine ideals that flourish in Harlequin Romances today.[41] In its derisive antipathy toward its subject the critique rivaled Nabokov's dismissal of Hemingway's novel *The Sun Also Rises* as a book about bells, bulls, and balls. In fact, when Petrushevskaia, Tolstaya, and Ivanova went on to assert that there is really only good and bad prose, it became evident that the negative epithet, for reasons suggested by the gender disposition in Russian society, was interchangeable with *women's*. Female authors vehemently dissociated themselves from "women's" writing, then, chiefly because the seemingly innocent terms did duty for evaluative (or, rather, devaluative) modifiers.

In their works, which favored the genre of the short story or novella, Russian women authors under glasnost, not surprisingly, tended to focus on what they knew best and what interested them most: human interaction, often heterosexual relations, family dynamics, generational conflicts, problems of self-fulfillment, and the conflicting claims of job and home. Hallmarks of Soviet women's prose during the last two decades include a subordination of plot to a preponderance of description; psychological exploration; a style that eschews modernist technique; and a fairly stable perspective, usually a female center of consciousness, conveyed through quasidirect discourse (*erlebte Rede*)—a limited viewpoint in which boundaries between author, narrator, and protagonist often become blurred.[42]

How have women's narratives differed from men's? Or, to cast the query in terms of the classic Freudian penal/penile test, one could ask: "What quintessential trait of male prose has women's fiction lacked?" Above all, a direct, focal treatment of political issues and an immanent impulse to universalize. A nakedly politicized system such as the Soviet Union's appreciated all too well that the personal *is* political, but not in the sense theorized by feminists and other Western intellectuals. According to orthodox Soviet principles, "retreat" into the private sphere signaled a repudiation of the obligatory participation in collective endeavors and thought mandated by a monolithic ideology. In effect, then, the personal was treasonable. But because of the a priori separation of masculine and feminine arenas of activity—public for men, domestic for women—male apostasy became female propriety. Women's literary forays into the private world followed so-called laws of nature (were a desideratum), whereas literary evidence of men's withdrawal from political involvement carried serious implications.

The discrimination paralleled official supervision of sexuality, with male "deviance" (i.e., homosexuality) punished by a law that left lesbianism unmentioned, for lesbianism was, presumably, inconceivable or socially unidentifiable. In other words, the exclusion of manifestly political matters from women's fiction and its emphasis on personal or familial aspirations coincided with establishment expectations. In that regard women's fiction could be considered conformist. Its place in the culture paralleled women's time, from a masculinist viewpoint, as a pause in the day's occupations when serious business was set aside for a lighter entertainment.[43] Moreover, the cult of maternity and self-sacrifice, the recurrent motif of guilt for striving to realize the self at the expense of the family (when the two proved incompatible), and the avoidance of formal experimentation all strengthened the impression that women's fiction was conservative, devoid of risk and color.

The Subversive Trio

The critical reception during the late 1980s of three women writers belonging to three different generations indicated that some readers might have felt more comfortable had their texts conformed to the bland dictates of the hypothetical genre of ladies' literature gleefully denigrated by one and all. These were Liudmila Petrushevskaia, Tatyana Tolstaya, and Valeriia Narbikova.

A playwright and prosaist in her fifties who, finally, after a quarter-century of professional struggles, has achieved public recognition, Liudmila Petrushevskaia ignites impassioned controversy. Her gritty plays and short stories, permeated with morbid humor and shocking grotesquerie, deal with the underbelly of adult relations—the nasty traffic in human desires and fears whereby everything carries a literal and metaphorical price. Suicide, alcoholism, child abuse, fictitious marriages, one-night stands, part-time prostitution to augment a miserable income, unwanted pregnancies, homelessness, abject crushing poverty, and physical and psychological violence constitute the stuff of her fiction and drama (and did so long before such concerns received the official stamp of approval under glasnost). This nightmarish world on the brink of existence testifies to Petrushevskaia's infallible instinct for instantly lighting on the darkest and most lacerating element in any situation. Life for her is the penalty we all pay for having been born. Although Petrushevskaia views children, pregnant women, the sick and the old as instantiations of the most vulnerable moments in human life, and tends to favor female narrators and protagonists, her writing is relatively free of gendered binarism.[44] It shows both sexes inflicting and experiencing pain in an unbroken chain of mutual abuse.

Devoid of nature and character description, sparse in dialogue and stripped of imagery, Petrushevskaia's prose relies for its effects on the distinctive language of its ambiguous narrators. Like the lives it expresses, that language is a triumph of incongruities, condensing urban slang, cultural clichés, malapropisms, racy colloquialisms, and solecisms, which stream forth in an effort to camouflage or to deter confrontation with what is most crucial and, usually, most painful. Petrushevskaia's familiarity with and enthusiasm for Freud is no accident. For her stratagems of deflection, transference, and avoidance Petrushevskaia early elaborated a highly individual style that disturbs readers almost as much as the seamy catastrophes in which her plots abound. Alienated by the monstrosities that quietly but implacably multiply in Petrushevskaia's fiction, few respond to the gnarled poetry of her language. Yet the gaps and collisions in that language are Petrushevskaia's chief means of destabilizing conventional perceptions and precepts that have congealed into coercive truths. Her resistance to accommodation and the unsentimental mordant tone—accentuated rather than relieved by flashes of grisly comedy—in which Petrushevskaia's narrators recount horrors explain why several commentators and Petrushevskaia herself have insisted that she writes "like a man" (optimism and passive resignation being women's obligatory province). Liberated from sexist prejudice, the phrase translates into "writes good prose" that bears a distinctive signature.

Particularly Petrushevskaia's longest story, "Our Crowd" ("Svoi krug," 1988), immediately after publication drew opprobrium on two counts.[45] Its unflinching, cynical dissection of an amoral coterie from the intelligentsia challenges the institutionalized image of that milieu as the stronghold of its society's conscience. Similarly, the female protagonist's physical violence against her son, though ostensibly exercised in his interests, overturns the enduring ideal of uncomplicated, nurturing maternity entrenched in Soviet ideology and sedimented in the nation's psyche. In other words, Petrushevskaia's morose emphasis on (self-)destructive human drives and intolerable external pressures, as well as her explicit references to sexual and physiological realia, violates the decorum of two gendered Soviet myths: the euphemistically couched personal concerns supposedly exemplified in ladies' literature; and the emotional affirmation of family life that official policy imposed upon women and cemented into the spurious national paradigm of femininity that for decades continued to stifle them.

Petrushevskaia's texts offer neither reassurance nor occasion for paternalistic condescension. Their aggressive and transgressive negation unsettles even the minority capable of appreciating their stylistic sophistication. According to Petrushevskaia, after the publication of "Our Crowd" acquaintances snubbed her on the street, while others upbraided her for "wallowing in filth" and questioned the "usefulness" of "maligning" the technically oriented branch of the intelligentsia that the story depicts. Such reactions expose the drawbacks of an enforced univocal critical tradition ruled by what Mary Jacobus calls the "flight toward empiricism," which naively assumes "an unbroken continuity between 'life' and 'text.'"[46] It allows scant room for imagination, ludic activity, and aesthetic transformation. And it reduces Petrushevskaia, a poetic talent with a tragic view of life, into a querulous journalist intent on degrading the (hypothetical but culturally promoted and inculcated) norms of her sex.

Most remarkable of all, neither Petrushevskaia, who considers her writing "masculine," nor the readers disquieted by her tough "unfeminine" literary manner perceive the flagrant contradiction between their sweeping claim that gender is irrelevant to literature, on the one hand, and the gendered terminology they apply to Petrushevskaia's specific case, on the other. If one accedes to the untenable logic operative in educated Soviet society, which customarily invokes "femininity" in discussions of all but the creative aspects of women's lives, one would have to conclude that as soon as a woman picks up a pen or sits at a keyboard she miraculously sheds the gender she apparently displays everywhere else. In other words, the woman writer is a Lady Macbeth, "unsexed" the moment she seizes her dagger/pen and prepares for action. According to the gendered binarism that has acquired the fraudulent status of objective truth through decades of systematic codification, Petrushevskaia *as a woman* betrays and/or jettisons her inherently feminine traits of emotion, compliance, nurturing, and pathos once she *as author* assumes the purportedly masculine desiderata of intellect, aggression, power, and Logos. Were one to credit such an unpersuasive scenario, the problem would still remain: how to reconcile the a priori essentialization of such a position with its simultaneous unproblematic endorsement of constructed or acquired gender-specific characteristics? No rhetoric can disguise the arbitrary premises or incongruous conclusions of the yoked syllogisms:

A. Woman is intrinsically feminine
Petrushevskaia is a woman
Petrushevskaia is inherently feminine;

B. Forceful prose is masculine
Petrushevskaia writes forceful prose
Petrushevskaia's prose is masculine.

Logic compels the inference that the very process of writing (well?) mysteriously metamorphoses the feminine principle into the masculine and reverses the transmutation the moment creativity ceases. Any Westerner versed in feminist theory recognizes this brand of "reasoning" as the "pen = penis" syndrome that Sandra Gilbert and Susan Gubar assailed in their study *The Madwoman in the Attic* (1979) and effectively laid to rest.

Tatyana Tolstaya's prose has little in common with Petrushevskaia's yet has similarly elicited unease for generally analogous reasons: complexity, stylistic distinctiveness, and self-assurance; and independence of dominant cultural trends as well as of expectations regarding women's writing. Although Tolstaya from the start enjoyed tremendous popularity in the West, where modernism had not been strangled by political conservativeness, during glasnost she provoked discomfort among both Soviet critics and readers, who not only confused her fiction with her journalism but also overlooked the primacy of poetry, metaphysics, and verbal play in her stories. Tolstaya relies on the transforming powers of the imagination to explode and construct worlds through the language into which, she maintains, we are all born. Her fiction celebrates the poetic possibilities of that language through a densely intertextualized, multivocal prose.

Tolstaya's apodictic pronouncements in articles and interviews ill prepare one for the quicksilver oscillation of her narrative among constant allusions, multiple unidentified voices, staggeringly bold tropes, and unresolved contrasting moods that revive the authorial practices of the 1920s and present a daunting challenge to the hermeneut. Few Russian writers of either sex breach realistic conventions more colorfully and creatively than Tolstaya, who withholds unequivocal guideposts from readers who comb her texts for meaning. Irony, decentering through a steady clash of synchronic perspectives and tones, the poetic devices of anaphora, rhyme, assonance, and developed metaphor, an amalgam of grotesquely comic and elegiacally lyrical—all make for an infinitely rich verbal play in which language ultimately displaces character as protagonist.

Tolstaya's acute sensitivity to the power of language enables her to pinpoint stock images and concepts neatly encapsulated in clichés. These include cultural myths about love, romance, and other ritualized aspects of heterosexual relations that she deconstructs in at least three of her stories: "Okhota na mamonta" (Hunting the Woolly Mammoth, 1985), "Poet i muza" (The Poet and the Muse, 1986), and "Ogon' i pyl'" (Fire and Dust, 1986).[47] Although in conversation, interviews, and articles Tolstaya adopts an impassionedly antifeminist position, her skepticism of systems and classifications leads her to dismantle all manner of constructs, including gender stereotypes. In two successive interviews Tolstaya confided that she conceives of the writer as ideally an androgynous being.[48] If one agrees with Carolyn Heilbrun that "androgyny seeks to liberate the individual from the confines of the appropriate,"[49] Tolstaya's ironic, allusive manner amply testifies to the creative androgyny that enables her to reproduce narratively the autonomy of a subversive subjectivity. Ambiguity, parody, and the incessant unresolved interplay among the competing discourses of diverse subjectivities invite readers to distance themselves from a single monological viewpoint and to recognize its limitations. Tolstaya's dethroning of authority, her awareness of the precariousness of a subject position, her mediating techniques of authorial self-elimination, and her subversive use of humor free her from the strictures of essentialist binarism that have corseted Russian women's fiction. One could profitably apply to Tolstaya what Susan Friedman has argued on H.D.'s behalf: that "[her] writing itself constituted her action against the dominant culture."[50]

Yet published and private responses to Tolstaya's fiction have tended to downplay its profundity, stylistic boldness, and originality by faulting it on "human" grounds or squeezing it into a domestic pigeonhole with a single subsuming voice of (s)mothering compassion. Just as Tolstaya's unusually outspoken refusal to genuflect before the sacred cows (bulls?) of the patriarchal literary establishment unleashed a flood of abuse and delayed her acceptance into the Writers' Union, so her unorthodox authorial practices incurred disapproval on the shaky grounds of "artificiality" or excessive "artistry," "aristocratism," and "flight from reality" or "from adulthood." Uncomfortable with Tolstaya's emphatic syncretism, critics and fellow literati have repeatedly addressed the ingenuous (and, strictly speaking, nonliterary) question of whether Tolstaya "likes" her characters and handles them "kindly"[51]—an issue of nurture, of metaphorical diapering and breast-feeding. Others have impugned the "appropriateness" of her ironic tonalities or found her prose overladen with "superfluous" tropes (echoing the rebuke of "too many notes" in Miloš Forman's film *Amadeus*). These reproaches register the vast expanses separating her prose from the ultimately conformist formulations of universally scorned ladies' literature. Instead of a steady flow of emotional self-revelation in a generic vein, consistent authorial identification with *porte parole* characters, and a monotonous language of vapid pastels or unabated hyperbole, Tolstaya's texts tackle metaphysical questions, favor flamboyant juxtapositions, and engage in linguistic imperialism. They demand not lachrymose empathy but, rather, intellectual effort, a ready command of cultural history, and an alertness to poetic strategies. In brief, the traditional masculine traits of undisguised voraciousness and freedom from external constraints, combined with disciplined organizing powers, distinguish Tolstaya's writing from *any* convention-bound prose.

Valeriia Narbikova, a young writer aged "thirty something" who since her debut in 1988 has published only a half-dozen narratives, won a reputation overnight as the "bad girl" of current fiction. (Inaccurately) dubbed the first Soviet woman author of erotica on the basis of her first publication, "The Equilibrium of Light in Diurnal and Nocturnal Stars" (Ravnovesie sveta dnevnykh i nochnykh zvezd, 1988), Narbikova conflates sexual with textual in narratives in which bodies, literary citations, and paronomastic elements copulate indefatigably.

Narbikova's blithe treatment of intercourse, her narrative sophistication, and her humorous debunking of authoritative male culture through, so to speak, the deflationary devices of inverted syllogisms, impudent inversion of intertexts, and cross-pollination of low and high culture have outraged a number of Soviet establishment critics.[52] Above all, Narbikova exposes the formidable power of language to construct systems that subsequently lay claim to reality and thereby murder authenticity, obstruct perception, and anesthetize mental processes. Her verbal play aims to defamiliarize a world congealed in inert formulas that have accreted unchallenged over time. "Equilibrium" operates on a matrix analogy between sexual and textual: just as the third member of a "love triangle" reconfigures the relationship of the original couple, so does the introduction of a new, illicit ingredient into a formulation numbing in its familiarity reanimate it, transforming one's perspective and awakening a fresh response or giving birth to an original concept. Drawing on cultural myths, fairy tales, and citations from literature and philosophy, Narbikova postulates language as the site of struggle, of co-optation, of seduction, of impotence and renovative power—to the extent that discourse becomes the ultimate intercourse. In a world of disjunction, in which language has drifted loose from lived experience but has contaminated it through imposition, the pursuit of an Edenic mode of expression, whereby phenomena are named anew, denotes a search for lost innocence. Hence the disrobings, the flights to nature, and the dismantling or restructuring of available configurations that proliferate in Narbikova's prose.

On the basis of the "theft" enacted in Genesis, Mary Daly has accused men of having stolen language from women.[53] Indeed, throughout Russia's history males have been the producers of language, especially of official discourse and its oppositional Aesopian code. It is therefore no coincidence that Petrushevskaia, Tolstaya, and Narbikova—three of the most challenging and original Russian writers during glasnost—heightened blood pressure among conservative Soviet critics and readers by their bold, unapologetic encroachment on that traditionally masculine terrain through their sui generis, irreverent use of language. If, to revise de Buffon's maxim, "Le style est la femme même," then their impenitently liberated authorial manner not only overturns Soviet preconceptions about women's fiction but potentially challenges the foundations on which Soviet culture has constructed womanhood. In the realm of gender, then, it is not via direct political agitation nor via the inauguration of new heroic or antiheroic models but, rather, through a linguistic coup d'état—a self-confident seizure of language—that Petrushevskaia, Tolstaya, and Narbikova became the (possibly unwitting) subversive "troika of perestroika" during the spectacularly self-contradictory period known as glasnost.

Notes

1. Liliya Nikolayeva, "To Love, Care and Cherish" (response to a questionnaire circulated on International Woman's Day), *Moscow News*, 1987, 16.
2. Sigrid McLaughlin, "An Interview With Viktoria Tokareva," *Canadian Woman Studies* 10, no. 1 (Winter 1989): 76.
3. Tatyana Tolstaya, "In a Land of Conquered Men," *Moscow News*, 24 September–1 October 1989, 13.
4. Opinion of Viktoriia Tokareva, reported by Beatrix Campbell, "Writer's Room With a View," *Guardian*, 21 February 1989, 35.
5. For a discussion of this story from such a viewpoint, see the competent survey of Baranskaia's oeuvre by Susan Kay, "A Woman's Work," *Irish Slavonic Studies* 8 (1987): 115–26.
6. Interview with Natal'ia Baranskaia in Moscow, conducted and taped by Helena Goscilo (13 May 1988).
7. See particularly the famous dialogue between Sergei Chuprinin ("Drugaia proza") and Dmitrii Urnov ("Plokhaia proza"), *Literaturnaia gazeta* 6 (8 February 1989): 4–5; Evgeniia Shcheglova, "V svoem krugu," *Literaturnoe obozrenie* 3 (1990): 19–26.
8. Gail Lapidus, *Women in Soviet Society* (Berkeley and Los Angeles: University of California Press, 1976).
9. Figures vary, depending on source. In 1990 one of the most frequently cited statistics was 86 percent of women were working outside the home. Broadcast by Ted Koppel, "Sex in the Soviet Union" (January 1991).
10. Statistics drawn from *Moscow News* (November 1988). For more specific data, broken down by specialization, see Helena Goscilo, "Russian Women Under *Glasnost*," *New Outlook* 2, no. 4 (Fall 1991): 45–50.
11. Kerry McCuaig, "Effects of Perestroika and Glasnost on Women," *Canadian Woman Studies* 10, no. 1 (Winter 1989): 12.
12. *Index on Censorship* 3 (1989).
13. Here, as elsewhere, discrepancies in statistics reflect different sources. The variously reported averages seem to range from twelve to fifteen. The highest figure I have encountered for abortions undergone by a woman is thirty. Ol'ga Lipovskaia, the founder and editor of the unofficial publica-

tion *Zhenskoe chtenie*, considers fourteen the national average (pers. comm., Moscow, 1990; also quoted in Francine du Plessix Gray, *Soviet Women: Walking the Tightrope* [New York: Doubleday, 1989], 19).

14. Nearly half of Russia's female workers engaged in unskilled labor. In agriculture manual labor remained women's province, for machinery tended overwhelmingly to be entrusted to men.
15. *Moscow News*, 30 April–7 May 1989.
16. Official government policy institutionalized gender identities in the Soviet Union through systematic campaigns. On this process, see Lynne Attwood, *The New Soviet Man and Woman* (Bloomington and Indianapolis: Indiana University Press, 1990); and Mary Buckley, *Women and Ideology in the Soviet Union* (Ann Arbor: University of Michigan Press, 1989).
17. I take femaleness to be a matter of biology, of possessing a body potentially capable of bearing and sustaining children. Femininity, by contrast, is understood here as a set of externally defined characteristics, a construct whereby cultural and social norms impose patterns of sexuality and behavior on women (hence de Beauvoir's assertion in *The Second Sex* [New York: Alfred A. Knopf, 1952] that "one isn't born a woman, one becomes one"). Hélène Cixous has illustrated how tradition has determined that identity as a symmetrical antithesis to the normative male paradigm, generating the familiar binary oppositions imbricated with the patriarchal value system, whereby *masculine* denotes culture, activity, intellect, aggression, power, and Logos while *feminine* denotes nature, passivity, emotion, gentleness, and pathos ("Sorties," *La Jeune née* (1975), trans. as Hélène Cixous and Catherine Clément, *The Newly Born Woman* [1986; reprint, Minneapolis: University of Minnesota Press, 1988), 63–132). In the 1990s most Russians of both sexes subscribe, with minimal modifications, to this binary paradigm.
18. While Russians fully appreciate how overt forms of political propaganda can brainwash even educated members of a society, their general conservativeness discourages them from interrogating more subtle, less visible, forms of mass manipulation. For instance, the cult of maternity, despite its complicity with official demographic campaigns and the heritage of Stalinist coercion, persists as an ineradicable fixture of Russian thinking.
19. The few lesbians whom I have encountered in Soviet and post-Soviet Russia, plus several gay men, would represent exceptions. I have yet to meet straight Russians who do not consider same-sex love abnormal.
20. Nina Belyaeva, "Feminism in the USSR," *Canadian Woman Studies* 10, no. 4 (Winter 1989): 17.
21. As the historian David Ransel astutely observes:

> "Feminism" is a thoroughly discredited notion in Soviet thought; the socialists of revolutionary Russia bound that signifier so tightly to bourgeois class interest that it has been virtually impossible to pry it loose and use it more creatively. Then the Stalinists destroyed the

> socialist program for women's rights [Zhenotdel, established in 1920 and headed by Inessa Armand and Aleksandra Kollontai, was disbanded in 1930], declared that the "woman problem" had been solved, and reimposed patriarchal authority with a vengeance. The resulting confusion of discourse and action left Soviet women without a language to discuss their grievances.

(David Ransel, review of Tatyana Mamonova, *Russian Women's Studies: Essays on Sexism in Soviet Culture,* in *Women's Studies in Indiana* [1990])

22. Many of these were published in *Moscow News,* a flagship of glasnost.
23. In 1988 *Moscow News* introduced a regular column entitled "She and We," dealing specifically with women's issues and featuring diverse items ranging from letter and opinion polls to editorials and "think pieces."
24. The center (Tsentr Gendernykh Issledovanii), attached to the USSR Academy of Sciences Institute for Socio-Economic Studies of Population, under the directorship of N. Rimashevskaia, had as its deputy the economist Anastasiia Posadskaia, one of the four founders of the League for Society's Liberation from Stereotypes (LOTOS) (and one of the few Russians with a thorough understanding of Western feminism). In 1994 the philosopher Ol'ga Voronina unofficially assumed the directorship of the Gender Center.
25. Members of the Moscow branch of the Soviet Women Writers' Association, constituted on the initiative of the poet Larisa Vasil'eva, met on a semi-regular basis to discuss professional issues, read from works in progress, and organize seminars, conferences, and other forums for women's creativity.
26. Such recent collections as *Ne pomniashchaia zla* (1990), compiled by Larisa Vaneeva, and *Novye Amazonki* (1991), organized by Svetlana Vasilenko, contain fiction of mainly younger-generation women writers (e.g., Svetlana Vasilenko, Nina Sadur, Valeriia Narbikova, Marina Palei, and Irina Polianskaia), who are more venturesome stylistically and sufficiently unidealizing in their vision of the world to have prompted unease among critics (see, e.g., the tirade masquerading as a review of *Ne pomniashchaia zla* by Pavel Basinskii, "Pozabyvshie dobro?" *Literaturnaia gazeta* [10 February 1991]; 10). For an analysis of the negative reception of this literature, see chapter 3.
27. The women's councils represented a revival of the Zhenotdely of the 1920s. While the campaigns for female candidates in the political arena on the part of the council headed by Ol'ga Bessolova proved unsuccessful, the efforts reflected a healthy recognition that political representation could lead to improved conditions for women.
28. *Moscow News,* 1–8 January 1988, 12. According to several feminists in Moscow, the press club smacked of frivolity and "coquetry," had no serious platform, and contributed little to the betterment of women's social status. Interview with Natal'ia Filippova, former member of Preobrazhenie (Moscow, May 1990), recorded by Helena Goscilo.

29. Elizabeth Waters, "Reading Between the Novosti Lines," *Canadian Woman Studies* 10, no. 4 (Winter 1989): 34.
30. Although women's issues received extensive coverage in the Soviet press during the late 1980s, and surveys and essays advocated a more liberal approach to gender issues, literary reviews tended to iterate precisely the kind of sexist formulas that Cixous's essay derides. See, for example, Basinskii, "Pozabylshie dobro?"; Shcheglova, "V svoem krugu"; and my discussion of them in chapter 3.
31. See, for instance, Susan Brownmiller, *Against our Will: Men, Women and Rape* (New York: Simon and Schuster, 1975); Andrea Dworkin, *Pornography: Men Possessing Women* (New York: Putnam, 1981), and Catharine A. MacKinnon, *Feminism Unmodified* (Cambridge, Mass.: Harvard University Press, 1987). For more extensive bibliographical data, see MacKinnon (231–36).
32. See the letter of protest by a fifteen-year-old male student in *Vecherniaia Moskva*, 25 April 1990, 2. Regarding film, see the review by Irina Pavlova, "Zachem svoboda?" *Ekran i stsena*, 26 April 1990, 4. Pavlova queries the value of an artistic and political freedom that yields such cheap results, for the absence of prohibitions in contemporary Soviet cinema does not vouchsafe improved quality and, in the specific cases of the films cited, merely breeds vulgarity. The views expressed in Igor' Dedkov's contribution to the Working Group on Contemporary Soviet Culture Conference (Moscow 1990) coincide in several respects with Pavlova's.
33. Pornography, violence in film and TV, etc., arose gradually out of the Western capitalist system that continues to sustain conditions hospitable to their development and in that sense may be called an "organic" part of Western society. The eruption of such phenomena in Soviet Russia after a lengthy tradition of puritanical suppression gave cause for unease, particularly because of the country's volatile atmosphere during the late 1980s. On the lively market in Soviet pornography, see Dmitry Sidorov and Dmitry Demidov, "Pillow Talk," *Moscow News*, 30 September–7 October 1990, 16. For a glance at pornography in Russia, see chapter 6.
34. A survey of attitudes toward sexual practices administered in 1988 reported that 15 percent of the males and 10 percent of the females canvassed by pollsters found premarital sex with any likable man acceptable for women, while 42 percent of males and 19 percent of females deemed premarital sex with any likable woman acceptable for men. Thirty-five percent of men and 43 percent of women considered premarital sex for women acceptable only with the "one she loved," but only 24 percent of men and 40 percent of women judged the criterion of love applicable to men. While respondents had mixed views on adultery, both sexes consistently condemned adultery more vigorously in women than in men. Figures indicated that women's views were more evenhanded than men's, the gap between what they allowed themselves and what they thought permissible for the other sex much narrower than in the case of male respondents

("What You Think about the Bedroom Revolution," *Moscow News*, September 1988, 11).

35. Such, at least, was the judgment of Posadskaia regarding her own research, fellow LOTOS member Ol'ga Voronina's, and such items as Tat'iana Klimenkova's survey of key aspects of Western feminism (T. S. Klimenkova, "Filosofskie problemy neofeminizma 70-kh godov," *Voprosy filosofii* 5 [1988]: 148–57). Members of LOTOS and of the new Center for Gender Studies actively pursued contacts with the West in the interests of strengthening their grasp on feminist principles and in the hopes of avoiding some of the pitfalls that American feminists have not circumvented. They therefore forged links with, for example, the Women's Dialogue USA/USSR, headed by Colette Shulman.
36. The editors of the otherwise liberal collection *Vest'* (News [1989]) and of the four-volume series *The Contemporary Moscow Novella* (Sovremennaia moskovskaia povest') supply the birthdates of all contributors except the female authors: Tat'iana Vrubel', Larisa Miller, Galina Pogozheva, and Anna Nal', as well as Nina Katerli (the sole female prosaist), in *Vest'*; and Irina Raksha and Viktoriia Tokareva, represented in volumes 3 and 4 of the *povest'* series, respectively. The latter two are the only women among the almost forty writers whose tales constitute the anthologies.
37. This is not to imply that Russian women should unthinkingly adopt Western feminism wholesale, but acquaintance with its basic principles and the history of its political endeavors would enable them to elaborate a version of feminism tailored to their specific circumstances. Westerners who impose irrelevant paradigms on Russian women, on the one hand, and Russians who protest that feminism might have been necessary in the West but has no application to their markedly different situation, on the other, both ignore what American feminists have increasingly stressed in recent years: the need to take into account the specifics of individual cases instead of embracing a universal model of womanhood. For a lucid and balanced overview of the fundamental conflict between American partisans of pragmatic progressiveness and French proponents of idealist radicalism (what Catharine Stimpson has called the "false ahistorical overuniversalizing of 'woman'"), see Betsy Draine, "Refusing the Wisdom of Solomon: Some Recent Feminist Literary Theory," *Signs* (Autumn 1989): 144–70.
38. Sigrid McLaughlin, "Contemporary Soviet Women Writers," *Canadian Woman Studies* 10, no. 4 (Winter 1989): 77.
39. Tatyana Tolstaya, "A Little Man Is a Normal Man," *Moscow News*, 1987, 10.
40. Natal'ia Ivanova, "'Kogda by zhizn' domashnim krugom . . . ,'" *Literaturnaia gazeta* 4 (1986): 72–74.
41. Natal'ia Il'ina, "K voprosu o traditsii i novatorstve v zhanre 'damskoi povesti,'" *Novyi mir* 3 (1963): 224–30.
42. Fairly well-known representatives of this fiction include I. Grekova, N. Baranskaia, M. Ganina, N. Kozhevnikova, G. Shcherbakova, and

L. Uvarova. For a sampling of their fiction, see *Balancing Acts*, ed. Helena Goscilo (Bloomington: Indiana University Press, 1989). See also the fine anthology entitled *Soviet Women Writing*, ed. Jacqueline Decter (New York: Abbeville Press, 1990).

43. Elaine Showalter, "Women's Time, Women's Space," in *Feminist Issues in Literary Scholarship*, ed. Shari Benstock (Bloomington: Indiana University Press, 1987), 31.
44. On gendered binarism, see Gillian Beer, "Representing Women: Re-presenting the Past," in *The Feminist Reader*, ed. Catherine Belsey and Jane Moore (New York: Basil Blackwell, 1989), 63–80.
45. Conversations with Petrushevskaia in May 1988 and with Liudmila Ulitskaia in May 1990 in Moscow.
46. Mary Jacobus, "Is There a Woman in This Text?" *New Literary History* 14 (Autumn 1982): 138.
47. On this, see Helena Goscilo, "Monsters Monomaniacal, Marital, and Medical: Tolstaia's Regenerative Use of Gender Stereotypes," in *Sexuality and the Body in Russian Culture*, ed. Jane Costlow, Stephanie Sandler, and Judith Vowles (Stanford: Stanford University Press, 1993).
48. Both during my visit to her at the University of Richmond in November 1989 and in Peter I. Barta, "The Author, the Cultural Tradition and Glasnost: An Interview with Tatyana Tolstaya," *RLJ* 147–49 (1990): 282.
49. Carolyn G. Heilbrun, *Toward a Recognition of Androgyny* (1964; reprint, New York: W. W. Norton, 1982).
50. Susan Friedman, "Modernism of the 'Scattered Remnant,'" *Feminist Issues in Literary Scholarship*, 210.
51. For a selected bibliography of Russian critical responses to Tolstaya's work, see Barta, "The Author," 283.
52. See Urnov; for an assessment contrary to Urnov's, see Nadezhda Azhgikhina, "Razrushiteli v poiskakh very," *Znamia* 9 (1990): 223–24.
53. Mary Daly, *Beyond God the Father* (Boston: Beacon Press, 1973); and *Gyn/Ecology* (Boston: Beacon Press, 1978).

2

The Gendered Trinity of Russian Cultural Rhetoric

> Alas! poor country;
> Almost afraid to know itself. It cannot
> Be call'd our mother, but our grave.
>
> —Shakespeare, *Macbeth*

> Their history, their stories, constitute
> the locus of our displacement.
>
> —Luce Irigaray, "When Our Lips Speak Together"

> Now here, you see, it takes all the running
> *you* can do, to keep in the same place.
>
> —Lewis Carroll, *Through the Looking Glass*

Indifference to Difference

Anyone examining virtually any process or comparing two phenomena or stages may read for sameness or for difference. Journalists and scholars, under the pressure of what Alexander Solzhenitsyn peevishly diagnosed as a fatal attraction to novelty, predictably favor difference (3, 17). Perhaps revelation seems intrinsically to possess more allure than affirmation partly because it intimates change or progress, the presumed desiderata of the modern technological age. Hence, when people encounter each other again after any temporal lapse, human instinct (trained by social habit and seduced by the promise of narrative) prompts the query "What's new?" rather than "Hello, what's the same?"

Reading contemporary Russian culture against the current, I contend that, notwithstanding the cataclysmic displacements effected by

Russia's partial transition to a market economy, one aspect of its current culture demonstrates sameness, subsuming ostensible or incipient difference. That aspect is gender—singled out by recent Western theory, ironically enough, as the locus of difference par excellence. Treatment of gender in Russian culture today suggests that in one respect, at least, post-Soviet culture is more Soviet than post-. Gender-specific Soviet hieroglyphics continue to glyph along, in the sense that, if part of what was formerly sacred (Greek *hiero*) now has been declared sacrilegious, the very concept of profanation still engages a "religious" system.

Mother Courage à la Russe, or Matreshki for Sale

From time immemorial the dominant Russian iconography has projected nationhood as female, its ethos and moral identity metaphorized as maternity. Whether the bathetic familial rhetoric of statehood casts the officially empowered ruler who oversees the country's politicomilitary fate as tsar-*batiushka* or as Stalin—Father of the Peoples—the territory that he disciplines, punishes, or glorifies with his "strong hand" invariably is the motherland.[1]

The pagan divinity of *Mat' Syra Zemlia* (Moist Mother Earth) venerated by the early Slavs as the fertile maternal body continued to figure prominently in folk rituals into the twentieth century, the durability of this worship prompting some scholars to postulate the primacy of "a great mother goddess in the early Russian pantheon" (Ivanits 15; also Hubbs 52–86). Life-giving soil for cultivation, like the dark continent awaiting discovery and "civilization" (or colonization), was troped as the female body ever ready to be tamed and impregnated.[2]

Accordingly, in Russia's predominantly agrarian and peasant society, motherland was *rodina-mat', Mat' Rossiia* (Mother Russia), a fecund source of self-perpetuation and nurture. Probably under this pagan influence Christian Russia likewise perceived the Virgin Mary (*Bogoroditsa* to the peasants) less as virgin than as mother—a compassionate agent of intercession with a higher authority (the male Godhead), attested in such texts as the twelfth-century apocryphal "Descent of the Virgin Into Hell" (Zenkovsky 122–29).

As the personification of stoic patience and all-forgiving self-abnegation, Mother Russia embraced her native or prodigal sons and, unlike her counterpart *Deutschland Bleiche Mutter* (Germany Pale Mother, 1979), glowed with robust color. Such, at least, is the visual image of her emblematic materialization—in the matreshka, the national folk symbol of fertility: a brightly (or garishly) painted wooden peasant doll whose rotund body encases another, smaller body, in which nestles a yet smaller one, and so on, in a potentially infinite series of *matreshki* spilling out of a peasant woman's stomach (Hubbs xi–xiii). A memento peddled in every souvenir store frequented by tourists to the Soviet Union, the self-replicating *matreshka,* which originated in the nineteenth century, symbolized the mysterious vitality of Mother Russia. The gaudy sturdiness of Matreshka Multiplex optimistically affirmed the continuity of generations in a culture pathologically committed to tradition. With the disintegration of that Russia, *patreshki*—significantly, not anonymous generic symbols but, rather, individualized as instantly recognizable political *male* leaders—appeared on the market.[3] As Evgenii Evtushenko recently declared, "the nation [*narod*] begins with women" (*Literaturnaia gazeta,* 11), but he neglected to mention that it is misgoverned by, hence ends with, men. If *matreshki* opened optimistic (i.e., unironic) Soviet parentheses, *patreshki* closed them.

Twentieth-century modernization, with its attendant shift to an urban, industrialized culture, only strengthened the maternal metaphor for nationhood, its pagan origins now harnessed to socialist ideology. Such an ostensible paradox becomes demystified if one recalls that during troubled historical periods the tendency to a conservative retrenchment of a traditional gender disposition is particularly pronounced. Maksim Gorky's protosocialist-realist novel *Mother* (Mat', 1905 [a turbulent year by any standards]) fashions the definitive archetype of the age in Pelageia Nilovna Vlasova. Refurbished for the new Soviet order, the "soft, melancholy, submissive" Vlasova (11) possesses a "large capacity for motherliness" (126). "Love," we learn, "is the mother of life" (143), a mother who embodies the socialist ethos: "We are all the children of one mother—the great, invincible idea of the brotherhood of the workers of all countries over all the earth" (38). Ultimately, Vlasova as mother, ideologically and anachronistically impregnated by her Christ-like son, breeds socialist ideals and nurtures Russian socialist youth.

If, as various commentators have maintained, issues of gender gain currency during political or national crises (van Buren 1), in Russia that pattern manifests itself specifically in an intensification of maternal metaphors. Thus, the trope of *rodina-mat'* flourished during World War II, as soldiers struggled to protect her and the future she vouchsafed. Aleksandr Tvardovskii's lengthy narrative war poem *Dom u dorogi* (House at the Road, 1942–46), for example, which interweaves female images of domesticity with scenes of battle and strife, portrays the birth of a baby boy (the future soldier-citizen) in the midst of war:

> I mal'chik zhil.
> Dolzhno byt', on
> Nedarom po prirode
> Byl russkoi zhenshchinoi rozhden,
> Vozrosshei na svobode.
>
> (Zhigul'skaia 42)[4]

> [And the boy lived. It can't have been
> By chance, that by nature
> He was born of a Russian woman
> Who'd grown/increased in freedom.]

An anthology titled *Mat': Stikhotvoreniia russkikh i sovetskikh poetov o materi* (Mother: Poems by Russian and Soviet Poets About Mother) plays countless variations on the same pseudo-inspiring theme,[5] while revealing that, as Russia's sense of identity grew threatened during the postwar era, the maternal image of nationhood became problematized. Especially the nationalist and chauvinist contingent of literati depicted the mother/motherland as embattled and devalorized. Such a reworking of the metaphor via hagiographical topoi may be seen in Alexander Solzhenitsyn's *Matrenin dvor* (Matrena's Home, 1963), which in biblical cadences extols the spirituality, capacity for selfless toil, and indifference to material acquisition in the eponymous Matrena, who embodies the quintessential Russian virtues now imperiled by encroaching "modern" (i.e., alien) elements. In the concluding encomium to her memory Matrena becomes synonymous with the martyred, soul-rich if goods-poor nation:

> She was the righteous one without whom, as the proverb says, no village can stand.

Nor any city.
Nor our whole land.

(Blake and Hayward 53)[6]

Thirteen years later Valentin Rasputin premonitorily expanded the element of martyrdom within the maternal metaphor in his elegiac *Proshchanie s Materoi* (Farewell to Matyora, 1976), which, as Barbara Heldt has correctly noted, portrays the squandering of a female ecology by guilt-ridden males (Buckley 167). Or, to phrase it differently, Rasputin laments the violence wrought by contemporary trends on old Mother Russia, with her rituals, traditions, and self-validating hierarchies. In an apocalyptic scenario that anticipates much of glasnost cultural production, his text predicts the extinction of Russia's sacrosanct heritage, the obliteration of nature through a dubious culture, as a consequence of which Russia's inhabitants lose their spiritual moorings and flounder helplessly in the darkness of nonbeing: "Only water and fog around them. Nothing but water and fog" (Rasputin 224).

It is no coincidence that Rasputin's story appeared during the purported demographic crisis of the 1970s in the Soviet Union—in actuality, little more than the culmination of racist fears on the government's part that the population in the Asian republics, with their traditionally higher birthrates, would eventually outnumber that of the European sections of the empire. Those misgivings prompted a campaign for larger families that urged women's return to the home, especially within the Russian republic. Ironically, that blueprint for the nation's moral deliverance, mutatis mutandis, resurfaced during perestroika, when Gorbachev vowed to liberate women by enabling their retreat into their proper domestic domain, where they could fulfill their preordained roles of mothers (Gorbachev 117).

Today articles, essays, and letters to editors echo these very sentiments at a time when unemployment has become a gendered problem in both Moscow and Petersburg, where women constitute more than 75 percent of those laid off from work.[7] According to a voluble faction of postcommunist Russian society, the solution to the country's anomie rests in mothers' tender hands. Crime would decrease, men would recover their masculine dignity (not to mention sobriety and sexual potency), disaffected adolescents would buckle down to meaningful activities, and the breakdown of the family would fade to a memory—

were women to reprise their predetermined function in the maternal metaphor of nationhood. Women's magazines, including not only the institutionally endorsed *Rabotnitsa* (Woman Worker) and *Sovetskaia zhenshchina* (Soviet Woman) but also newer post-perestroika publications (e.g., *Sudarushka* [Little Lady] and *Delovaia zhenshchina* [Business Woman]) assert that "motherhood is woman's fundamental function and her chief predestination" (*Rabotnitsa*, 7).[8] Anxious that men not suffer identity crises through joblessness, proponents of women's unemployment cum domestication in Russia may even outnumber health zealots proselytizing against smoking in the United States.

The Bad Mother: Revamped and Retroversed

Post-glasnost literature and film have tackled this moth-eaten gendered rhetoric of national identity in a number of ways. Several works elaborate the metaphor, only to reorient it, extending its vertical implications by troping Russian social history as multigenerational families of women in an environment that relegates men to the periphery (Goscilo, "Petrushevskaia's Vision," 5, 14). Viacheslav Krishtofovich's signally titled film *Rebro Adama* (Adam's Rib, 1991), Liudmila Petrushevskaia's novella *Vremia noch'* (Night Time, 1992), and Galina Shcherbakova's *Ubikvisty* (Ubiquists, 1992) all operate on the principles of *vremia vpered* (time forward) and *vremia nazad* (time back) in the interests of synchronization, whereby maternity absorbs both past and future, collapsing them into a paradoxically timeless image of stasis in the "present" of the viewer's and reader's experience.

These works belong, in a sense, to a more general tendency ushered in by glasnost—that of pinpointing the origins of and deviations in what Russians perceive, somewhat linearly, as the developmental course of their history. Since the mid-1980s, articles by historians, journalists, and philosophers (e.g., Vladimir Seliunin, Aleksandr Tsipko, Vladimir Kozlov), as well as belles lettres, took up with a vengeance Trifonov's earlier quest for roots and causes of the catastrophic present—unfailingly characterized as a consequence of earlier decisions, policies, events, and personalities. Crediting the past with enormous explanatory power, these publications tacitly embraced a pre-Tolstoian view of history and a mechanical concept of temporality. In this respect Mikhail Kuraev swam against the tireless tide, inasmuch as his atypical

Kapitan Dikshtein (*Captain Dikshtein,* 1989) denarrativized "history as master plot" into random components, not only alinear but also ultimately unknowable (with both *fabula* and *siuzhet* eluding certitude). Replacing causality with fortuitous sequentiality, blurring lines between fact and fiction, Kuraev interrogated the primacy of "big events" and the unitary concept of history that shaped the treatment of historical topics in scholarship, journalism, and literature of the period. Glasnost "fiction" and drama by Dudintsev, Grossman, Shatrov, and others intent on recuperating an officially withheld past not only sustained the fictional pretence poorly but also reduced history to the transparency of fully accessible facts inertly awaiting incorporation into a comprehensive Truth. By contrast, perhaps the most fascinating aspect of the pertinent works by Krishtofovich, Shcherbakova, and especially Petrushevskaia is the complex, paradoxical way in which they trope temporality as female physicality, to produce an ambiguous, dispiriting view of Russian history that merits analysis.

The Feminization of History

An appropriate subtitle for all three works—*Adam's Rib, Night Time,* and *The Ubiquists*—might be "Materi i deti" or "Materi i docheri" (Mothers and Daughters):[9] in each, women are reproducers and survivors, those who outlive men and enable other women's continued existence. Mothers all double as daughters (hence, are figures simultaneously representing the past and future), and family genealogy defines itself in female terms (in some cases paternity is not even conclusively established). Yet, whereas generations in Sergei Aksakov and Tolstoi, for instance, figure continuity, in these works the ceaseless conflicts between mothers and daughters that might elsewhere connote development, change, progress, etc., become meaningless, in a sense, robbed of significance by the realization (on the reader's/viewer's—and in Shcherbakova's case, a character's—part) that the daughter, despite her too visible rebellion, actually replicates her mother. Daughters seem less future bearers of the torch than imperfect Xeroxes of the past. Their life plot duplicates their mothers'; their weaknesses and desires pull them back into the protofemale pattern of their forebears' existence (in Krishtofovich, physical/flesh frailty, whether it be sexual susceptibility or incontinence). Hence, the peculiar end effect of stasis, of a *perpetuum mobile* within the temporal space that produces "history"—conceived as rote repetition without significant change or momentum.

Imagery contesting generational development emerges strongly in Krishtofovich's film in the grandmother's (i.e., "first" mother's) paralysis and the centrality of her bed (a coffin of sorts, in which she "tolls the bell" and wordlessly releases bodily fluids); in the almost complete overlap Petrushevskaia's novella installs between key aspects of Anna Andrianovna's character and biography and those of her mother and daughter; and in Nina's total identification with her mother, Niura, in Shcherbakova's *The Ubiquists,* in specific psychophysical terms that grammatically denote not affinity but sameness ("v etoi poze na malen'koi skameechke pered otkrytoi pechkoi, vygrebaia zolu . . . ona vdrug oshchutila—ona Niura. I koleni u nee postavilis' tak, kak byvali u materi pri etom dele. . . . I shchepochki ona razlamyvala tak, kak delala mat' " [in that pose on the little bench in front of the open stove, scooping out the ashes, she suddenly felt that she was Niura. Even her knees were placed just the way her mother's used to be during that task. . . . And she broke up the chips just as her mother used to, 55]). In kindred fashion Nina's daughter Lizon'ka unexpectedly perceives the sameness between her mother and Lelia, the sister who superficially seems Nina's polar opposite ("I tut vdrug Lizon'ka uvidela, chto oni, okazyvaetsia, i pokhozhi. Sestry-sestrichki. . . . Nikakoi, okazyvaetsia, raznitsy ottogo, chto odna domokhoziaika, a drugaia partiinyi rabotnik" [And at that moment Lizon'ka suddenly noticed how alike they were, after all. Sisters through and through. . . . The fact that one was a housewife and the other a Party worker made no difference, it turned out, 63]). Immobility, repetition, and the centrality of a fixed site in which rituals are enacted (the bathroom and the grandmother's bed in Krishtofovich, Anna Andrianovna's apartment in Petrushevskaia, and Niura's kitchen in Shcherbakova) all spotlight the adynamic nature of history—defined à la Pushkin and Tolstoi not as extraordinary battles but, rather, as everyday prosaics[10] and troped as successive generations of women.

One might conceivably bracket these works within Russia's sweeping tendency today to reinstate the past into its future, and not only among the predictably regressive supporters of what used to be called Village Prose. Essaying new beginnings by recouping former traditions seems the current way of life in Russia (its re-era), most apparent in the political groups advocating a modern tsardom, the rebirth of religious "faith," the revival of Cossack activities, the reissuing of early works formerly prohibited by Soviet ideology, and the restoration of prerevolutionary names to towns, streets, and organizations: the return of Leningrad to St. Petersburg, Gor'kii Street to Tverskaia, Frunzenskaia Street to Znamenka, etc.—transformations that not only confuse visitors, inhabitants, and even experienced taxi drivers[11] but also normalize such flagrantly contradictory terms as *new old, former future,* and so forth. By moving forward into the past, Russians intent on replacing recent orthodoxy with distant Orthodoxy have profoundly historicized their present moment.[12]

Of the three works that entropize history only Krishtofovich's offers relief from a pervasive aura of degrading struggle and gloom by occasional injections of humor. Yet the visual image of a mute, paralyzed matriarch as an incontinent but despotic "animal"; the ringing bell (a relic of the past) that at any moment may summon her daughter, Nina Elizarovna, and granddaughters, Lida and Nastia; the persistent pull of all dramatis personae to the matriarchal vortex that unremittingly demands service yet produces solely excrement—all these not only reduce the daughter and granddaughters to the status of appendage but simultaneously infantilize the grandmother, proleptically equating her with the baby that Nastia is expecting. Moreover, by associating all of the women with such motifs as crime (crippling/robbing), sexual betrayal, and physical need, the film collapses them into a single Womanhood. Their interchangeability is emphasized visually in scenes of role reversal (e.g., when Nina Elizarovna docilely obeys her daughter Nastia's order to switch on the TV for the motionless grandmother) and doubling (e.g., when Nina Elizarovna tries on Lida's new bikini as both women, standing first one behind the other, then side by side, study their reflections in a mirror).[13]

If the title of *Adam's Rib* automatically conjures up misogynistic biblical dicta about women's derivative status vis-à-vis malehood, the film actually subverts that stereotype.[14] For it is men whom Krishtofovich relegates to secondariness, to the status of incidental (or accidental) figures. Having served their purpose of impregnation, they maintain little contact with their biological offspring and are merely invited to "play father" when festive occasions demand their presence at the apartment that A. Kurchatkin, in the novella from which the film derives, pointedly dubbed "women's home" (*babii dom*).[15] Since *dom* for all intents and purposes defines the sphere of human activities in the film, those outside that sphere fall outside of life processes. Choices and decisions, moreover, reside in the hands of women: Nastia resolves to have her child, even as she permanently dismisses the half-witted Misha, who fathered it; Lida does not join her philandering married boss at a resort for the romantic interlude they planned mainly because of her encounter with the man's wife; Nina Elizarovna's mother, we learn, persuaded her to shed her first husband, etc. Plans regarding the addition of a new member to the household receive serious attention only after the drunken, rowdy men leave Nina's name day party.

The film's closing scenes, wherein a freak accident restores speech and mobility to the grandmother in a veritable "recovery ex machina," may be interpreted as heralding an abrupt, unmotivated (and unconvincing) opportunity for radical change—a change that the remainder of the film has removed from the realm of probability.[16] If Nastia's pregnancy and the expected baby point to a future generation that finally will "mobilize" Russian history in a spirit of "free speech," then the last-minute resurrection of the matriarch makes sense. For the promise of such a development should at the very least qualify the historicized metaphor of muteness and paralysis or eliminate it altogether.[17] But perhaps this interpretation assumes too much about the grandmother's condition, the true nature of which Krishtofovich leaves weightily enigmatic at film's end. Until that juncture history assumes the form of a changeless configuration through which generations pass in meaningless succession.

Petrushevskaia also depicts three generations of women, focusing, as does Krishtofovich, on the middle-aged protagonist-narrator, who likewise must attend to an incontinent, bedridden mother (hospitalized) and a daughter given to extramarital pregnancies. Furthermore, "Night Time" also ultimately elides three females into a single persona by a duplication of familial scenarios, biographical patterns, and mother-daughter dynamics.[18] All of Anna Andrianovna's narrative stratagems calculated to enshrine her "difference" serve only to expose her ineradicable kinship with her mother, Sima, and daughter, Alena. Moreover, Petrushevskaia's complicated scrambling of time sequence privileges uniformity over distinctions. Like *Adam's Rib*, the narrative ends on a highly ambiguous note susceptible to several readings. In consigning her mother to a psychiatric home, Anna Andrianovna gains a "freedom" of sorts, just as Alena does by escaping with her offspring from the psychic prison of the maternal apartment. Yet, by synchronizing these moments, Petrushevskaia reinscribes sameness and neurotic pattern even as she hints at their potential termination. Alena's seeming liberation from the disabling family blueprint is orchestrated with the kind of cryptic qualifications that Petrushevskaia habitually employs to arouse readers' skepticism.

Shcherbakova's text, while more openly concerned with history in its traditional (undomestic) mode, filters "historical" events (collectivization, war, Stalin's reign of terror and repression, etc.) through the experiences of a multigenerational family presented chiefly through its female members. The novel's title, which Shcherbakova explains in a footnote, alerts the reader to what precisely the family ultimately achieves. That achievement, as in Krishtofovich and Petrushevskaia, is survival.[19] Yet, as the terms of Shcherbakova's own definition of *ubiquists* imply, that capacity to endure comes at the price of humanity: "Ubikvisty—rasteniia i zhivotnye, obitaiushchie povsemestno, sposobnye zhit' v samykh raznoobraznykh usloviiakh. Naprimer, trostnik i volk" (Ubiquists—plants and animals that may be found everywhere, capable of living in the most diverse conditions. For example, the reed and the wolf) (11). Shcherbakova entertains no illusions about the endless cycle of reproduction, which she presents as no more *than* reproduction. In the novel's cheerless conclusion, which parallels that of *Night Time,* An'ka leaves her mother and country for Canada, on a visit that undoubtedly will become emigration. Although her escape may intimate the possibility of individual fulfillment, the novel strongly suggests that the millions who remain "at home" will continue to experience life as "survival" amid an infinite series of pointless repetitions. The last paragraphs of the novel record her mother Lizon'ka's visit to the cemetery where Lizon'ka's grandparents are buried. Significantly, her final dialogue takes place with their imagined voices projecting from the youthful photographs adorning their graves in Soviet fashion.[20] Losing all sense of place and time, Lizon'ka in a moment of existential despair poses the un-Soviet, Karamazovian question: If human existence is the random chaos she and her family have known, why live "Zachem? Zachem?" (For what? For what?) (88)?

One might reasonably object that these works, rather than offering a fresh perspective, actually perpetuate the dusty habit of equating women with body, reproduction, domesticity, and conservative attitudes. Indeed, to some extent they do. Moreover, in troping history along gendered lines, they implicitly supply to the imperishable question "Who is to blame?" (Kto vinovat?) an ominous answer that attributes moral responsibility to Russian womanhood. Their originality, therefore, exists less in their representation of gender than in their refurbishment of the maternal trope—now an inimical and destructive force—and, above all, in their concept of Russian history. All three works erase the commonplace Soviet separation between the private and the public, between the everyday and the historical. If read as narratives of national history (and they encourage such a reading), the works propose a disturbingly somber view of Russia's past at odds with the glasnost phase of cultural commentary. That view originates in the conviction that Soviet Russian history has had no course but has merely undergone a fundamentally static replaying of the same elements, even as its propaganda trumpeted the revolutionary change that its surface appearance sometimes confirmed. In that sense Soviet Russia has been not the optimistic nurturer but, instead, what Melanie Klein calls the "Bad [or incapacitated] Mother," giving birth but also blighting one's life. Through this bleak, revisionist image of motherhood the works document, as Krishtofovich remarked in an interview, "not how we lived . . . [but] how we survived" (Fein 22). By extending the conventionally vertical trope of motherhood, the works posit Soviet history as a grueling, mechanical reenactment of a limited set of paradigms—paradigms that turn experience upon itself with a pleonastic futility that diminishes life into mere prolongation.[21]

Whore as Homeland

In another recent complication of the maternal metaphor artists have conflated motherhood with another hackneyed female trope—that of the prostitute. Contrasted to the mother metaphor on account of its horizontal qualities (in all senses), the image of the prostitute normally conjures up antifamilial values, social degeneration, and the readiness to sell for money what presumably should be freely yet selectively given. It stands to reason, then, that the trope would proliferate during the transition to market, when, indeed, the myth of boundless Russian generosity has collapsed under the grim reality of the huckster, the *valiuta*-hungry bargainer.[22]

Nikolai Shmelev's "Vizit" (Visit, 1988), Galina Shcherbakova's "Tri 'liubvi' Mashi Peredreevoi" (The Three 'Loves' of Masha Peredreeva, 1990), and Victor Erofeyev's *Russkaia krasavitsa* (Russian Beauty, 1990 [written in 1980–82]) reflect this trend, as does Tofik Shakhverdiev's semidocumentary video *Umeret' ot liubvi* (To Die of Love, 1990) and Razika Merganbaiba's twenty-minute Uzbek film *Dostoinstvo* (Dignity) on prostitution in Tashkent (Buckley 164). In Erofeev's pointedly titled *Russian Beauty* the pregnant heroine, prostitute Irina Tarakanova (Cockroach), represents the new Russia ("two fates were to be decided: Russia's and mine" [227]) and voluntarily (if only temporarily) assumes responsibility for the country's moral salvation via a self-sacrificial Joan of Arc death (236). The novel, while parodying a host of Russian myths, nonetheless enthusiastically resorts to the malestream rhetoric that tropes nationhood as mother and, more recently, prostitute. As Irina elegantly formulates it, "My beaver is bigger than my brainbox, and that, you must admit, is as it should be for a woman" (300). Ultimately, Erofeev's *Russian Beauty* proves a pretentious-existentialist *Intergirl* in reverse: tropologically speaking, the solution to Russia's travails potentially lies in Irina the Cockroach's "beaver," the repository of Leonarchik's life-giving seed. Or, to unpack the lightweight metaphor, the re/birth of Russia necessitates its vastly belated recuperation of a Renaissance that bypassed it but now, in the overdetermined figure of old Leonardo (da Vinci), may inject new life into a semibarbaric culture finally open, so to speak, to congress with invigorating foreign elements.

A key metatext in this regard is Vladimir Kunin's novella *Interdevochka* (Intergirl, 1988), which Petr Todorovskii transformed into a huge cinematic box office success the following year.[23] The double image of womanhood fashioned by current Russian cultural rhetoric is personified in Tania, a hard-currency hooker, and her mother, a schoolteacher. The tropes interact simultaneously along sequential and relational planes: both icons of the modern Russian ethos are erased in a scenario of mathematically calculated formulas, the mother committing a symbolic suicide to restore violated honor (Kunin 158), while the prostitute daughter perishes, appropriately, in the spoils of her profession (a foreign car—a Volvo) as she belatedly races to rejoin saintly mother and sacred motherland (with a penitential death cry of "Mama, Mama, Mama!" [153]).[24]

In their choice of whore as organizing trope these works respond simultaneously to the new permissiveness (which allows the portrayal of Russian prostitution) and to the dislocation of national mythologies (Russians nowadays pragmatically charge for what under the "kinder, gentler" conditions of tsardom and pseudocommunism the "great Russian soul" disbursed gratis). As both Florence Nightingale and Trick-turner, Tania emerges as the "perfect imperfect" transitional synthesis: her role of nurse and loving daughter, as well as her verbatim recall of high culture poetry and affection for animals, is inherited from her mother (old Russia); her economically motivated sexual services are symptomatic of the new capitalistic drives overrunning a nation seduced by evil foreign influences.[25] Her corrupt aspect recalls the iconography from a recent issue of *Literaturnaia Rossiia* (Literary Russia, 4 December 1992), which boasts a cover that portrays "hospitable democracy" (a Western import) in a sexualized sadomasochistic image—as a woman (shown only from the waist down) with transparent gauzy gloves, lacy gartered stockings on legs exposed by a waist-high slit in her dress, holding a whip in one hand and opening an animal cage with the other.[26]

Apart from unprecedented explicitness in physiological detail, then, the troping of nationhood along feminine lines as mother and whore—Body, Nature, Reproduction—has not undergone revolutionary change. Modifications exist primarily in the details.

All Things to All Men: Troping Pushkin

But what of the rhetorical representation of Russian culture itself, traditionally viewed as the supremely male arena of artistic activity? Unsurprisingly, it likewise continues to rely on its hardiest metatrope: the metonym that is Aleksandr Sergeevich Pushkin. Whereas maternity (biology/body) ensures historical continuity and safeguards or neglects national morality (praxis), creativity (aesthetics) and governance remain inherently masculine talents (intellect and imagination; activity and theory). Biological utility constitutes women's principal asset, whereas men's expertise encompasses multiple spheres: art, philosophy, administration. Women procreate—produce babies. Men create—generate art and ideas. Most Russians do not question the gendered binarism that feminizes nature and masculinizes culture. Accordingly, flanked by the metaphors of mother and prostitute, the metonym for "high art" that still reigns supreme is Pushkin, the protean Prometheus. These strange bedfellows constitute the gendered trinity of current cultural rhetoric, not unlike Mary and Magdalene alongside Christ.[27] As Mary Ellmann ironically notes in her witty study *Thinking about Women:*

> Christ honored only the mother who conceived without intercourse and the prostitute who resigned from it. So they [Mary and Magdelene] were alike, after all, and both at fault in the sexual form which God the Father had presumably designed for them. (179)

To the question "Why Pushkin?" my answer is threefold: (1) Russia's peculiar penchant for ideological legitimation through "high" art—and no artist in Russia is "higher" than Pushkin;[28] (2) the specific demands of any cult formation, for which Pushkin's relatively brief biography is eminently suited;[29] and (3) Pushkin's reluctance to foreclose a text or an issue, which renders him a multidexterous image (to modify and transpose Gerald Graff's term [Graff 603]), inviting multiple, even mutually exclusive, extrapolations. In possibly the most stunning appropriation black Americans adopted Pushkin as one of *their* glorious native sons, popularizing a highly selective version of his biography (as "man of color") in a series of comics documenting "Great Men" in black history ("The Life").[30]

For Russians not idolizing Pushkin is tantamount to betraying Russia, abrogating all human values, or involuntarily revealing crass imperviousness to aesthetics. The process of the poet's canonization launched by the Pushkin celebration of 1880 was consolidated in the ensuing hundred-odd years by official campaigns orchestrated to capitalize economically and politically on Pushkin's name and its totem powers (Levitt, esp. 154–75). Despite appropriative gestures by Valerii Briusov and Marina Tsvetaeva—both named their *professions de foi Moi Pushkin* (My Pushkin, 1929 and 1937, respectively)—the state ensured that the poet became and remained *our* Pushkin, a national treasure, not only the fountainhead and acme of Russian art but also the slippery signifier invoked to legitimate whatever ideology dominates at a given moment.

Notwithstanding Solzhenitsyn's somewhat quixotic claim that in Russia literature functions as an alternative government,[31] Pushkin's case vividly illustrates the state's preemption of literature and its producers for the purposes of forced unification via pseudo-artistic self-vindication. Pushkin's aesthetic attitude to ideas made him the ideal candidate for co-optation by radically divergent interest groups. Hence, the liberal press hoped to use the Pushkin Celebration of 1880, which unveiled the Opekushin monument in Moscow, as an argument for constitutional reform (Levitt 120), while conservative nationalists (e.g., Dostoevskii) used the occasion to stimulate nationalist pride by eulogizing the writer's universality and messianism.

During the 1880 celebration Dostoevskii's apotheosis of Pushkin as "panhuman" and yet quintessentially Russian, as well as the political rivalry that accompanied the festivities, set the course for future Pushkin rituals and marketing strategies.[32] The year 1887, the fiftieth anniversary of Pushkin's death (when the copyright to his works expired), witnessed the sale of approximately two million copies of Pushkin's works, amounting to 12 to 18 percent of all books published that year nationwide (Levitt 155). The 1899 Pushkin jubilee and subsequent rituals unleashed a Pushkinomania that reached its apogee under Stalin in 1937—not insignificantly, coinciding with the height of the purges. At the Party's behest publishers printed nineteen million copies of Pushkin's writings; the president of the Academy of Sciences declared that interest in Pushkin among soldiers in the Red Army surpassed that of the pre-Soviet bourgeoisie; and the poet was officially pronounced *the* model for the "new Soviet man" (Levitt 164–65). The cult of Pushkin in belles lettres, in short, mirrored Stalin's "cult of personality."

Since then the wave of memorials, monuments, museums, "Pushkin places," postcards, and reissues of his works has swelled to tidal proportions. Recognizing the hyperbole and near hysteria of this canonization, fascinatingly, does not curb the wild excesses of Pushkin worshippers. In 1987, at the peak of perestroika, Sergei Zalygin announced that *Pushkinology* is synonymous with *Russianology, humanology, history,* and *futurology,* while the Petersburg poet Aleksandr Kushner resorted to Christological analogy by calling Pushkin the "bread we eat, the wine we drink" (Levitt 173). While one divinity after another has toppled in the last decade, Pushkin as cultural metonym has withstood all the vicissitudes of glasnost and has emerged intact.[33]

Not only literati but also literature itself has enthusiastically colluded in the Pushkinization of whatever political, moral, and aesthetic values a given text espouses. In Evgenii Zamiatin's *My* (We, 1920), Pushkin is synecdochically equated with free, imperishable art, in diametrical opposition to the mechanical, state-serving oratory disgorged on demand by poets of the Single State. Boris Pasternak's *Doctor Zhivago* (1954) glorifies Pushkin as the genius of unpretentious simplicity. Mikhail Bulgakov's *Master i Margarita* (The Master and Margarita, 1928–40) implicitly makes Pushkin synonymous with an Art that accesses transcendent Truth, while Solzhenitsyn's *V kruge pervom* (*First Circle*, 1968), written from 1955 to 1964, figures Pushkin as the ultimate criterion for "art" and the exemplar of a timeless universal ethics. Andrei Bitov's *Pushkinskii Dom* (Pushkin House, 1978) (the cradle of Russia's cultural-artistic heritage, as opposed to the humble domesticity of *Matrena's Home*) deconstructs the Pushkin myth but, in the process of dismantling the "artifact," reinstalls the Pushkin who transcends all categorization by his "divine right of genius" (the Christ analogy recurs in Bitov's reference to the locale of Pushkin's duel as the "sacred place, watered by *his* blood" [338]—a return of sorts to Lermontov's earlier outrage at d'Anthès's spilling of the "blood of the righteous" [*pravednuiu krov'*] [Lermontov 1:9]).[34]

And now? Even amid the postcommunist general disavowal of Soviet sacred cows, Pushkin remains the saintly steer. Glasnost and post-glasnost texts whose links with postmodernism elicit expectations of partial debunking, though they ironize myths, tellingly opt for Pushkin as the myth of choice: the most colorful examples include Bitov's story "Fotografiia Pushkina (1799–2099)" (Pushkin's Photograph [1799–2099]); Valeriia Narbikova's "Probeg—pro beg" (Running through the Run, 1990); Dmitrii Prigov's "Zvezda plenitel'naia russkoi poezii" (The Captivating Star of Russian Poetry, 1991); and Tat'yana Tolstaya's "Noch" (Night, 1987) and "Siuzhet" (Plot, 1992).

The impulse shared by all of these texts to contest or demythologize, while inevitably also reinscribing (Hutcheon 129), is exemplified in Iurii Mamin's film *Bakenbardy* (Sideburns, 1990)—whose domestic circulation, significantly, was blocked, presumably because of an organized boycott cum payoff by ultraconservative factions of precisely the sort satirized by Mamin (Lawton 220). A carnivalesque dystopia that explores how totalitarian institutions appropriate art (metonymized as Pushkin) for their coercive aims, the film cleverly exposes the perils of cultism and single-minded politicization.[35] By simultaneously portraying Pushkin fanatics as advocates of phallic power (they tread unsoftly and carry a big stick), Mamin, whether intentionally or not, underscores the masculinist roots of the Pushkin trope. Likewise, Andrei Siniavskii's idiosyncratic but often commonsensical *Progulki s Pushkinym* (Strolls with Pushkin, 1975, written from 1966 to 1968), which enraged Russians by its deconstruction of their cultural icon, detropes Pushkin in the interests of humanization yet manages to retain its own brand of idolatry. Not unlike the corpse of Stalin/Varlam in Tengiz Abuladze's film *Pokaianie* (Repentance, 1984), Pushkin as trope cannot be laid to rest, his ubiquity cutting across political lines, generations, and national borders. Russians who may agree about nothing else become united in proclaiming Pushkin their "all," their Genius, their divinity, the "soul" or "spirit" of Russia, and Art incarnate: in short, the transcendental signified. The only element powerful enough to dethrone Pushkin, after sharing cultural space with him, is the American hamburger—aka McDonald's. The selection of Pushkin Square (with its revered monument of the Great Poet) for Russia's first McDonald's symbolically captures a defining aspect of Russia's present moment: the rivalrous and sometimes rancorously debated coexistence of high cultural traditions and pragmatic entrepreneurial innovation.[36] In short, as long as Culture retains its lofty perch, Pushkin reigns supreme. When Culture slips irrevocably to the lower case, Pushkin's status will be lowered accordingly.

What does all of this suggest? If cultural rhetoric offers eloquent clues to the mores of a given society—and I believe it does—then anyone seeking a reconceptualization of gender roles in postcommunist Russia will enjoy more success if she looks for snow in Africa. For the last few years have not noticeably modified, let alone overturned, the misogynistic mental habits shaping and shaped by the ironclad cultural rhetoric I have outlined. Attempts by Russians to revise notions of gender—such as the formation of women's groups and clubs, feminist publications, conferences on gender, and the establishment of the Gender Center in Moscow as well as the introduction of women's advanced studies at the Russian State Humanities University (RGGU)—represent isolated, miniscule islands of activity and change in a sea of sameness. Familiarity with the work of the Gender Center scarcely extends beyond the narrow circle of its members, consisting of a handful of scholars; communication and exchange between the center and faculty or students involved in gender or feminist studies at Russian National Humanities University verge on nil; unsystematic or delayed distribution of announcements about conferences on gender results in erratic attendance; publications addressing gender issues appear in insignificant runs, tend to depend on Western financial support,[37] and are vastly outnumbered by the infinitely more popular pornography, mysteries, adventures, and romances disseminated throughout the capitals;[38] and some of the unscholarly "women's publications" themselves are code affirming, reinforcing all too familiar sexist binary oppositions.

A case in point is the Petersburg publication *Natali,* named, grotesquely, after Pushkin's wife, presumably the uxorial ideal whose fame derives from the country's chief cultural icon.[39] The two issues of *Natali* I have perused focus on cosmetics, gossip, babies, and ads for beauty contests and nursing jobs. Moscow's most recently founded monthly women's paper, *Zhenskie dela* (Women's Affairs), with a current run of 450,000 copies, boasts a naked woman on its front cover's logo, reports on scandals and material borrowed from pornography, and on the back cover of its November 1994 issue dwells lip-smackingly on the Miss Sis'-94 (Miss Tit-94) contest, won by a pneumatically endowed nineteen-year-old student improbably called Zena Fulsom.

In the sphere of gender, then, analysts of postcommunist Russian society discover copious evidence of continuity rather than rupture. Perhaps that explains why the tiny minority of feminists active in Moscow and Petersburg have turned increasingly to their Western counterparts in hopes of finding moral and financial support, learning from precedents, and elaborating some program that eventually will trigger a genuine perestroika not only in women's lives but also in the dominant cultural rhetoric of their country.[40]

Notes

1. Russia's emotional attraction to leaders with a penchant for brutality and mass murder, exemplified by Ivan the Terrible and Joseph Stalin, has been commented on by numerous scholars. The cult of Stalin especially has been the subject of recent films, including Semen Aranovich's *Ia sluzhil v okhrane Stalina* (I Served in Stalin's Guard, 1989) and Tofik Shakhverdiev's *Stalin s nami?* (Is Stalin With Us?, 1989), both of which examine contemporary Russians' "fond" [*sic*] attachment to Stalin's memory and utter obliviousness to his inhuman methods. See Lawton 143–45. Nostalgia for a "strong hand" has captured segments of post-glasnost society partly because of the chaos and perceived lack of united leadership in the country.
2. Mikhail Iampol'skii, an astute critic indifferent, at best, to gender issues, has acknowledged, nonetheless, that women's bodies in early Russian films such as Dovzhenko's *Earth*, for instance, function exclusively as metaphors. See video by Iampol'skii.
3. With only isolated exceptions the "male dolls," dubbed *patreshki* by Vladimir Padunov and Nancy Condee, represent the country's leaders from Lenin to Yeltsin. Recognizable historical referents confer an individual identity upon the male figures, whereas their female counterparts continue to dwell in universalized anonymity.
4. See also Zhigul'skaia 45.
5. This collection has its ironic masculine counterpart in the anthology *Sto stikhotvorenii o Staline* (Hundred Poems About Stalin) (Moscow: "Vasanta," 1993).
6. On the national-religious elements in Matrena's portrait, see Jackson (esp. 69–70).
7. For statistics on the role of gender in unemployment in today's Russia, see Anatasia Posadskaya, ed., *Women in Russia* (London and New York: Verso, 1994), xii.
8. Susan Larsen at Yale University has also noted the persistence of dusty misogynistic stereotypes in both recent film and the current press. My appreciation to her for our various exchanges on the topic and for her generosity in pointing me to several sources.
9. Both Petrushevskaia's and Shcherbakova's interest in mother-daughter relations is evident in some of their other works, including: Petrushevskaia's "Doch' Ksenii" "Strana," "Medeia"; Shcherbakova's "Tri 'liubvi' Mashi Peredreevoi," *Chistye prudy* (1990) 214–53; "Dochki, materi, ptitsy i ostrova," *Soglasie* 6 (1991): 82–89; *Anatomiia razvoda* (Moscow: Molodaia gvardiia, 1990).
10. I borrow the term *prosaics* from Gary Saul Morson, who elucidates usage of the word in a historical context at considerable length in his study of Tolstoi's *War and Peace*.
11. During a recent stay in Moscow my efforts to locate a bookstore on Zna-

menka (formerly Frunzenskaia) were complicated by the "aid" of a driver whom I had flagged down. An official driver for the police, neither he nor the six [*sic*] policemen whom he asked for directions had any notion where Znamenka was located. When I happened to spot a roadsign bearing the street name as the driver was racing past it, he sheepishly confessed his ignorance of most of the "new old" names—that is, of "today's history."

12. That moment shows Russia poised to embark on its "real" history, whose unfolding presumably was thwarted by the perverse imposition of Sovietization.
13. The backward rhythm that finds expression in the grandmother's hold on the younger generations is reinforced by numerous details in the film—the Vorgeschichte that elides World War II, sexual infidelity, the maternal bed, and mother-daughter relations; Nina Elizarovna's employment in a museum; and the retrospective cast to the name day party, at which Nina's two ex-husbands "go back over old territory." Retrogression is buttressed by the repetition of actions and situations: Nastia's constant appropriation of others' possessions (Lida's gloves, her scarf, some tongue for the party) and the appropriation of Lida's lover by her "friend" Marina—a lover whom Lida has appropriated from his wife (in an echo of the Vorgeschichte); Nastia's dismissal of her child's father, which resonates with Nina's "throwing out" Lida's father, Viktor (at her mother's reported urging).
14. Krishtofovich originally opposed naming the film "Adam's Rib" because he considered the biblical connotations too recondite (!) and pretentious but with time grew enamored of the title (Fein 22).
15. The title of Anatolii Kurchatkin's novella, published in *Oktiabr'* 6 (1986): 3–54, underscores the link between women and home that Krishtofovich's film can establish directly by the simple visual expedient of confining the film's action almost exclusively to the "closed space" of the women's apartment.
16. It is characteristic of the film's passion for paradoxes and generation reversals that Nastia's implicit reference to the grandmother's anticipated death ("But surely this will end some time?") coincides with the moment of the old woman's "rebirth."
17. Interestingly, Krishtofovich in an interview reportedly disclaims interest in "politics" and "big" topics, choosing to focus on "ordinary lives and minds." That the issue of generations fascinates him may be deduced from the material he has used in his films, for example, the 1984 TV film he based on Lev Tolstoi's story "Two Hussars."
18. As in *Adam's Rib,* parallels between generations emerge most vividly in sexual matters: both Sima and Anna Andrianovna engage in shouting matches with their daughters, whom they suspect of usurpation (Petrushevskaia 101); both make life unendurable for their sons-in-law, whom they denigrate as "parasite" (*darmoed*) and "bloodsucker" (*krovopiets*) and

unfit to shoulder responsibilities as head of the family (100–101); both lock themselves in their rooms when they feel threatened (102); both terrorize everyone in their orbit so as to assert their rightness (99). Anna Andrinovna similarly shares with her daughter a desire to punish her mother, a checkered sexual history, and an association with the sexually loaded motif of symbolic animals (dog, stallion)

For a more detailed analysis of the story, see Woll; and Goscilo, "Petrushevskaia's Vision."

19. The notion of survival as a significant achievement, of course, belongs to the genre of war and camp literature and current Western feminist writing on abuse, rape, battering, etc. That the discourse of heroic survival may be unproblematically invoked for women's "private" suffering indicates the West's greater progress, perhaps, in validating women's experience. (I am grateful to Bozenna Goscilo for drawing my attention to this point.)

20. As do Krishtofovich and Petrushevskaia, Shcherbakova both emphasizes time's passage and negates or problematizes it, here through the paradox of Lizon'ka's speaking with the dead (shades of Lucian and Menippean satire in general), whose decrepitude, moreover, is belied by their visual representation in snapshots taken of them in their youth (Shcherbakova 88).

21. Curiously enough, contemporary American therapy increasingly approaches a number of psychological problems manifested in physical disorders (especially those diagnosed as gender-specific, e.g., bulimia and anorexia) from a multigenerational perspective that addresses issues of fusion or replication, transmission of obsessive patterns, individuation, etc. On this topic, see Root et al., especially chap. 5, "Multigenerational Issues."

The perception that "*plus ça change, plus c'est la même chose*" animates a recently published poem by Vladimir Kornilov:

> khren s toboi, zolotaia rybka!
> Plavniki svoi unosi . . .
> Nikakogo ne budet rynka
> Na ogryzkakh vseia Rusi.
>
> Bylo khudo i stanet khudo.
> Ubiraisia, i Bog s toboi . . .
> Zhdali chuda i netu chuda—
> Snova nevod s morskoi travoi.
>
> (*Konets veka*, 146)

22. On the resignification of the prostitute during this period, see Katerina Clark, "Not for Sale," *Stanford Slavic Studies* 7 (1993): 189–205.

23. It is, of course, no coincidence that Vladimir Kunin wrote the film script for *Adam's Rib.*

24. For additional analysis of the film from the standpoint of gender and pornographic values, see the chapter titled "New Members and Organs: The Politics of Porn" in this volume.
25. To what extent a prostitute is presumed to be female and Western market practices signal the sale of sex is illustrated by such post-glasnost phenomena as the sexual peddling of boys dressed and made up as girls. One journalist reports the lucrative business of a Muscovite who sells the sexual favors of three boys, aged eight and nine, to foreign and domestic clients. The boys, "transformed" into girls by dresses, skirts, and cosmetics, readily service customers for twenty dollars a day or more. On this, see Serrill.
26. "Gostepriimnaia demokratiia," *Literaturnaia Rossiia,* no. 49 (4 December 1992); cover.
27. Lev Tolstoi in his later renunciation of "pure" art's value in *Chto takoe iskusstvo?* (What Is Art? 164) implies Russian culture's paralleling of Pushkin and Christ. For instances of such homological thinking and for an overview of the early phases of mythmaking around Pushkin, see Debreczeny 270 and passim.
28. Inspired by Madame Tussaud's, a group of theatrical artists under the leadership of Nikolai Zelenetskii established the Theatrical Museum, a wax museum in Moscow's Sokol'niki Park. Among the various tableaux of fifteen historical figures, an orthodox yet peculiarly eloquent juxtaposition links Stalin with Ivan Groznyi, who holds in his arms not the son he killed (as depicted in Repin's famous painting) but, instead, the culturally overdetermined figure (in both senses—body and metonym) of Pushkin. See Freeman and Berton 63–64.
29. Marcus Levitt correctly observes that the comparative brevity of Pushkin's life conveniently enabled "a relatively close succession of 'large' ('All-Union') jubilee dates" (168). The frequency with which the Soviet establishment could organize Pushkin anniversaries manifestly benefited its program of ideological reinforcement.
30. My gratitude to Nancy Condee and Volodia Padunov for acquainting me with this fascinating publication.
31. In *The First Circle,* in which Pushkin's verses serve as a moral ur-text.
32. Pushkin's purportedly "purely Russian" nature had already been stressed by Nikolai Gogol's article "Neskol'ko slov o Pushkine" (A Few Words about Pushkin, 1834); by Mikhail Lermontov's "Smert' poeta" (Death of a Poet, 1837), excoriating the foreigner who had killed him; and by practically all subsequent votaries at the Pushkin altar. See Debreczeny 272–73, 276.
33. For more examples of pre-glasnost Pushkin idolatry among such literati as Tiutchev, Platonov, and Kaverin and for commentary on the 1987 special January issue of *Novyi mir* (New World), see Debreczeny 283–90.
    Metatexts have started appearing recently, such as *Legendy i mify o Pushkine* (Myths and Legends about Pushkin), which concludes with the

editor's signally titled essay "The Cultural Hero of the New Times" (Virolainen).

34. The preoccupation with Pushkin's blood (aristocratic, African, pure, Russian, spilled, etc.) reflects its boundless potential for figurative purposes, whereby Pushkin's blood becomes a martyr's sacramental "essence."

35. The commonality between cults of the poet and the political leader is illustrated with witty economy in a scene in which a few strokes by a sculptor suffice to transform a statue of Lenin into Pushkin's likeness. The process of petrification is identical.

36. Were the monumental Pushkin to glance over his shoulder, he could conceivably peer into McDonald's. In fact, whenever the crowds of hungry hopefuls patiently waiting in line to eat at McDonald's become long enough, they snake around the block, winding up at the Pushkin monument.

37. Of the several studies by scholars from the Gender Center published in 1992, *Zhenshchina v meniaiushchemsia mire* (Nauka) had a run of eleven hundred copies; *Zhenshchina i sotsial'naia politika* (ed. Z. Khotkina), five hundred copies; and *Feminizm: Perspektivy sotsial'nogo znaniia* (ed. Ol'ga Voronina), five hundred copies. The last two were in-house publications. At least two other projects, including translations from Western feminism, were funded in part by Katrina vanden Heuvel. The most recent such sponsored publication by members of the center, plus colleagues from outside, appeared in the West: *Women in Russia*, ed. Anastasia Posadskaya (London: Verso, 1994).

38. At the same time, pornography itself seems to have lost the broad popularity it enjoyed a year ago. The numerous porn publications that randomly overran stands in 1991 and 1992 either have found a more specialized audience (i.e., one motivated by more than a general curiosity), and therefore a genre-specific sales space, or have lost their appeal and diminished in number. For the most recent dramatic shifts in sales patterns of printed material in Moscow, see Condee and Padunov.

While few would deny that popular culture is ousting Culture from the contemporary Russian market, that revolution should not blind one to the strong link between high and low culture—namely, the misogyny that reduces women to physiology, irrationalism, and mother/whore troping in the first, and to cat (cunt-ass-tit) in the second.

39. No spouse of any writer in Russian (or possibly world) history has inspired such impassioned interest as Natal'ia Goncharova. Despised as the ball-obsessed philistine incapable of appreciating Pushkin's verse and as the empty-headed cause of Pushkin's demise or defended as the innocent, honorable wife of a Great Man, Goncharova in her lifetime elicited comments above all about her shapely figure. For an intelligent discussion of Russia's contemporary and posthumous imaging of Goncharova, see Sandler.

40. The new women's prose, which includes fiction by Svetlana Vasilenko, Marina Palei, Larisa Vaneeva, Nina Sadur, and Elena Tarasova, and which

sundry Russian commentators have berated for its unwomanliness (see chap. 3 of this volume), represents the first revisionist step in literature. Such publications as the bilingual issue of *Heresies* entitled *IdiomA*, fulfill a kindred function in art. For that reason their appearance marks a significant moment in Russia's cultural development.

3

Ona-ism Despecularized: The Grammar of Womanhood as Revisioned by the New Grammarians

> What had happened to the marvelous mirror of her enthusiastic admiration in which he had once discovered his uniqueness?
>
> It was all so enchanting, this journey over a woman's body, an invisible, anonymous, unreal body, free of any blemish, without imperfections or disease, a totally fanciful body—an idyllic playground.
>
> —Milan Kundera, *Life Is Elsewhere*

> *The commodity of exchange—of desire—is man's business.* For two reasons: the exchange takes place between masculine subjects, and it requires a *plus-value* added to the body of the commodity, a supplement which gives it a valuable form.
>
> —Luce Irigaray, "Women on the Market"

Texts Produced

As Tatyana Tolstaya once accurately observed, logic does not enjoy pride of place in Russian culture. Indeed, Russian philosophy has no counterpart to the analytical tradition that produced, for example, Bertrand Russell, who exerted a decisive influence on even such geographically remote thinkers as the Polish logicians Ludwik Borkowski, Jerzy Slupecki, and Maria Kokoszyńska. In this self-conscious outpost of Western civilization neither the Cartesian rationalism nor the Lockean empiricism that met in Kant ever took firm hold. The West European revival of classical logic in the twelfth and thirteenth centuries bypassed Russia, where the rationalistic tendencies of the Russian

Judaizers in the sixteenth century were stamped out by the Orthodox church and the ruling princes.[1]

While those strains have dominated Anglo-American philosophy, in Russia their modern systematization belongs almost exclusively to the realm of mathematics. The majority of well-known Russian philosophers, such as Solov'iev, Berdiaev, and Florinskii, as well as the Ukrainian Skovoroda, are religious thinkers and, furthermore, mystically inclined. Tellingly, Russian literary texts, journalism, and personal interviews tend to denigrate logic as a German trait—symptomatic of the pragmatic burgher (Stolz, not Oblomov)—over which they privilege the allegedly Russian characteristics of mystical faith, irrational passion, and unique expansiveness (the cliché of the broad Russian soul to which Dostoevskii's jingoistic novels have lent intellectual respectability).

That flaunted national illogicality operates ubiquitously, irrespective of education, it seems, flourishing among the intelligentsia and the uneducated alike. And, particularly in issues of gender, it manifests itself in extreme and noxious form. For, while mainstream Russian tradition (i.e., male "thought") has equated "woman" with illogicality and sublated her from culturally significant arenas of activity, it has done so in illogical ways that contradict her empirical reality. Russian critics' response to innovative recent women's fiction illustrates the extent to which a profound, widespread, but unexamined essentialist bias persists in Russian critical discourse in the late 1980s and early 1990s.[2]

In the male-forged grammar of conventional Russian gender identity, malehood is largely synonymous with the nominative case (the subject); with transitive and intransitive verbs (denoting action of which woman is object or from which she is excluded); with capitalization (the Beginning, the defining category); with the period and the exclamation mark (as the last word [final authority] and the assertive register); with the complex sentence (as an index, presumably, of intellectual intricacy); and with the indicative and imperative mood (the declarative mode and the command-supply or order-issuing system of male-constructed hierarchies). Womanhood, consequently—and in Russia womanhood traditionally *has* been a consequence—means the oblique case: the accusative (object), dative (passive recipient), or instrumental (means to a goal); those reflexive verbs that denote passivity or self-ministration; the question mark, ellipses, and parentheses (signaling tentativeness or uncertainty, internalized censorship, and subordination or irrelevance); the sentence fragment (incomplete without a male); and the subjunctive or conditional mood (awaiting confirmation by the male subject and suspended in the limbo of hypothetical desire).

Grammar, like other aspects of language, is subject to evolution, and, among the myriad changes now sending shock waves throughout Russia, probably those of greatest interest to feminists are instances of revision in the grammar of gender. These developments have occurred on a tiny scale in multiple cultural spheres. The work of Kira Muratova and Lana Gogoberidze in film, of Irina Nakhova, Bella Matveeva, and Mariia Konstantinova in art, plus such exhibitions as ZEN (Moscow 1990) and the publication of *IdiomA*, suggest that transformations in conceptualizing and representing gender are not confined to a single area of cultural production.

In her hard-hitting film *Astenicheskii sindrom* (The Asthenic Syndrome, 1990), for instance, Kira Muratova endows the female protagonist's startling aggression, violence, verbal obscenities, and casual sexual coupling with a psychological/metaphysical weight normally reserved for "complicated" men given to existential conflict. In fact, Mikhail Iampol'skii has astutely discussed the film as pivoting on a series of gender inversions (Drozdova 205). Bella Matveeva in her canvases pushes the conventional male portrayal of women's bodies as seductive objects for presumably male delectation to a near-parodic extreme, lovingly painting her own slinky, sensually stretched and clothed form with a kind of ironic defiance that stylizes the temptress/seductress into a remote Turandot-like figure self-sufficient in her own beauty. Matveeva simultaneously reverses stereotyped gender roles, as in her diptych of a naked, languorously lounging male opposite a partially clothed female in a more active, aggressive pose. Elsewhere she blends female and male forms into androgynous figures that recall Sasha in Sologub's *Petty Demon* and evoke such "trouser parts" in opera as Mozart's Cherubino (*Le Nozze di Figaro*) and Richard Strauss's Octavian (*Der Rosenkavalier*), in which the combination of female dress and male body or soprano voice and male garb weakens or dissolves conventional gender distinctions.[3] Formulaic gender identities, images, and codes of behavior early enshrined in Russian culture, however, have undergone most far-reaching transformations at the hands of new grammarians in prose fiction.

Western feminism has long grappled with the vexed question:

How can a woman writer intent not only on dissociating herself from her culture's dominant assumptions about gender but also on postulating gender as socially mediated go about her task? How can she avoid complicity in the prevailing myths of her society and inscribe her independence of them? As several recent Russian publications attest, one effective solution is a deconstruction or cross-gendered revisionism that ironizes or anatomizes the very process of mythmaking. Such an approach marks not only the paintings of Irina Nakhova, for example,[4] but also several works of recent women's fiction—by Nina Sadur (b. 1950), Marina Palei, Tatyana Tolstaya, and Nina Gorlanova—that expose the prevailing cultural sign system as a mastadonic outgrowth of self-serving masculinist ideology. That exposure relies on the rewriting of seminal cultural myths, using irony and inversion as a major narrative stratagem. And, curiously, at least two of the relevant texts resonate with recent Western interrogations of cultural paradigms—paradigms that the pre-gender-conscious era equated with self-evident truths and inviolable authority.

Nina Sadur's poetic yet blisteringly unsettling story cycle *Pronikshie* (Touched, 1990) cleverly preempts modern cultural myths by creating the illusion of an animistic universe seemingly predating or overpowering modern civilization. In this folklore-steeped environment both sexes are prey to inexplicable forces and passions utterly beyond human control. Driven by primal urges, hounded by mysterious powers, women intent on shaping their own destinies resort to magic and spells so as to defend themselves against hostile elements. Against this background of demonologized individual and collective psychology, malehood is specifically equated with blind egotism and destructiveness.

In this regard Sadur's narrative "Chervivyi synok" (Worm-Eaten Sonny) is a key text, for it undermines conventional role assignment according to gender by radically and blasphemously revising one of the Western world's most venerable myths: that of the Fall. The biblical story places the burden of mortality on female fallibility, inasmuch as Eve succumbs to the snake's blandishments, violates divine prohibition, and in turn seduces Adam into biting the fatal apple. The original woman, then, is identified with sexuality, temptation, and weakness—traits that have tinged virtually all subsequent portrayals of her sex ("daughter of Eve," the "weaker sex").[5]

Sadur's text expands on the message broadcast by a bumper sticker exhibited on numerous American cars during the late 1970s and 1980s: it showed a half-bitten apple, accompanied by the inflammatory statement: "Eve was framed." Whether God, Adam, or the pseudochroniclers who wrote the original myth into history "set Eve up," males presumably devised and enacted the frame-up for their own self-serving purposes. Such is the implied message of the sticker, whose (probably unintentional) paronomasia (pictorial "frame") adverts to the masculine penchant for "portraying" women according to their own unacknowledged needs. In a parallel move Sadur reverses the gender roles of the lapsarian myth by implicitly casting woman as the defamed victim of male greed (the apple). In Sadur's sacrilegious scenario, Man, chosen as God's son (here degraded to "sonny" [*synok*]), is explicitly the voracious consumer, the death-bearing agent (hence "worm-eaten" [*chervivyi*]) who saps the life out of Woman, concealing his rottenness behind masks and subordinating all around him to his undifferentiated appetite.[6] Throughout the story Sadur resorts to hyperbole and catalog so as to stress Man's predatory insatiability and his links with the snake, the devil, and beasts. The stylized simplicity of Sadur's treatment evokes dictionary entries that define phenomena in minimal objective terms:

> He himself is the tempter. . . . he's a boor. He's a goat. A servant.[7] A mercenary. . . . He summons to destruction. . . . Men . . . gobble us up with our innocence, our future, our bones. They corrupt us and infect us with death. They drink us up and crush us like a milk carton. . . . God knows that man was bitten by the demon of betrayal. Of lust. Of flight. Of will. Of freedom. Of betrayal. Only, how could the demon have bitten such a reptile[?] . . . He's a beast. He swallowed a scorpion. He stings. He tramples woman down, poisons her, teaches her everything, then hates her for learning all his dirty games so well. (Sadur 234–35)

Sadur's narrative initially posits a hackneyed image of male strength and physical magnetism ("Men are strong. They're tall, dark and handsome"), only to demolish it subsequently via an accretion of "contrary evidence" that culminates, at story's conclusion, with a vividly repulsive counterimage of Man as dissoluteness and dissolution:

> Because of all his dangerous life, worms breed in man's brain. And they gnaw at his brains in all the convolutions and suck at the grey matter, they make man even more brutish. . . . Vanity and cruelty. And the mercenary-man sleeps without a mask, and his face is horrible, and the worm-suckers peep out and squeeeak, how tasty he is. (Sadur 235)[8]

Sardonically switching the gender roles in the drama of the Fall, Sadur attributes the consequent tragedy of human suffering and mortality not to the wily Eve but, instead, to the fatally flawed Adam. By remythologizing origins—in a text, moreover, that fashions a wholly credible folkloric dimension—Sadur urges a fundamental reinterpretation of subsequent history. Man here gets demoted from his authoritative role of word bearer (Logos legislator) to that of worm carrier (source of psychic and bodily decay), his fabled authority travestied as ruinous petty tyranny. For Sadur, Man is vulture, not culture, and, instead of answering Freud's query "What do women want?" she reveals what men have insisted on getting.

The brief story "Svidanie" ("Rendezvous," 1991) by the young Petersburg prosaist Marina Palei (b. 1955) likewise discredits a ready-made immemorial scenario. Evoking the timeless literary (and, more recently, cinematic) topos of the romantic encounter,[9] Palei satirizes the clichés of this overdetermined literary moment while simultaneously deconstructing the traditional relationship between male "creativity" and the female body/beloved/Muse so extensively documented in Russian and other literatures.[10] She unmasks this mainstay of romantic aesthetics as one-way traffic between a solipsistic subjectivity (the male) and an object (the female) denied not only all humanity but also any identity apart from instrumentality. To emphasize the gendered morphology of male-female relations, the narrative, appropriately, proceeds from the male viewpoint:

> Ah, beloved! What wouldn't he do for her sake! She's precisely what his soul has yearned for. In general, he's certain that a woman—the one and only, of course—shouldn't have anything that's particularly expressive, for that's tiring. Here she is, then, his one and only, and that's because she's wonderfully neither this nor

> that, neither beautiful nor ugly. He perceives her as he does himself in a mirror, she's his creation, the crowning achievement of his many efforts and experience. (Palei, "Svidanie," 174)

"Rendezvous" reads like a fictional gloss on John Berger's *Ways of Seeing,* a pioneering analysis of gender politics in visual male presentations and perceptions of the female form.[11] It vividly illustrates Luce Irigaray's notion that

> the mirror that envelops and paralyzes the commodity specularizes, speculates (on) man's "labor." *Commodities, women, are a mirror of value of and for man.* In order to serve as such, they give up their bodies to men as the supporting material of specularization, of speculation.[12]

Palei "frames" the protagonist's tryst with a "real-life" woman in his perusal of landscape paintings. This visual exercise stimulates recollections of artistic portrayals of the female nude, which Palei uses to satirize the undeconstructed masculinist habit of dismembering and "reshaping" the beloved woman in conformity with male-generated criteria of femininity—criteria shared and circulated, mutatis mutandis, by men alone. For, as Irigaray notes,

> Reigning everywhere, although prohibited in practice, hom(m)osexuality is played out through the bodies of women, matter . . . or sign, and heterosexuality has been up to now just an alibi for the smooth workings of man's relations with himself, of relations among men. (172)

Palei caps her satirical survey of Western male artists' homo-bonding hypostatization of the ideal female body parts as objects of contemplation and representation (Botticelli, Leonardo, Velásquez, Ingres, Picasso) with a radical realization of metaphor: the "living" female body becomes quite literally a mechanism to be dismantled once its Purpose—as speculum for male Angst—has been fulfilled, or, more accurately, exhausted. She then proceeds to objectify the male by distancing him from the reader through a shift in viewpoint, a strategy that, predictably, reveals his "mechanical" nature, functioning no differently from the female's, and "assembled" according to identical principles:

> But his weariness doesn't leave him. He's now in such a state, as if he'd been ordered to divide by zero. His protective relay switches off. The servomechanisms under the casing sag helplessly. His eyes fade.
>
> The view from the window fades automatically. (Palei, "Svidanie," 175)

Transformed from representing subjects into represented objects, males as exemplars of vaunted objectivity diminish into insecure seekers of self-affirmation. Whereas in the West marketing strategies and literary depictions of women presuppose woman as the consummate consumer, both Sadur's and Palei's revisions transfer the lust for possession and consumption onto men. Whether the target of possession/consumption be object or woman is immaterial, since woman automatically *becomes* the object—of self-serving male desire.

Just such an unorthodox view of the male as arch consumer is also at the heart of Elena Tarasova's unusual story "Ty khorosho nauchilsia est', Adam" (You've Learned Well How to Eat, Adam, 1991), which methodically inventories all of the natural phenomena ravaged in the service of man's merciless self-gratification. Indeed, in a startling reversal all three texts show *male* identity as contingent, deriving from the reassuring instrumentalization of women and other forms of alterity that populate "Man's kingdom." They illustrate how, in this sexual imaginary, woman "is only a more or less obliging prop for the enactment of man's fantasies" (Irigaray, *This Sex*, 25).

Male (and female) fantasies are a commonplace in the prose of Tatyana Tolstaya, who, despite the notoriety of her voluble antifeminism in the West, has written several stories that encourage a feminist reading. One of the most successful, "Ogon' i pyl' " (Fire and Dust, 1987), subverts, through irony and cross-gendering, stereotypical icons of womanhood and female sexuality. Tolstaya's targets are two related gendered clichés: the notions that women's sexuality is most productively sublimated into maternity and, as a corollary, that domesticity is her proper domain. In a quintessentially Tolstayan narrative that operates by binarism while simultaneously discrediting it, the paradigmatically programmed Rimma—a married pragmatist whose aspirations revolve around husband, home, children, and comfort—supplies the bourgeois blueprint, contrasted to the freewheeling Svetlana, the epitome of psychological, sexual, and social individualism. Through the objectified protagonist, Svetlana, and the contrasting center of consciousness, Rimma, the narrative dramatizes the stultifying limitations of formulaic homemaking (the dust of the title) and the rewards of female sexuality cum imagination (the fire of the title). By story's end woman's physical appetite and lust for diverse experience (both anathemized in no uncertain terms by the Soviet establishment) have been amply vindicated by Svetlana, who bears the eloquent nickname of Pipka (Cunty), appears naked or near-naked for much of the narrative, enjoys improbable adventures (sexual and geographical), trails fascinating legends behind her, and—what is particularly critical for Tolstaya—has a vibrant imagination that produces spellbinding narratives.

Curiously, Pipka's sexuality and narrative powers instance Irigaray's punning dovetailing of mouth and labia in her essay "When Our Lips Speak Together." In fact, Pipka's flair for spinning outrageous and seductive stories (analogized with the *Thousand and One Nights*) partly accounts for her sexual allure; her talent magically attracts males who appear not to notice or value those physical traits that standard ideals of female beauty would deem deficiencies (a "horrible black mouth," tooth stumps). While weaving an aureole of enticing mystery around Pipka, Tolstaya's story celebrates uninhibited female pleasure. Lacking caution and calculation, Pipka passionately pursues experience, and that passion systematically shades into sexual energy, freely indulged with a staggering array of fortuitously encountered males.

In contrast to Rimma's code-affirming values and static existence, Pipka's way of life entails risk and constant peregrinations away from a dubious pied-à-terre (the "semi-fantastic Perlovka") that sooner resembles a male harem than a domestic haven. Pipka's periodic returns to Rimma's apartment, in fact, echo the structure of masculine movement in the majority of nineteenth-century Russian novels, in which the arrival of the footloose male as the active principle triggers plot action. To cast the conflicting options in terms of literary genre, Tolstaya posits the tale of adventure—with its multiple sexual encounters, spatial and psychic expansiveness, unexpected twists in plot, and a "larger-than-life" protagonist—and not bourgeois drama, as a viable feminine narrative model.[13] In Tolstaya's scenario the latter as instantiated in Rimma's example ends with a dreary sense of loss, of life's tendency to repeat, diminish, and disillusion, while the former unfolds in a colorful succession of libidinal encounters.

Elan takes precedence over moralism: instead of following the timeworn pattern of punishing a female protagonist for "loose living," Tolstaya as author rewards her for living—to the full. Pipka's life culminates in a transcendent death, fittingly troped as a potential metamorphosis into a "higher existence": the "flame on the highway" that may metaphorize Pipka's enigmatic final fate. Thus, the conclusion of the story dissolves the ancient opposition of body and soul by implying that Pipka's bodily "largesse" is on a continuum with her spiritual capacities.

Insofar as it narrativizes with zest and humor the sexual energy of a "bad girl," to which, moreover, it harnesses spiritual and creative expansiveness, Tolstaya's "Fire and Dust" echoes Nina Katerli's "Polina" (1984) and anticipates Marina Palei's more recent novella *Kabiriia s Obvodnogo kanala* (Cabiria from the Bypass, 1991).[14] Not unlike Tolstaya's story, "Polina" relies on the prolific, venerable Russian genre of the contrastive character sketch made famous by such "classics" as N. Karamzin's "Chuvstvitel'nyi i kholodnyi. Dva kharaktera" (The Sensitive and the Cold. Two Characters, 1803), I. Turgenev's "Khor and Kalinych" (1852), and A. Chekhov's "Tolstyi i tonkii" (The Fat and the Thin, 1883). Upon its publication, however, Katerli's gynocentric polarization of two alternate life options ruffled orthodox critics' feathers, for Katerli's treatment challenges the value system of Soviet ideology. The novella pits the proclaimed if specious security of institutionalized domesticity against the uncertainties of a single, sexually active life—to the detriment of the former. Maia's ostensibly perfect family life, complete with influential husband, indulged daughter, and material comfort bordering on affluence, unexpectedly unravels, leading to her nervous breakdown; Polina's anomalous, sexually open style of existence on the fringes of mainstream Soviet society unexpectedly proves more attuned to the unpredictable ebb and flow of life.

It is difficult to imagine how those readers who expressed disapproval of Katerli's heroine Polina on moral grounds responded to

Palei's Raimonda/Monka, a woman whose lifelong primary—indeed, almost exclusive—focus falls on sexual pleasure. Even in these incomparably more permissive times in Russia a woman's enthusiasm for copulating with virtually any man she meets inevitably elicits condemnation or at least dismay among a broad segment of the Russian public. Not only Palei's ironically tolerant treatment of Monka, mediated through the perspective and narrative voice of Monka's "proper" younger cousin, but also her enthusiastic recognition of female sexuality and her skepticism of what she calls "eta vsroslaia, krivodushnaia . . . igra, imenuemaia Institutom braka" (this adult, dishonest game called the Institution of Marriage, 52) make "Cabiria" one of the most transgressive Russian texts in recent memory. And, in contrast to semi-journalistic "social realist" fiction, exemplified by the stories of Nikolai Shmelev and Nadezhka Kozhevnikova, Palei's novella seduces neither by its plot dynamics nor by its reassuring moral stance but, rather, through the evocative richness of its language. With its allusions to Fellini, the ancient deities worshiped in the Greek islands, and the earth/fertility goddess Ceres,[15] the very title of "Cabiria" alerts the reader to the complexity of Palei's design. Moreover, the ambiguities generated by such paranomastic formulations as "porok serdtsa" (a defect, vice of the heart) to describe the heroine's condition point to Palei's concern with reexamining the most overworked and overdetermined human organ in literature—the heart that lends itself too easily to troping. If feminist narratives attempt to destabilize the binarism that serves as a foundational principle in misogynistic constructs, then Palei's sophisticated efforts to reconcile the ancient division of body and mind/spirit justify characterizing "Cabiria" as a thoroughly feminist piece of fiction.[16] In that respect her novella overlaps with Tolstaya's "Fire and Dust" and has much in common with Liudmila Ulitskaia's fictional explorations of women's sexuality, as, for example, in "Gulia" and "Lialin dom" (Lialia's House).[17]

Whereas Sadur, Palei, and Tolstaya debunk universal myths, subject-object relations, and role assignments, Nina Gorlanova in her "Novella" (as she calls her story) ironizes a specific, highly influential "classic" of Russian literature: Mikhail Lermontov's *Geroi nashego vremeni* (Hero of Our Time, 1840).[18] Gorlanova's treatment of Pechorin, the late Romanticist masculine ideal that subsequently underwent endless variations, is irreverent at best. Her version of this male-fantasy text, and, specifically, the "Kniazhna Meri" (Princess Mary) segment of the cycle, which highlights Pechorin's role of irresistible but disillusioned, rootless heartbreaker, reduces tragic demonism to buffoonish egotism. Gorlanova's treatment, in a sense, elaborates into a fictional text Milan Kundera's perspicacious deflation of male posturing: "Lermontov is not afraid of death, but he is afraid of ridicule. He longs to jump from the balcony, but he dares not, for he knows that while suicide is tragic, unsuccessful suicide is absurd" (Kundera 282). Just how beguiling the portrait of Pechorin appears not only to the adolescent but also to a presumably more mature male imagination may be gauged by the rather overwrought summation of his traits by Vladimir Nabokov, no less:

> a fictional person whose romantic dash and cynicism, tigerlike suppleness and eagle eye [cf. heroes of Harlequin romances], hot blood and cool head, tenderness and taciturnity, elegance and brutality, delicacy of perception and harsh passion to dominate, ruthlessness and awareness of it, are of lasting appeal to readers of all countries and centuries—especially to young readers. (Nabokov xvii)

Instead of following Lermontov's example of contrasting the Romantic "genuine article" (Pechorin) with the superficial imitation (Grushnitskii), Gorlanova pairs two Grushnitskiis, called, in assembly-line fashion, "Pervyi Grushnitskii" (the First Grushnitskii) and "Vtoroi Grushnitskii" (the Second Grushnitskii). Their dissimilarities are subsumed by their common name and their shared trait of genuine imitation: that is, adherence to a threadbare formula of masculinity.[19] They become Man Redux, for the pluralization of an individual name is a familiar and effective technique of derisive debasement.[20]

Throughout, the text travesties the Grushnitskiis' typically masculinist pretensions, which assume the concrete form of dissipation for Grushnitskii No. 1 and of pseudo-witticisms and Don Juanism for No. 2 (pointedly called Gospodchikov [Lordstone], the Lord of Creation). For both, women serve as the testing ground for, and confirmation of, their sexual prowess, on which their identity hinges. *Così fan tutti,* as Mozart might have said and as Gorlanova, indeed, shows.

Gorlanova satirically inventories the stale male repertoire of gestures calculated to enhance Man's image as a sexual athlete: a mathematical approach to sexual experience, governed by numbers; bragging that "on mozhet 'dva raza ne vynimaia' " (he can do it "twice without taking it out"); trading reminiscences in all-male company about "u kogo i skol'ko zhenshchin bylo" (who's had how many women, 187); resorting to physical violence when feeling impotent "Prishlos' nemnogo pobit' i etu zhenshchinu, kotoraia ne mogla ego sdelat' polnotsennym" (He had to beat this woman a little too, who couldn't make him completely whole, 190), etc. Beneath these ritualistic flourishes lurk insecurity and performance panic, which Gorlanova slyly embellishes by means of deglamorizing or trivializing physical details: hernias, baldness, impotence, childish fits of rage accompanied by slipper throwing.

Placing her reader in the highly charged space that marks the distance between the glamor of masculine self-presentation and the pathos of men's terminal self-preoccupation, Gorlanova invites the reader to view the former through the latter. Her parody of a parody (Grushnitskii) ultimately diminishes Man by recasting him into material more suitable for farce than tragedy. In fact, her text illustrates the fatal effect of humor on posturing and self-importance. Laughter transforms *A Hero of Our Time* into *A Self-Deluded Poseur of All Time.*

Perhaps the most remarkable aspect of the fiction I have discussed here is its ability to maintain a high level of narrative interest while striking at the very core of sexist mythmaking. Until recently women's writing in Russia has tended, however unwittingly, to reinforce imposed gender paradigms by working pliantly within their boundaries. By contrast, in the process of structuring an absorbing tale, these works self-confidently demote those paradigms from the claimed status of Truth to objects of skeptical examination. Instead of naturalizing misogynistic values by embedding them unobtrusively in the very sign system of a text, so that they appear as the immovable furniture (i.e., the unassailable given) of the text/world, these more self-conscious treatments "estrange" the signs into plot material that is then subjected to ironic scrutiny. The process not only leads to a skeptical dissociation from a relatively predictable male perspective on gender but, more broadly, urges a fresh, more critical reading of texts that unquestioningly embrace that perspective. As the new grammarians of gender, then, Sadur, Palei, Tolstaya, and Gorlanova succeed in subjectivizing objects and objectivizing subjects, in removing the predictable predicate that automatically follows the pronouns *on* (he) and *ona* (she). Their achievement may augur the birth of the eventual death of "onaism"—a phenomenon that the signs of the times may yet relegate to antiquity.

Texts Perceived

Russians' reception of texts such as these, which belong to the category of "novaia zhenskaia proza" (new women's prose), demonstrates not only the inflexibly irrational nature of gender bias among the country's intellectual elite but also those features that, owing to the society's prolonged exclusion of multiplicity, still parochialize literary criticism: (1) a virtual absence of intellectual self-consciousness, whereby critics equate their overt or implicit advocacy of a particular position with a perception of Truth; (2) a prescriptive, dogmatic concept of literature as a repository of moral values, its teleological function that of exemplification; (3) neglect of the ludic component in literature or its relegation to "empty" game; (4) a declarative critical tradition that favors unsubstantiated pronouncements over carefully reasoned argument, hence lapses into illogicality and self-contradiction; and (5) largely unexamined essentialist assumptions about "human nature," "Russia," "literature," and "woman" that close multiple doors to discussion.

While all too readily acknowledging that their society has been dominated by the superimposition of official political ideology, Russians discount the less blatant manifestations and effects of mandated orthodoxy. It has proved easier to detect and therefore to dismiss, however belatedly, naked propaganda about socialism, the heroism of the country's leaders, and the evils of Western exploitation than to challenge the sacrosanct premises invisibly underpinning an entire way of thought that deconstruction has undermined in the West: for example, History as Truth, Literature as a specific body of canonical high culture works, Character as unitary, Nature as prelapsarian, and Language as transparent. In short, most Russians continue to embrace as essences what Western critics acquainted with the scholarship of Michel Foucault, Roland Barthes, Jacques Derrida, and Jacques Lacan may perceive as primarily social constructs abetted by psychological processes and needs.[21] Those Russian scholars who are conversant with deconstruction and postmodernist theory, such as Mark Lipovetskii and

Andrei Zorin, belong to the younger generation, constitute a miniscule minority, and, significantly, rarely address questions of gender.[22] Of the proliferating current Western-*isms*, it is precisely feminism that they ignore. Since reviews of women's literature fall mainly to Russian critics oblivious to contemporary developments in Western intellectual circles, their commentaries resemble exercises in nostalgia, resuscitating an era that predates all of our current post-*isms*—a paradise lost of epistemological innocence.

Reviews of women's collections by Natal'ia Ivanova, Natal'ia Startseva, Evgeniia Shcheglova, Alla Latynina, Svetlana Alieva, and Pavel Basinskii appeared between 1986 and 1991 in such central, highly reputable publications as *Literaturnaia gazeta* (Literary Gazette), *Literaturnaia Rossiia* (Literary Russia), *Literaturnaia ucheba* (Literary Studies), *Literary obozrenie* (Literary Review), and *Moskovskii literator* (Moscow Litterateur).[23] Untouched by theoretical considerations, they represent mainstream perspectives and styles of commentary on questions that inevitably surface in discussions of female authorship. They therefore provide eloquent insight into the range of likely responses by "typical," or "average"-educated Russians both to women's writing and to women as writers.

Taxonomical Dilemmas

A cardinal premise of contemporary Russian criticism is the vehemently asserted extraneousness of gender to artistic production. According to this widespread view, women's purportedly inherent femininity, which ineluctably manifests itself in all other spheres of private and public life and for decades has been promoted vigorously through state campaigns,[24] miraculously evaporates the instant a woman picks up a pen. The symptomatic repudiation by Natal'ia Ivanova and Evgeniia Shcheglova of women's literature as a discrete corpus stems from their credence in this involuntary loss of gender at the portals of creativity. Mary Ellmann has characterized this wonder as "the hermaphroditic fallacy," whereby "one half the person, separating from the other self[,] produces a book by binary fission" (41–42).

Like many Western skeptics of gendered taxonomies, none of the reviewers apart from Svetlana Alieva seems prepared to envisage gender as, *minimally*, a convention, no different from geography ("Spanish versus Italian literature"), chronology ("the Romantic Age versus the Age of Realism"), language ("poetry versus prose"), tone ("epic versus mock-epic"), race ("African-American writers"), religion ("Catholic novelists") or other categories long accredited as contingent principles for organizing discussion. Yet common sense alone suggests that it is no more arbitrary to group texts by gender than by scale or generation. And, more important, perhaps, is the necessary realization still awaiting the majority of Russian critics that classification per se represents a convention susceptible to endless modification.[25] When Shcheglova analogizes literature and science, in order to declare their shared independence of gender ("Just as 'male' and 'female' sciences do not exist, so these categories of literature do not exist" [21]), she is operating unreflexively within the hallowed convention that reveres science as an "objective discipline"—a convention challenged, among others, by Evelyn Fox Keller and Donna Haraway, whose scholarship has documented what they perceive as the systemic androcentricity of scientific research.[26]

After proclaiming the primacy of quality (as an immutable, immanent universal criterion) and the irrelevance of gender to literature, these review essays nonetheless proceed to discuss women's fiction as an identifiably distinct entity. Moreover, they do so in unambiguously essentialist terms. Thus, Ivanova speaks of "age-old feminine curiosity," the "markedly feminine" subject matter of Marina Kretova's story (8) and the "traditionally 'feminine' frame of the narrative plot" (11), and endorses the passage she cites from Max Frisch calling for a uniquely gendered style (*gynesis*) commensurate with women's "'specific way of thinking'" (12). Shcheglova notes "a truly female—maternal—attitude toward the world" (23), defines *woman* as the "embodiment of warmth, kindness, and love" (29), maintains that "a woman's view is altogether different from a man's" (23), that the "genuinely feminine [*sic*] and the humane are indivisible" (32), and that "nature was wise and farsighted in dividing humanity into two sexes, giving to each its own" (45). Alla Latynina considers much of contemporary women's prose "thoroughly masculine in confidence and clearheadedness" (53), while Alieva endorses its "natural talent, intuition, and purely feminine insight" (54). Quite predictably, Pavel Basinskii—the only male reviewer included in my discussion—speaks of "masculine businesslike efficiency" (77), contends that "femininity can be revealed only in the presence of a man as the necessary enzyme" (76), and, echoing

Plato, finds "the 'masculine' spirit" synonymous with "the spirit proper" (78). These pseudo-truths sound all too familiar to readers of Joanna Russ's sobering study of strategies for suppressing women's writing, which catalogs numerous examples of such essentialist formulations, from Robert Lowell's ambiguous praise of Sylvia Plath to Ursula Le Guin's reflection that the "Creator Spirit is more masculine than feminine, but on the deeper levels is both at once" (Russ 23).

As proponents of "intrinsic femininity," these critics subscribe to the stereotype of womanhood conceived in antinomian terms that Hélène Cixous dismantled in "Sorties": within the hierarchized binary oppositions that preside over Western patriarchy, the activity, culture, Logos, reason, form, clarity, and authority that constitute the male Norm predicate the antithetical female Other of passivity, nature, Pathos, emotion, matter, mystery, and submission (or nurture) (Cixous 63–132). Indeed, Russian critics perpetuate this dichotomous structure in fully expecting women writers to "cherish and console" their literary personae and their readers, while simultaneously despising them as "lowbrow" for doing so. Tatyana Tolstaya, for instance, elicits mixed reactions largely because of what Shcheglova, typically, calls "icy coldness" and an "indifference to a protagonist's inner life" (42), a movement away from "feeling" that postpones and ultimately robs of conviction Tolstaya's "pity" for her "heroes" (43). The compassion and self-abnegating subordination to more comprehensive needs that presumably inhere in Russian womanhood extend to female authors, who may be (in fact, must be) *literarily* inferior to their male counterparts but rest secure in their *moral* superiority ("destined by nature to safeguard [ethical . . .] principles in the family," as the Program for the Association of Women Writers within the Writers' Union announces). Conceived as domestic/cultural mothers, nurses, helpmates, and enablers, fictional heroines likewise exist primarily to fulfill readers' and society's expectations of optimistic support and self-denial in a higher (male-defined) cause. The most appropriate icon for emulation by writing and written women, then, is Florence Nightingale.

Sentiment and Woman's Social Role

While forcibly cast in the social, hence literary, role of maternal martyr and reassuring nurturer, and judged by those criteria, women are judged only to be found wanting, for the criteria themselves invite scorn from the self-appointed authorities who posit them. Shcheglova ridicules the lachrymose tendency of "conservative" women's prose, which plays upon (presumably female) readers' emotions (22). Assuming a neither-nor stance, her article lambasts the lowbrow comforting aspects of women's literature, even as it conveys, conversely, the author's unease at the bleakness of vision in recent women's fiction. Sentiment, of course, has not enjoyed an enviable reputation in Western civilization, on account of the long-standing privileging of cerebral (i.e., purportedly male) aspects of human endeavor, stretching from Aristotle to the New Critics. Soviet Russian literature has relied on affect to a greater degree than most Western literatures, and, when Mikhail Sholokhov, practitioners of "village prose," and jingoist ideologues such as Boris Polevoi and Nikolai Ostrovskii make unabashed appeals to audience emotions, no one raises objections. After all, their "moment of weakness" occurs in a text demonstrably saturated with masculinist values and so may dissolve within that larger context.

When women authors indulge in sentiment, however, they betray their "irrationality" and violate some unspecified law of measure apparently inapplicable to male writers.[27] Whereas Western feminists (notably Jane Tompkins)[28] have made considerable headway in the rehabilitation of sentiment, Russians denigrate "excess of emotion" or pulling at heartstrings as a feebleness endemic to the "weaker sex," excusable *only* so long as it does not encroach upon literature. This derailed pseudo-reasoning leaves little space for women writers, trapped between the Scylla of "ladies' novellas" (exaggerated sensibility), on the one hand, and the Charybdis of "usurping male modes" of writing (tough impersonality), on the other—two accusations leveled at them throughout the essays that greeted the publication of anthologies of "new women's fiction."

The Stigma of Ladies' Literature

Latynina correctly pinpoints the provenance of the label "ladies' prose" or "ladies' novella" that critics attach to women's fiction in order to belittle it. Coined by Vladimir Lakshin in his revealingly titled essay "Eve, Having Taken a Bite of the Apple" (1962), the purely dismissive term has congealed into an ineradicable cliché of Russian critical discourse. Reinforced, first, by Natal'ia Il'ina's ironic send-up of the female "genre" in the prestigious journal *Novyi mir* (New World) ("On the Question of Tradition and Innovation in the Genre of the Ladies' Novella" [1963]) and by Kornei Chukovskii's "On Arguments about the 'Ladies' Novella'" (1967),[29] it subsequently received a boost from the impassioned disdain for the "genre" voiced by such influential writers as Liudmila Petrushevskaia and Tolstaya in the course of interviews. Ivanova's essay, in fact, summarizes the flaws ascribed to ladies' novellas by her predecessors: "coquetry, affectation, and narrowness of purview"—an inordinate preoccupation, in other words, with such "feminine" concerns as love, marriage, betrayal, divorce, and domesticity, at the price of "socially significant problems" (11). The presumption here is that a significant problem is by definition social or that only a social problem is significant.[30] Latynina likewise corroborates the ignominious paradigm of *ladies' novella,* citing "sentimentality, conservative style, and an abundance of melodramatic passions" as its distinguishing features (53).

Yet the satirical condescension toward this putative genre fails to disguise the sexist irrationality of its disparaging users. As Shcheglova correctly states, it is a tired maxim of Russian criticism that the rubric *ladies' novella* need not identify an author's gender (21). If, as Latynina and Tolstaya concede, numerous male authors produce ladies' novellas, why does roundly despised, mediocre writing of this type merit a gendered label? Because for Russians feminization per se constitutes derogation: *Ladies'* or *women's* by definition means secondary or second-rate. Ivanova subscribes wholly to the masculinist valorization of high culture's exalted address when she faults Marina Kretova's "The Fellow Outside" for lacking "a loftier flight and a more sweeping wingspan" (9).[31] A "typical story precisely for a 'woman's' magazine," it suffers from a "range of vision circumscribed by the 'woman's' principle . . . , for the operative principle should be universally human [*sic*] instead of narrowly feminine" (9). This devaluation of female experience (automatically "narrow") equates *human* with manhood—"universal" because of an a priori elevation to normative.[32] It therefore comes as no surprise that Ivanova singles out Raisa Polomova's story as the "least 'feminine' and therefore [*sic*] most distinct" (10) in the collection under review, and commends the author's attempt to overcome "the canons of 'women's prose.'" Ivanova's unproblematic readiness to endow with "canons" a literary category that she deems nonexistent instances the curious mental lapses of Russian commentators summoned to analyze women's literature.

Gendered Indiscretions

Following in Lakshin's and Il'ina's timeworn footsteps, the reviewers unanimously concur, then, that ladies' novellas or feminine prose guarantees formulaic banalities. All too aware that any association with that brand of writing automatically consigns them to the status of disenfranchised secondariness, women authors disavow the role of gender in art.[33] Viktoriia Tokareva and Petrushevskaia, in fact, unwittingly postulate transvestite authoring when they announce that they write "like [as?] men" (McLaughlin, "Interview" 75–76),[34] while Tolstaya advances a theory of neuter or androgynous creativity (Tolstaya "A Little Man," 10; Barta 277, 282). By an ironic paradox the older generation of women (i.e., those over forty) distance themselves from female prose, only to be frequently linked with precisely that discredited form of writing,[35] whereas the younger generation programmatically embraces its identity of woman writer yet impresses reviewers (e.g., Shcheglova and Basinskii) as striving above all to divorce itself definitively from the stigmatized "genre." Latynina's observation that nowadays "it's women who more often than not, as if fearing accusations of excessive sentimentality, etc., create prose that is thoroughly masculine in confidence and clearheadedness" (53) sets the direction and tone for Shcheglova's and Basinskii's review articles.

Shcheglova divides recent women's literature into three types: a refurbished version of ladies' writing (the palliative of "comforting" narratives, "false, grandiloquent, and, because of this, lacking any real love of people" [32]); a continuation of "naive suffragism" carried over from an earlier era; and the "new wave," characterized by "antiaestheticism" and "provocatively 'antifeminine' épatage" (34). The last she interprets as an attempt to sidestep identification with the bathos that trivializes comforting prose (35). What she singles out for opprobrium in this—what Chuprinin has called the "Other"—prose[36] is its profoundly physiological bent ("gross naturalism" [45]), its focus on the "external effect," and the self-elimination of a clearly defined authorial voice. Ignoring Petrushevskaia's and Tolstaya's sophisticated use of rhetorical devices, Shcheglova perceives only an empirical transfer of biologically grounded *realia* from life to page in their prose. Beneath her dismay at their ostensible reduction of life to biologism in a style of "superfashionable 'avant-gardism'" (44) lurks the standard Russian conviction that artistic complexity, sexual explicitness, and pessimistic vision are unnegotiable male prerogatives.

Such a conviction indisputably fuels Basinskii's haranguing review of *Ne pomniashchaia zla* (The Woman Who Remembers No Evil), a model of misunderstanding couched in misogynistic truisms. The female authors' collective introduction to the anthology is less a manifesto, as Basinskii reads it, than a proleptic polemical response to the questions customarily provoked by women's anthologies. Whether deliberately or not, the anticipated questions coincide with those posed in Ivanova's, Shcheglova's, and to some extent Natal'ia Startseva's essays. Part of Basinskii's petulance doubtless stems from his subliminal realization that the two-page introduction marks a watershed of sorts in the history of Russian women's writing. It does so on three counts: its authors not only unequivocally assert their identity as specifically women writers but also pinpoint the shifting yet circumscribed options in permissible social roles for women from the eighteenth century to the present. Furthermore, they illuminate the recurrent circle in women's texts and titles (which so taxes Shcheglova's imagination and patience) as a polysemous image of imprisonment, infernal suffering (a nod to Dante), and endless continuity. The contributors' acute awareness and foregrounding of their gender, with all its attendant ramifications, prepare the intelligent reader for such motifs in the collection as female sexuality, bodily experiences, rape, abortion, male violence, etc. Basinskii, alas, is not that reader. His revulsion at the contents of the anthology hinges on three disabling factors: the "frankness" of the texts, which violate "taboos" regulating "naturalistic" detail and manifestly bruise Basinskii's sensibility; the "antiteleological" nature of the anthologized prose; and his own incomprehension, which he inadvertently betrays at one juncture in a classic maneuver of projection that lays the responsibility for his hermeneutical limitations at the author's door ("If I understand anything at all in the labyrinths of the prose of Valeriia Narbikova . . ." [77]).

The physiological explicitness of contemporary Russian fiction in general has sparked heated controversy in recent years, but Basinskii's objections concentrate on graphic descriptions of bodily experiences undergone exclusively by women to which males have no access: birthing, in Nina Gorlanova's "Istoriia ozera Veselogo" (The Story of Lake Cheerful), and abortion, in Svetlana Vasilenko's "Shamara." Both stories depict women grappling in isolation with the act of birth, with, Basinskii indignantly complains, the reader as sole witness, "forced to watch with repugnance the convulsions of *giving birth* as a purely physiological act" (75). "Why," he demands, "try the nerves of the reader who's harried enough by our life without this? Is this the task of 'women's prose'?" Basinskii here eliminates the mediating agencies governing fiction, placing himself on the same level as the text, which he confuses with palpable everyday reality.

If, for the sake of argument, we provisionally accept such a dubious positioning, which conflates fiction with life, his reading still leaves several problems unresolved. One of the story's major points is precisely that women have learned to cope with life-threatening hardships in solitude because of Russian society's cavalier attitude toward women's needs. The struggle to survive a delivery in brutal circumstances does not conduce to poeticizing the act of birth. Male authors, with no personal knowledge of birthing, are hardly equipped to document the event in painstaking detail, though they may lyricize it in abstract paeans to the perpetuation of human life. That Russia's maternity homes and the conditions under which women have abortions (the country's chief means of "contraception") are criminally negligent and unsanitary is no secret, even if Russian males find it more comfortable to remain ignorant of the deplorable inadequacies. In other words, the suffering portrayed by both Gorlanova and Vasilenko is *part* of that life which "harries" Russian readers—above all, its female half. Uneuphemized female physicality, however, repels the fastidious Basinskii, for whom woman's "nature" derives solely from the authoritative center of the normative male paradigm, either reflectively ("Mechanically, . . . a woman's soul *reiterates* the hellish circles of a man's spirit" (76; emphasis added) or via prepositions (beside, beneath, or versus man).[37] Hence, for Basinskii, Tarasova's "gloomy irony" and "discouraging prognoses" instance the imitative unnaturalness of what he quaintly dubs "existentialism in skirts" (76)—a philosophical dress code unacceptable in a movement that decidedly came clothed in trousers.[38] Ultimately, Basinskii's vituperative reduces to an aggressive discomfort with an opaque language untrammeled by the mimetic imperative and with female subjectivity as a center of consciousness different from and patently incompatible with his own.[39]

Basinskii's naively empirical bias leads him to simplistic readings of narratives whose originality and complexity utterly elude him. Unable to identify the clearcut "aim" of the collection,[40] he bypasses or downplays its stylistic innovations. For instance, Nina Sadur's inspired creation of a personal quasi-folklore in the cycle *Touched* hardly resembles the "simple-hearted children's genre" of fairy tales (74) but endows her macabre distillations of ominous psychic drama with intense poetic power. Similarly, the symbolic dimension in Tarasova's "The Woman Who Remembers No Evil"—a young woman with Boyle-Mariotte syndrome—transforms a physiological disfigurement into a modern, gendered replay of Christ's passion (Basinskii's diagnosis: "This kind of stuff shouldn't be published!" [75]). Perhaps most surrealistic is Basinskii's "interpretation" of Narbikova's tongue-in-cheek paronomastic playfulness, which explores the creative power and limits of language, as "masturbation by the masculine spirit [sic] in the face of the cold indifference of the woman's soul" (77). Nietzsche's notoriously misogynistic generalizations from *Thus Spake Zarathustra* provide the momentum for Basinskii's illogical leap from women's "barbarism" to the conclusion that a "woman's soul" is "the invention of man, a kind of artistic trick in the interests of his own creativity" (75). A familiar strategy of repression, the specious "Adam's rib" technique of casting everything female in terms of male categories casts doubts on the sincerity of Basinskii's concluding plea for a "new word" from women writers.

That exhortation to women writers ("find your own voice")—which presupposes their present accommodation to Echo's fate—reticulates throughout these articles. Latynina laments women's willingness to "give an incomparable imitation of another's [i.e., male's] voice" instead of "talking with . . . [its] own," (51), and Ivanova ascribes the "secondariness" of women's prose to its "attempt to outdistance men on their own ground" (11). Basinskii bluntly accuses today's women writers of "usurping" male traditions through their "unprecedented daring" in infracting taboos (74).

As I noted earlier, the dilemma of creative female autonomy has also vexed many a Western feminist. Laura Mulvey's query neatly encapsulates the predicament: "How does an independent aesthetic evolve out of confrontation with a dominant one?" (Mulvey 191). Her sensible answer: through the creation of works that will be read and achieve meaning in the reflected light of the aesthetics they negate (192). Julia Kristeva, exploring the intersection between the crisis that produced the language of modernism and the "feminine," essentially agrees, contending that transgression is played out through language. Indeed, the command of language by some of today's women writers is precisely what individualizes their prose. One must be deaf not to hear the distinctiveness of, for example, Tolstaya's literary voice or that of Petrushevskaia, Narbikova, Sadur, Palei, and Vaneeva. Even critics not particularly attuned to their authorial practices or sympathetic to their concerns have singled out language as Tolstaya's and to a lesser extent Petrushevskaia's inimitable creative signatures.

In short, the problem lies not with women writers but, rather, with their critics, who still remain impervious to the originality of women's fiction because they approach it in hackneyed fashion that levels out differences. Criticism on current Russian women's fiction confutes George Berkeley's philosophical argument for the inconceivability of things existing absolutely unperceived.[41] If that criticism is to overcome its intellectual myopia, it must broaden its theoretical horizons and refine its modes of analysis. Commentators dealing with women's writing need to educate themselves out of their knee-jerk rejection of anything seemingly or genuinely associated with feminism.[42] I am not advocating the imposition of Western variants of feminism on Russian thought, for to do so sanctions a cultural imperialism that denies the value of specific experience and glosses over meaningful distinctions. I am suggesting, however, that an increased willingness to interrogate essentializing Truths might make for a less pallid and predictable criticism whose chief interest will not be confined to the zoological. Reexamining naturalizing procedures might free women to contemplate alternatives to (as well as to *consciously* opt for) the multiple coercive duties in which delusory notions of innate femininity have trapped them. In addition to texts by Liudmila Ulitskaia and Larisa Vaneeva, Katerli's *Polina*, Tolstaya's "Fire and Dust," and Palei's *Cabiria from the Bypass* offer fictional treatments of just such alternatives.[43] One can only hope that Russian criticism will finally catch up with the salutary subversiveness of its indiscreet, "unladylike" women's writing.

Notes

1. On this, see James Billington, *The Icon and the Axe* (1966; reprint, New York: Vintage Books, 1970); and Dmitrij Tschizewskij, *Russian Intellectual History* (Ann Arbor: Ardis, 1978).
2. See the second section of this chapter.
3. On Matveeva and other contemporary female artists, see the excellent article by Isaak 28–29.
4. See ibid., 30–31. Nakhova's deconstructive technique makes wide use of diptychs that suggest time's passage and reveal the contingent, temporally determined aspects of phenomena traditionally perceived as timeless.
5. Although, according to the modern interpretation of Genesis by biblical scholars, Eve represents "not her sex but the whole of humanity," outside of such specialist circles the image of Eve is that of inherently wily femininity. See John A. Phillips, *Eve: The History of an Idea* (San Francisco: Harper and Row, 1984), esp. 55–57.

   It is surprising that feminists who have written on women's relationship to food have not paid more attention to the First Woman's defiance of God's prohibition regarding its consumption and to the cultural consequences of that act, particularly for women. See, for instance, Helena Michie, *The Flesh Made Word: Female Figures and Women's Bodies* (New York and Oxford: Oxford University Press, 1987).
6. The motif of unappeasable human hunger (and man's destructive submission to it) finds thematic elaboration in Elena Tarasova's story "Ty khorosho nauchilsia est', Adam," in *Novye Amazonki*, ed. Svetlana Vasilenko (Moscow: Moskovskii rabochii, 1991), 277–301.
7. A pun typical of Sadur's style here, *knekht* in Russian means a post on a ship's deck, while in Russian slang it is the equivalent of marauder, and in German it signifies servant.
8. Characteristic of the paranomasia in the cycle, the verb for "squeak" (*pishchat*) puns on the word for "food" (*pishcha*).
9. In fact, *Svidanie* is the title of a novella (1879) by Nadezhda Khvoshchinskaia (pseudonym V. Krestovskii) that V. Uchenova adopts for the volume of fiction in which the novella appears. See V. Uchenova, ed., *Svidanie* (Moscow: "Sovremennik," 1987).
10. For the best-known instances from Russian Romantic prose, see V. Odoevskii's "Sil'fida" (The Sylph), N. Gogol's "Nevskii prospekt" (Nevsky Avenue), and Iu. Lermontov's "Shtoss." The topos is particularly exploited in poetry, from A. Pushkin's "Ia pomniu chudnoe mgnoven'e" (I remember the wondrous moment) to A. Blok's cycle of *Stikhi o Preskrasnoi Dame* (Verses on a Beautiful Lady).
11. Berger's by now classic study tackles many of the ideas that have become fundamental to feminist thought: for example, the conventionalized differ-

ences in male and female presence, the concept of female internalization, the voyeurism of male artistic depiction/spectatorship, the distinction between nakedness and nudity (John Berger, *Ways of Seeing* [1972; reprint, London and New York: BBC and Penguin, 1977]).

12. Irigaray, "Women on the Market," *This Sex Which Is Not One*, trans. Catherine Porter (Ithaca: Cornell University Press, 1985), 177. Citations from Irigaray's other essays (e.g., "This Sex Which Is Not One") refer to this volume and will be identified by page numbers in parentheses in the body of the chapter.
13. For a more detailed commentary on this story and two others by Tolstaya from the standpoint of gender, see Helena Goscilo, "Monsters Monomaniacal, Marital, and Medical: Tatyana Tolstaya's Regenerative Use of Gender Stereotypes," in *Sexuality and the Body in Russian Culture*, ed. Jane T. Costlow, Stephanie Sandler, and Judith Vowles (Stanford: Stanford University Press, 1993), 204–20.
14. Nina Katerli, "Polina," *Neva* 1 (1984): 11–60 Marina Palei, "Kabiriia s Obvodnogo Kanala," *Novyi mir* 3 (1991): 49–81. A translation of the first twenty pages of *Cabiria* is available in English (trans. Ronald Meyer, "Cabiria from the Bypass," in *Present Imperfect* [Boulder: Westview Press, 1995]).
15. For Cabiri and Ceres, respectively, see J. Lempriere, *Lempriere's Classical Dictionary* (London: Bracken Books, 1984), 126, 155–56.
16. Curiously, Katerli's less vividly sensual protagonist Polina also suffers from a heart defect.
17. In general Ulitskaia credits women with a rich range of sexual appetites, her stories teeming with the kinds of sexual encounters that under the Soviet regime would have been unimaginable for a woman. The eponymous protagonist of "Lialia's House," for instance, not only enjoys but becomes addicted to sexual intercourse with her son's closest friend and becomes traumatized to discover him also engaged in sexual intimacy with her daughter. "Gulia" portrays a woman in her sixties, if not older, who seduces the son of her closest friend and then indirectly brags about it. Ulitskaia treats female sexuality with generosity and humor. Collections of Ulitskaia's prose appeared in France and Germany before Russians saw fit to publish a volume of her fiction (1994).
18. Only desperation or a wicked sense of irony can account for the inclusion of this story in the anthology entitled *Eros, syn Afrodity* comp. S. Markov (Moscow: Moskovskii rabochii, 1991), 185–91.
19. Gorlanova here is also working within the genre of the character sketch. Despite its satirical tone and its ultimate collapsing of the two Grushnitskiis into a masculine type, the story is reminiscent of Karamzin's sober sketch of two authentically different "types" in "Chuvstvitel'nyi i kholodnyi."
20. Vasily Aksyonov recognized as much when during a conference in California in 1981 he referred to his having been trivialized through such a pluralization. See *The Third Wave: Russian Literature in Emigration*, ed. Olga Matich and Michael Heim (Ann Arbor: Ardis, 1984), 31.

21. Russian articles on Western theories of deconstruction and postmodernism, which for a while were few and far between, have increased in the last few years. Early examples include V. Ivbulis, "Ot modernizma k postmodernizmu," *Voprosy literatury* 9 (1989): 256–60; and O. Vainshtein, "Leopardy v khrame: Dekonstruktsionizm i kul'turnaia traditsiia," *Voprosy literatury* 12 (1989): 167–99. For an assessment of the two pieces, see Harriet Murav, "The Postmodern and the Post-Utopian: Some Problems in Contemporary Soviet Criticism," *Contention* 2 (Winter 1991–92): 47–63. The "Lacunae" section of the new journal *Novoe literaturnoe obozrenie,* founded in 1992, regularly contains translations of Western theorists, from Riffaterre and de Man to Deleuze.
22. Others, such as Mikhail Epshtein and Mikhail Iampol'skii, now reside and teach in the West. Epshtein's major interest lies in postmodernism, and, while he includes Tolstaya, Valeriia Narbikova, and the poets Ol'ga Sedakova and Elena Shvarts in his discussions of metarealism and other aspects of new wave writing, his perspective so far has seemed impermeable to gender. See Mikhail Epshtein, "Iskusstvo avangarda i religioznoe soznanie," *Novyi mir* 12 (1989): 222–35; and "Posle budushchego. O novom soznanii v literature," *Znamia* 1 (1991): 217–30 (trans. as "After the Future: On the New Consciousness in Literature," *South Atlantic Quarterly* 90, no. 2 [Spring 1991]: 409–44). Iampol'skii, a sophisticated comparatist fluent in French and French theory, tends to omit mention of gender even in his work on the politics of body discourse, as does the equally impressive but even more male-oriented Valerii Podoroga. See Mikhail Iampol'skii, "Vina—pokaianie—donos," *Stanford Slavic Studies* (1992): 206–37; and Valerii Podoroga, "Znaki vlasti (zapisi na poliakh)," *Kinostsenarii* 4 (1991): 179–91. Some of Iampol'skii's writing, however, such as his discussion of Kira Muratova's *Aesthetnic Syndrome,* opens up his criticism to the possibilities of a gender deconstruction.
23. For a translation of these essays, with a foreword on which my comments here expand, see *Skirted Issues: The Discreteness and Indiscretions of Russian Women's Prose, Russian Studies in Literature* (Spring 1992). All citations from these reviews are identified by page references to this issue.
24. On sex-role socialization in the USSR, see Lynne Atwood, *The New Soviet Man and Woman* (Bloomington and Indianapolis: Indiana University Press, 1990). For an examination of the influence theoretical writings and official programs exerted on gender formation and women's status in Soviet Russia, see Mary Buckley, *Women and Ideology in the Soviet Union* (Ann Arbor: University of Michigan Press, 1989).
25. On the conventions guiding classification and on the saliency of the "semiotic nature" of texts to any taxonomical enterprise, see Gary Saul Morson, *The Boundaries of Genre* (Austin: University of Texas Press, 1981).
26. See Evelyn Fox Keller, "Feminism and Science," *Signs* 7, no. 3 (1982): 589–602 (reprinted in *Women, Knowledge and Reality,* ed. Ann Garry and Marilyn Rearsall [Boston: Unwin Hyman, 1989], 175–88); also Donna Har-

away's two articles in *Signs* 4, no. 1 (1978): 21–60; Emily Martin, "The Egg and the Sperm: How Science Has Constructed a Romance Based on Stereotypical Male-Female Roles," *Signs* 16, no. 3 (1991): 485–501; and Helen E. Longino, "Can There Be a Feminist Science?" in Garry and Rearsall, *Women, Knowledge and Reality*, 203–16.

27. Mikhail Zolotonosov addressed this issue in connection with Liudmila Ulitskaia's novella *Sonechka* (1992), in a review article that rescues what he calls Ulitskaia's neosentimentalism from the hackneyed vapidness of "women's prose" (Mikhail Zolotonosov, "Chuvstvitel'nost' s pristavkoi 'neo,'" *Moskovskie novosti* 6 [7 February 1993]: 5).
28. See Jane Tompkins, "Sentimental Power: *Uncle Tom's Cabin* and the Politics of Literary History," *Feminisms*, 20–39. See also Mary Kelley, "The Sentimentalists: Promise and Betrayal in the Home," *Signs* 4, no. 3 (1979): 434–46.
29. Chukovskii's essay returns to his earlier review, published in 1910, of A. Verbitskaia's prose, which tried to map out the generic traits of the ladies' novella without actually using that label. Il'ina's better-known article borrows Chukovskii's tone and style of sardonic devaluation. See "Verbitskaia," in Kornei Chukovskii, *Sobranie sochinenii*, 6 vols., (Moscow: Khudlit., 1969), 6:10–21.
30. On the "social invisibility" of women's experience, see Russ 39–48.
31. Some eighty years ago Virginia Woolf ironized this entitlement of masculine values through what Russ calls the "double standard of content": "This is an important book, the critic assumes, because it deals with war. This is an insignificant book because it deals with the feelings of women in a drawing-room. A scene in a battlefield is more important than a scene in a shop" (Virginia Woolf, *A Room of One's Own* [New York: Harcourt, Brace and World, 1929], 77).
32. On this, see Phyllis Chesler, *About Men* (New York: Simon and Schuster, 1978), 106–7.
33. In this regard, see the disclaimers by Rimma Kazakova reported in Elaine Feinstein, "Poetry and Conscience: Russian Women Poets of the Twentieth Century," In *Women Writing and Writing about Women*, ed. Mary Jacobus (London: Croom Helm, 1979), 136–37.
34. Interview with Liudmila Petrushevskaia, taped by Helena Goscilo, Moscow 1988.
35. Reviewers have tended to discuss the works of I. Grekova, N. Baranskaia, M. Ganina, and V. Tokareva within the context of "typical women's writing." Tolstaya and Petrushevskaia have escaped this fate, but not without penalties: Soviet Russian critics routinely point to Tolstaya's coldness and cruelty and Petrushevskaia's grim harshness.
36. Shcheglova's polemic with Chuprinin ("I refuse [*sic*] to see in this literature the 'important sociopsychological, worldview embracing, artistic phenomenon' that he has found in it" [34]) recalls the original debate about the

"other," or "alternative," prose between Chuprinin and Dmitrii Urnov in *Literaturnaia gazeta* 6 (8 February 1989): 4–5.

37. On women's prepositional relationship to men, see Elaine Showalter, "Review Essay: Literary Criticism," *Signs: Journal of Women in Culture and Society* 1, no. 2 (Winter 1975): 452.
38. The concept of cross-dressing in both literal and metaphorical senses is, of course, alien to Russian critics, despite such famous cases as Nadezhda Durova's enlistment in the "all-male" army during the Napoleonic Wars. In this connection, see her memoirs; Nadezhda Durova, *The Cavalry Maiden*, trans. Mary Fleming Zirin (Bloomington: Indiana University Press, 1988).

    It requires the omission of Simone de Beauvoir from histories of existentialist thought for the sartorial metaphor to work, but overlooking Beauvoir as anything more than an appendage to Sartre has not overly troubled Western specialists in existentialism, let alone Basinskii. On this, see Margaret A. Simons, "Sexism and the Philosophical Canon: On Reading Beauvoir's *The Second Sex*," *Journal of the History of Ideas* 51, no. 3 (July–September 1990): 487–504.
39. On kindred male responses to female fiction in turn-of-the-century England, see Elaine Showalter, *Sexual Anarchy: Gender and Culture at the Fin de Siècle* (New York: Penguin Books, 1990). Showalter argues that, since for the new women of the 1880s and 1890s, feminine "difference" was the basis of a "developing Female Aesthetic," writing fiction was regarded as a "political act of sexual solidarity." That fiction sought new narrative modes for its explorations of female sexuality, marriage, divorce, and single motherhood, availing itself of such alternative fictional forms as dream narratives, fantasies, utopias, allegories, and fragments (64).
40. Basinskii operates within the confines of a goal-oriented social realism, which adheres to a moralized concept of literature and a hypermoralized view of womanhood.
41. A proponent of immaterialism, the Irish philosopher, in his *Three Dialogues Between Hylas and Philonous* (1713) and *A Treatise Concerning the Principles of Human Knowledge* (1710), argued that the mind or experience is essential to the universe.
42. The publication of a recent volume of essays, *Women in Russia: A New Era in Russian Feminism*, ed. Anastasia Posadskaya (London and New York: Verso, 1994), constitutes a tiny but essential step in this process. Although some of the essays indicate ignorance of Western scholarship on Russian gender issues, the fact that the collection has appeared in the West paradoxically will likely increase its prestige in Russia, drawing broader attention to the research of the scholars at the Gender Center, who constitute the majority of contributors.
43. On the fruitfully destabilizing aspects of Tolstaya's narrative, see Goscilo, "Monsters Monomaniacal."

4

Inscribing the Female Body in Women's Fiction: Stigmata and Stimulation

> In the novel I wanted to compensate for the absence of corporeality in Russian literature.
>
> —Vladimir Sorokin, Interview

Some time in the 1980s Russian women's fiction shed its threadbare Romantic habits for new modes of gendered representation. Until then the idealizing impulse of Platonism, bequeathed by the Romantics, had shaped literary treatments of women's physicality. As the incarnation of the sublime ideal that tantalized and tormented the male subject, woman (the dis- or misplaced Goal) was inscribed metaphorically or metonymically according to the dictates of the unitary aesthetic that Paul de Man justly attributes to the Romantic imagination. Hence, her appearance intimated the transcendent mysteries of that vague "beyond" that so beguiled Shelley, Coleridge, Hoffmann, Lermontov, Gogol, and Odoevskii,[1] while also permitting the Lavaterian observer to "read" and interpret her physiological "text" according to conventions that unhesitatingly extrapolated character traits from individual physical features.[2]

Generalized into a vague blur of ethereal beauty, in Russia as elsewhere, woman's form was reduced to symmetry, delicacy, and harmony, its specifics carefully confined to large, expressive eyes ("mirror of the soul"), porcelain pallor, and clouds of hair.[3] While religious icons (angel, Virgin Mary) dominated the conceptualization of womanhood, euphemism and lyrical effusions desexed any bodily part associated with potential sensuality (e.g., breasts, hips, feet). In that respect women's writing of the 1830s intersected with men's, as amply evidenced by the narratives of Nadezhda Durova, Elena Gan, Evdokiia Rostopchina, and Mariia Zhukova.[4] For the psychological process of internalization shaped women's self-perception in conformity to the gendered binarism that rules malestream Russian thought in the spheres of social, political, and cultural activity. While acquiescing to their relational identity as lesser antithesis, female authors for the most part opted for a double interiority, fictionally inscribing themselves from within and, moreover, primarily as vessels of thought and above all emotions.

The totalizing aesthetics of Romanticism demanded that female virtue assume a correspondingly attractive external form ("beautiful inside and out"), and vice signal its presence through obverse (comparably visible) clues. That morally polarized code entrenched itself so firmly that, as late as the second half of the century, it dictated the descriptive particulars of the contrast between Turgenev's transparent innocents ("turgenevskaia devushka" [the Turgenevian girl]) and his experienced sexual predators, for example, the snake-haired Polozova (*Veshnie vody* [Spring Torrents]); or between Tolstoi's girlish, "truthful-eyed" Kitty Shcherbatskaia and Anna Karenina, whose lush figure, springy step, and riotous curls collectively implied an excess of sensual appetite.[5] According to this economics of the female body, minimalism conveyed morality; voluptuousness evoked voluptuariness.[6]

If the 1890s witnessed a belated readiness to extend literary possibilities for inscribing women's bodies,[7] any developments achieved by the 1920s were abruptly curtailed in the ensuing decade. The imposition of puritanical caveats by the caretakers of Soviet ideology, together with systematic official campaigns for population increase, led to the exaltation of women's maternal and uxorial capacities at the expense of their sexuality. Accordingly, Soviet literature adapted the Romantic aesthetic of the preceding century to the pseudomodern Russian context, now highlighting the maternal instead of the virginal aspects of the Madonna paradigm. Unlike her fragile Romantic counterpart, the new Soviet heroine exhibited superhuman resilience and strength but shared with her swooning predecessor traumas that novelists invariably cast as emotional, sometimes physical, but rarely sexual.

In the (post)glasnost era the young generation of female authors producing so-called new women's prose has reversed that protracted trend. Writers such as Nina Gorlanova, Marina Palei, Nina Sadur, Liudmila Ulitskaia, Larisa Vaneeva, and Svetlana Vasilenko have elaborated a strategy of externalization, of maximal palpability, whereby not tearful lamentations but the female body—as the text's physical and tropological center—testifies to women's experience. Female bodies "document" their owners' suffering and degradation: they bruise, hemorrhage, and break; they endure rape, childbirth, abortion, beating, and disease; they succumb to substance addiction, incontinence, and sundry dehumanizing processes—all painstakingly detailed in slow motion. Hence, the fastidious distress among Russian critics that current women's prose has betrayed women's fabled uplifting mission of defleshed inspiration—*das ewig Weibliche* or the *Prekrasnaia dama*—by sinking into the muck and mire of physiology. From this viewpoint the reassuringly euphemized connotativeness of the female body has degenerated into the literalized dysphemism of gross, violated flesh. Whereas the Romantic heroine's defleshed body projected the harmonious bliss of a paradise to be attained or regained, the body of today's heroine inscribes the torments of a living hell—hence, the recurrent motif of the Dantesque circle (*krug*) in recent women's fiction.[8]

As the site of a unitary aesthetic ideology, women's earlier corporeal self was generalized and sanitized into the classical body—closed, disciplined, and permitted only two forms of effluvia: picturesque tears of sorrow (with the Pietà as iconic precedent) and maternal milk (nurture). The fluids now entering and exiting women's orifices, by contrast, are blood, semen, mucus, bile, urine, and alcohol (Emma Bovary's death sequence magnified to the *n*th power and systematically intercalated throughout a text). If earlier visual insignias of reformative immaculate beauty such as marble-white foreheads, modestly downcast eyes, and ethereal grace elicited the distanced aesthetic pleasure of contemplation, current details of bruised faces, bloated stomachs, and bloodied thighs provoke moral outrage or visceral revulsion on readers' parts. Whereas modified deviations from propriety-bound conventions formerly reinforced those very conventions, inasmuch as they invariably signaled infractions of a (putative) norm, those erstwhile infractions now constitute the norm.

New women's prose spotlights the grotesque body, the uncensored, disruptive body of apertures and appetites—Bakhtin's lower bodily stratum. It opens up the female body to "unsanitary" activity.

And it raises several related issues: (1) the possible functions of body inscription in literature, (2) the probable motivation for the current displacement of the classical body with its grotesque counterpart, and (3) the potential benefits of the new modes of fictionalizing female physicality as manifested in the prose of women writers.

What You See Is What You Get?
The Palpability Trap

> Seeing is believing. —Thomas the Apostle

As Wendy Steiner, among others, has observed, "painting until very recently has been taken as mimetic, a mirror of the world" (Steiner xii). Accordingly, visibility purportedly vouchsafed verisimilitude, a transparent means of conveying the "truth of reality" through the palpable medium of paint (a kindred accuracy was later attributed to photography). Translated into the verbal—thus presumably more labile—form of fiction, the illusion of visibility was rendered primarily through accretion of concrete physical detail that consorted with other modes of characterization, such as action and dialogue, to produce the credible image of a person as well as of place and time.

Within this sphere the body, quite predictably, constituted the chief information center or locus of verification, particularly after the influential publications of Lavater's physiological and Gall's phrenological studies. Hermeneutics of the body presupposed a continuity between outer (visible) and inner (invisible) self to such an extent that any disjunction carried shock value and warranted commentary.[9] Physical portraits as "speaking pictures" of individuals, whether genred simply as physiological sketches (e.g., Lermontov's "Maksim Maksimich") or meta-genred as *ekphrasis* (e.g., in *Anna Karenina*),[10] attest to the saliency of a materialized "body language" for the construction of fictional human identity.

The body language that proliferates in current Russian women's fiction, however, serves different ends. Rarely invoked in order to characterize or to reinforce credibility along a continuum of increasing verifiability (from intangible to material), it sooner fulfills the rhetorical function of metonymically installing authorial and authoring premises instead of pseudoconcretizing authored beings. In other words, alcoholism in Liudmila Petrushevskaia and Vaneeva, rape in Vasilenko and Tat'iana Nabatnikova, abortion in Palei and Gorlanova do not so much index the moral laxity of individual fictional personae as they inscribe the epistemological and conceptualizing habits that produce specific fictions or texts.

Given the extraordinary power of body rhetoric in Russia today, to read the debased body in women's fiction as merely body and thus symptomatic of physical brutality under deteriorating living conditions is to ignore both the tropological properties of the body and the highly differentiated interpolation of the body as rhetorical device by various practitioners of women's prose.[11] Petrushevskaia, for instance, reverses discursive traditions by tabooing the emotional-spiritual dimension of experience privileged in nineteenth-century prose and replacing it with a lexicon of physiological processes as the sole permissible (unadulterated) mode of discourse (Goscilo, "Petrushevskaia's Vision"). Tolstaya à la Paul de Man explodes the assumptions behind totalizing readings by positing a definite disjunction between body and soul (physical versus imaginary or spiritual; outer versus inner).[12] Valeriia Narbikova employs sexual acts to spotlight textual practices, and so forth.

What I wish to consider first in this tripartite examination is the fictional body use of two relatively unknown writers, Larisa Vaneeva and Svetlana Vasilenko, who in the last few years have captured Russian readers' attention partly through their unorthodox approach to female corporeality. Unlike the older generation of women writers who disavow the traditionally discredited rubric of "women's writing," both Vaneeva and Vasilenko assert their specifically female personal and authorial identity; both draw on visual forms (painting and film) conceived in a modern(ist) vein: that is, they favor ellipses, temporal and spatial discontinuity, juxtaposition of ostensible incompatibles, uneven emphases, and all manner of crossovers and lacunae; and both incorporate multiple aspects of formerly tabooed physicality into their texts in a provocative manner.

Passionately committed to ecological causes and inclined to lyricize nature and the cosmos in sometimes hyperbolic purple prose, Vaneeva presents women's bodies from a worm's-eye perspective that makes pastel-hued sentimentalists out of Zola and onanistic Peeping

Toms. "Parad planet" (Parade of the Planets) is a quintessential Vaneeva text, inasmuch as it proceeds through an imperfectly meshed alternation via quasi-direct discourse of passages steeped in transcendent exaltation, on the one hand, and seamy physiological "naturalism," on the other.[13] The story's narrative follows the zigzags of Vaneeva's typical protagonist—an intensely reflective but doomed woman—in this case, Saveleva, as she records experiences that may have occurred in empirically corroborated reality or merely figured in her substance-abused imagination.

Saveleva's identity is established initially through her limbs—swollen, painful, squashed into boots intended to render her physically appealing (although her nicotine abuse might eventually necessitate amputation of her legs, doctors warn her). That identity of apocalypticized seductiveness becomes elaborated through references to her "most exquisite Chardinesque bust" and "Tatar Mongolian" lower parts (326); her short plump legs; her hair, from which she plucks the grey; and her long neck, meant for "kisses and axes" (322)—indeed, her husband attempted to strangle her several times. A sexually experimental alcoholic, Saveleva has a drug-addicted seventeen-year-old daughter whom she used to beat regularly but now accepts into her own bed, even though afterward she feels compelled to sterilize the bed linen and disinfect the bathtub.

In rapid succession Vaneeva tosses her protagonist as well as her reader between the two extremes of "rank physiology" and elevated abstraction. Saveleva's fragmented recollections of last night's odyssey of epic drinking and three-way sex are interspersed with philosophical ruminations about (and inner flashes of) spiritual bliss, extraterrestrial invasion, and inexplicable nirvanalike moments of universe-embracing ecstasy. Not unlike Venedikt Erofeev in *Moskva Petushki* (Moscow to the End of the Line), Vaneeva shades alcoholic haze into creative transports—as if conventionally perceived corporeal debasement were inseparable from visionary powers and a yearning for transcendent cosmic unity: *in vodka sanctitas.*

With no psychological depth to anchor Saveleva's character, her actions and thoughts are insufficiently individualized to be predictable, consistent, or, minimally, even subject to analysis along conventional characterological lines. *Faute de mieux,* Saveleva becomes the sum of her body details and her semimystical tirades, with empty space in between. Such emphatic omissions regularly mark Vaneeva's texts, whose jagged, disconnected lines of "information" require input from the reader willing to reconstitute a radically segmented form. In fact, the title of Vaneeva's collection, *Iz kuba* (From a Cube), adverts to her links with modernist art, with its collation of disparate spheres in reduced, two-dimensional fragments.

Since in "Parade of the Planets" bodily foul play appears to provide access, possibly, to quasireligious vision, *body* may be read as a "celestial body" of sorts and simultaneously as the overwhelming presence of flesh, relentlessly addicted to a ritualistic engorging and disgorging. Despite the depressing squalidness of habitual physical abuse and overuse, which drive the text, the distance between vodka-soaked flesh and incandescent imagination and visionary power seems so effortlessly traversed as to undergo erasure. In short, the body functions as the ambiguous locus of Vaneeva's binary polarity: meat and mysticism. The body in Vaneeva is central not only to physical appetite but also to "out-of-body" experience.

In Vasilenko's fiction, by contrast, the female body resists stable identification with any single phenomenon. It functions, in fact, as the field through which passes every conceivable experience, open to endless signification. A source of joy and suffering, the corporeal self is both metaphor and material entity, subject and object, depending upon the specifics of the given moment. As signifier, it floats more freely than any other body in current women's prose.

Although, in light of this multiplicity, to make claims for the typicality of any Vasilenko text would be misguided and misleading, her fictional body use emerges perhaps most *forcefully* in her novella "Shamara," a latter-day women's revision of Nikolai Leskov's "Ledi Makbet Mtsenskogo uezda" (Lady Macbeth of the Mtsensk District).[14] Set in a labor camp polluted by radiation (Vasilenko's literary version of her native Kapustin Iar), the tale, tellingly and tautologically labeled *videopovest'*, is profoundly visual. In the course of its forty-odd pages the eponymous heroine's body undergoes every conceivable violation in an environment ruled by "animal life": married to the convict Ustin (one of the eight men who earlier gang-raped her), Shamara is terrorized by a hard-drinking albino soldier in an armored troop carrier, has intercourse with him to save Ustin, terminates the resulting pregnancy in her own bathtub, and gets brutally beaten by Ustin, slapped by her coworkers and the local authorities, accidentally almost killed on a rollercoaster by her hermaphroditic friend Lera, and almost murdered by an escaped sexual psychopath. The entire world of the narrative consists of people's holding knives to each other's throats, randomly fondling others' bodies, spying voyeuristically on copulating couples, attempting murder and suicide, succumbing to alcohol, and so forth.

Vasilenko, however, does not single Shamara out as victim, thereby differentiating between her and other convicts and their mates: Shamara herself resorts to violence, thievery, bullying, alcohol, and magic spells (in the style of Nina Sadur), to prevent Ustin from straying. And, more important, Vasilenko inscribes Shamara's body not only as an ambulatory testament to stoic suffering but also as a center of pleasure and aggressive appetite. Collapsing the world with her own subjectivity, Shamara recognizes in both a kindred primordial, unappeasable will—a will that Vasilenko vigorously sexualizes. Acknowledging her own needs, Shamara forthrightly articulates her sexual desire for a man, enjoys a drinking spree, and takes sensual delight in her own and others' physical appearance; in addition she perceives her surroundings in terms of sexual energy. Although shifting viewpoint within quasi-direct discourse complicates the attribution of perspective, within Shamara's character zone, inanimate objects become actively sexualized. Hence, the sun kisses her, the armored troop carrier, driven by lust for her ("*okhvachennye pokhot'iu*" [83]), flaunts itself, almost touching her with its hot flank ("*zharkin bokom*" [83]), and tears and soils her dress. Indeed, this opening scene of the novella metaphorically foreshadows the albino driver's later sexual demands on her.

In "Shamara," as elsewhere (e.g., her first story, "Za saigakami" [Going after Goat Antelopes]), Vasilenko resists both conventional narrow troping and simple materialization of the female body. Neither antithetical to mind or emotion nor a visible emblem of them, woman's body in Vasilenko has a capacity for multiple signification, including nonsignification.

As these and other women's texts evidence, the heart has lost its status as the privileged organ of women's experience, displaced by the uterus and the bodily lower stratum[15] that are the locus of women's pain and pleasure. And the specific terms and significance of that displacement in recent women's texts attest to the rehabilitation of female physical appetite, which traditional concepts of femininity stigmatized morally and aesthetically, regardless of whether that appetite was alimentary or sexual. Fictional women have regained their bodies and the expressive potential of their flesh.

Cross-Gendered Passion à la Holbein

> Suffering is permanent, obscure and dark,
> And shares the nature of infinity.
>
> —William Wordsworth, *The Borders*

Bodily discourse has acquired formidable political and rhetorical powers in Russia through the longevity and inflexibility of the comprehensive interdictions against it (Foucault 6). By contrast, official abuse of lofty abstractions has wholly discredited "idealization." Thus, while eloquent flesh "speaks," the conventional voice stays mute or elusively deflective. What formerly may have occurred behind the scenes of textual representation now solidly occupies center stage: rape in Tat'iana Nabatnikova's "Shofer Astap" (The Bus Driver Astap), Ulitskaia's "Bron'ka," and Vaneeva's "Antigrekh" (Anti-Sin); prostitution, alcoholism, and addiction in Vaneeva's "Parada planet" (Parade of the Planets) and Petrushevskaia's "Takaia devochka" (A Girl like That); prolonged, agonizing childbirth and/or abortion in Elena Makarova's "Na sokhranenii" (To Be Brought to Term), Vasilenko's "Shamara," and Palei's "Otdelenie propashchikh" (The Losers' Division); loss of control over body functions in Petrushevskaia's "Ali-Baba," "Gigiena" (Hygiene), and *Vremia noch'* (Night Time), and Palei's "Den' topolinogo pukha" (The Day of Poplar Down).[16] In visual terms women's prose has shifted from Botticelli to Daumier and Toulouse-Lautrec. Rose-petal complexions bedewed by tears—the sole permissible bodily effluvium in an age of sublimation[17]—have ceded to eyes rolling out of sockets, supurating wounds, blood trickling down thighs, and buttocks smeared in excrement.

This poetics of gross externalization was pioneered by Petrushevskaia, universally acknowledged as the patron saint of the "new physiology."[18] Indeed, if all nineteenth-century male authors came out from under Gogol's overcoat, then today's young female prosaists have emerged from under Petrushevskaia's skirt. The vividness and wealth of concrete physical detail (regarding bedwetting, defecation, brutal violence, etc.) in her works and theirs have elicited revulsion, opprobrium, and bemusement from critics accustomed to the decorum of omission, periphrasis, or euphemizing tropes.[19] To dismiss this phenomenon—what Russians call "*chernukha*" (grime and slime)—as merely a vulgar flaunting of newly acquired freedom in the interests of *épatage* is to underestimate the profound metamorphosis in psychology and aesthetics that women writers have sustained and written into their texts.

To illuminate further what energizes this volte-face in women's fiction, I shall analyze two stories, by Ulitskaia and Elena Tarasova, in light of three discrete moments in Russian culture that my reading brings together: (1) literary representations of Jesus Christ; (2) a key scene in Dostoevskii's *Idiot;* and (3) a comment by Tatyana Tolstaya during a conference on contemporary women's writing.

Jesus

Apart from the reactive roles of the grieving Virgin Mary (Mater Dolorosa) and Mary Magdalene (the whore redeemed by a "good man"), Christ's Passion is an all-male drama. Not only its Pater-Director, central hero, secondary characters, and apostle-reporters but also the literati who subsequently interpolated or recast "the greatest story ever told" (Andreev, Belyi, Blok, Bulgakov, Pasternak, Aitmatov, Shukshin, Slapovskii) are men. The complex persona of Christ provided Western letters with an endlessly evocative symbol ideally suited for a formidable range of metaphysical and psychological dilemmas explored in male fiction, poetry, and drama. By contrast, Christ's Passion has scarcely figured in women's texts, which, for obvious reasons, have not drawn suggestive parallels between the Son of God and their female protagonists, despite Luce Irigaray's contention that the human incarnation of the Son of God is the "most feminine of all men" (Irigaray 249).[20] Although, as exemplars of self-sacrifice, Russian women would seem perfect candidates for cross-climbing apotheosis, their culture's misogynistic habits nailed them to the pedestal, not the Cross, thereby safely removing them from the spotlight of a cosmic tragedy into the wings of a domestic farce.[21]

The Idiot

In a deceptively understated passage in Dostoevskii's *Idiot* (a novel that, significantly, questions whether beauty can vouchsafe spiritual salvation), as Myshkin and Rogozhin contemplate a copy of Holbein's painting *Christ Taken from the Cross,* Myshkin voices the paradoxical insight that the artist's depiction of Christ could make one lose faith (pt. 2, bk. 4). Although the remark goes unexplained, the reason for the painting's effect lies in its physiological treatment of a "sacred topic"—Christ's mutilated, suffering flesh gainsays his divine aspect.[22] Instead of the prettifying idealization mandated by traditional iconography, Holbein opts for an emphatically demystifying rendition of unendurable *human* agony inflicted upon a body subject to the laws of nature. For Myshkin, Holbein's Christ conjures up not the promise of eternal life but the palpable terrors of mortality.

Tolstaya

During a conference discussion of Petrushevskaia's work,[23] Tolstaya astutely observed that Petrushevskaia's (fictional and dramatic) world is devoid of God, an absence that, presumably, partly accounts for its atmosphere of relentless, irreparable despair.

The convergence of these three moments yields a plausible explanation for the strategy of enfleshment in current Russian women's fiction: female authors' turn to the paradigm of the Cross[24] for their portrayal of womanhood signals both a loss of faith in any transcendent redemption and a categorical disavowal of the woman-as-Madonna complex. The sublimated role of the Madonna (whose immaculate chastity constitutes the staple antidote to earthly love [Warner 159])[25] has proved grotesquely incommensurate with women's real-life experience as well as their literary aspirations and means. It falls short as metaphor by ignoring not only women's subjectivity but also the brutal immediacy of the manifold physical sufferings they have stoically endured. The sanitizing metaphor operates, so to speak, in bad faith. Why the male-gendered paradigm of the Cross—with its automatic evocation of filiality, *kenosis,* and paradoxical dualities—offers more auspicious tropological material for women writers becomes clear when we examine two texts that best illustrate the paradigm shift: Ulitskaia's "Narod izbrannyi" (A Chosen People) and Elena Tarasova's highly controversial "Ne pomniashchaia zla" (The Woman Who Remembers No Evil), which mark two successive stages on the route to disillusionment.

By evoking the culturally overdetermined image of the Jews, the title of Ulitskaia's story prepares the reader for victims singled out, either randomly or by some incomprehensible higher authority, for cruel hardships. Indeed, the all-female narrative explicitly tackles the issue of religious belief in the midst of colossal physical suffering via two disenfranchised groups traditionally associated with the biblical Christ: church beggars and the physically deformed. The protagonist Zinaida, her savior Katia, and the exemplary nun Evdokiia all belong to both categories, and Ulitskaia presents them sequentially—in the order of increased affliction—so as to highlight the "parable" of the story: the crippled and maimed serve a consoling function by involuntarily reminding others of their comparative good fortune. That principle of relative blessing governs the device of augmentation used to introduce the narrative's focal trinity and their mothers: however pitiable, the obese, witless orphan Zinaida, with her adrenal glandular disorder, swollen legs, and uncontrollable gluttony,[26] is less unfortunate than the streetwise Katia, a destitute, hard-drinking cripple on crutches, whose mother not only steals her husband while Katia is incarcerated on his account but refuses to register her daughter, leaving her homeless. Katia's afflictions, in turn, pale beside those of Evdokiia, a mouselike creature whose miniature, blasted body—a torso without legs, arms, or control over her movements—is carried about by her mother (also a nun). Contemplation of that devastated body inside the church as Katia is "returning God's ticket"[27] effects the epiphany that lays the cornerstone of Katia's philosophy, which she divulges to Zinaida. Ulitskaia suggests that Katia's insight, not unlike Christ's lessons, fulfills the *psychological* promise of a "new life," its efficacy as inspiration presumably corroborated, at narrative's end, by Zinaida's ability to mentally resurrect her recently deceased mother. Whether Zinaida's momentary blissful vision will be repeated or integrated into her future existence and what consequences Katia's practical faith will have for Zinaida in the long run remain open questions.

Ulitskaia boldly casts the three protagonists as regendered surrogate Christs (carrying the New Word within their crucified bodies), their suffering teleologized *not* within a domestic formula that inevitably requires women's self-sacrifice but, instead, in a broader, more philosophical context that resonates with Dostoevskii's novels. Furthermore, we see sacred motherhood desanctified and, in Katia's case, profaned, while the sufferers, whatever their spiritual achievements, are radically deglamorized: at story's end Zinaida is still fat, stupid, and ungainly; Katia lapses into a drunken stupor, her "masculine-looking" hand suffused with blood; the dehumanized Evdokiia remains as grotesquely deformed as before. The stigmata, in other words, do not disappear. What faith the text posits is born of desperation, at the lower depths (*na dne*) of human possibility, not facilely invoked as the blind, automatic optimism prescribed for women's fiction that retroactively bathes the text in a roseate nimbus. Suffering here serves a pragmatic, not exalted, purpose. And the interplay between its psychological and physical aspects profits immeasurably from Ulitskaia's skill in avoiding bathos and the formulas of gender stereotype.

Elena Tarasova's "The Woman Who Remembers No Evil" shares with Ulitskaia's story a frank treatment of female bodily dissolution and its concomitant psychological traumas; a bleak view of human (especially familial) relationships; a submerged polemic with Romantic modalities;[28] and a productively ambiguous handling of the Passion. Its gloomier perspective, however, posits no redemptive "goal" for physical suffering, which is envisioned as arbitrary and purely destructive. The emotional wasteland charted by Tarasova holds out no comfort, however fleeting, that is not delusive. Truth, John Keats notwithstanding, proves separate from beauty, if one confronts lived experience instead of capitulating to the seductive reassurance of a totalizing aesthetics.[29] The relentlessly futilitarian tenor of Tarasova's story derives from a number of related strategies: spatial manipulation; hyperbolic accretion of physiological detail; doubling and analogy; and a decrowning of the Crucifixion.

Spatial Manipulation

Tarasova's treatment of space communicates an acute sense of claustrophobia. Stasis—as a correlative for an existential "no exit"—frames the story, whose narrated time span is restricted to part of a single day, during which the heroine crouches immobile beside the oven.[30] Although retrospection temporally and spatially extends the narrative (which proceeds exclusively via quasi-direct discourse), events resuscitated through memory squeeze so tightly into the story frame as to overwhelm it. By threatening to burst its seams, the narrative mimics the uncontrollable biological forces that cause eruptions in the protagonist's flesh.

References to her experiences in the outside world likewise reinforce a stifling impression of crampedness: people press up against her on the bus, passersby constantly bombard her with inquisitive glances, the staff in the mental asylum straps the patients to their beds, etc. These devices, together with the repeated image of the circle (e.g., "*porochnyi krug*" [213]), convey the protagonist's desperate sensation of entrapment within the monstrous hulk of her blighted body.

Physiological Detail

In the grip of an unnamed syndrome analogized with Boyle-Mariotte's law, that body has undergone almost complete dehumanization: limbs swollen and twisted, the flesh distended to gargantuan proportions, veins ruptured in the scaly skin, eyes inflamed. Loss of hair and teeth and the acquisition of a beard[31] further diminish the protagonist's visual recognizability as a woman. Tarasova supplements these grisly particulars with a graphic catalog of discrete corporeal violations:[32] the heroine's loss of a finger, chopped off by a slammed car door; her father's beating her into unconsciousness; the messiness of her suicide attempt, accompanied by blood dripping from her slit wrists and regurgitation from an overdose of tablets; the bedclothes reeking of urine in the mental asylum, where patients tied to their beds helplessly soil themselves. This obsessive focus on the physiological aspect of things—psychologically motivated (in quasi-direct discourse) by the protagonist's own appearance—foregrounds the body.[33] It lends an immediacy, a concreteness, to the traditional problem, explicitly addressed by the text, of the relationship between body and soul and their respective roles in our earthly existence. Moreover, it rescues women from their association exclusively with the body in the standard binary opposition between body and soul traceable to Aristotle's contention that, "while the body is from the female, it is the soul that is from the male, for the soul is the reality of a particular body" (Agonito 43).

Doubling and Analogy

Tarasova generalizes the protagonist's condition through doubles whose deviations from physical norms offer variations on her plight: Kandalarova, a victim of gigantism and a fellow resident at the mental home; the dwarf, who slings mud at her, recognizing in her visible self his own twisted mirror image; and the ungainly hippopotamus at the zoo, with whom she overtly identifies. All represent "nature" gone awry, materialized in the abnormal body that renders its possessor a pariah among humans. By the epistemological principles that turn all subjects into the objects of others, Tarasova's protagonist, as the unwitting target of countless gazes, becomes the superobject, her maximally heightened awareness of her object status eroding her subjectivity.[34]

Indeed, in her reflected perception the aberrancy of her corporeal self ultimately drains her humanity, degrading her to a beast. That state is ruled by animal instincts—what she calls the blood's summons (*zov*). These base impulses the asylum exposes through the inmates, who, their veneer of civilization jettisoned, revert to primordial habits: they bay and howl, crawl on all fours, unselfconsciously enact their atavistic panic at the thunderstorm that primitives endow with supernatural powers,[35] and have no control over, or memory of, their irrational, potentially destructive acts (hence, the story's title, which allies the protagonist with the mental patients).[36] With the constraints imposed by social decorum (conventional appearance) removed, humanity reveals its irreducibly animal nature.[37] The hierarchy implied by such a scenario locates the human mind between the (lower) animal body and the (higher) divine spirit.[38] Since one of the richest cultural signs implicated in such an ordering is Christ's Crucifixion, Tarasova makes extensive use of it throughout.

Decrowned Passion

The narrative engages Christ's Passion directly: the protagonist compares herself to Christ, notes that it is her thirty-third birthday, refers to her own and others' crucifixion, and so forth. Furthermore, the text specifically raises the paradox inherent in the cross-drama that distressed Dostoevskii's Myshkin—the reliance of spiritual faith on a specific visual aesthetics:

> Yes, she was now the age of the man-God. But they crucified him graceful and healthy at thirty-three. In all his portrayals, he's not so beautiful in the face, but he's lean and youthfully graceful, and with his whole body, not yet grown cold, he wants to live, live! She not only didn't want to live, but couldn't. Yet there was no way she could die. If only they'd crucified her instead of him, the man-God. But no one would bow to such a deity: gods shouldn't elicit revulsion. . . . A purplish-red, bloated carcass hanging down from the cross. . . . People probably believe only in the beautiful and healthy. (212)

Through contrast within parallel, the passage confronts the philosophical, psychological, and artistic dilemma of the presumed (or desired) congruence between the visible and the intangible, the body and the psyche, the animal/human and the divine.

Christ's salvatory mission required the accommodation of two contradictory imperatives: one evidentiary (pragmatic), the other aesthetic. On the one hand, palpable proof of Christ's agony (as man) necessitated recognizable signs of corporeal pain according to some human measure—hence, the blood and the stigmata, to convince the doubting Thomases of the world. Yet to convey the sublimity of Christ's self-abnegation and his ability to transcend mortality (as god) required a degree of spiritualized beauty. Historically, the dominant iconographic solution to this two-pronged dilemma has been the reassuring idealization via denial of brutal body disfigurement that Holbein's painting abjures and Tarasova's text deconstructs.[39] Only beauty, as Tarasova's protagonist bitterly argues, can captivate an audience so as to make the argument for faith and compassion (the lure of unitary aesthetics). "Ugliness" or anomaly, by contrast, fails to get a broad hearing, for at best it breeds skepticism and unease, at worst hatred and revulsion. The Word that Tarasova's protagonist disseminates, in tune with the body it inhabits, proclaims corrosive negation to a miniscule audience—specifically, a neighbor's naive daughter, whom she "infects" with her bile. Unlike Ulitskaia's Katia, Tarasova's protagonist discounts any "legitimate" purpose, however vestigial, in physical deformation. Indeed, the very belief in such a purpose rests on an assurance vested in beauty itself.

Although Tarasova's narrative seems to valorize body aesthetics in a manner alien to Ulitskaia, "The Woman Who Remembers No Evil," in fact, deliberately complicates the relationship of body and soul by blurring chronology. The protagonist's insistence that the soul reflects ("repeats" [*povtoriaet*]) the body appears, on first glance, merely to reverse the weary formula of "beautiful inside and out." Tarasova, however, firmly anchors that ostensibly familiar mirroring principle in a "realistic" psychology that ultimately bifurcates body and soul: physical injuries leave their mark on the soul, but, whereas the body can heal completely, the soul retains permanent scars. In that sense it has memory, which the animal-like inmates of the mental hospital where "prosto vse obnazhennoe i goloe, vse—obnazhennaia plot" ([simply everything is bared and naked, everything is bared flesh], 205), lack.

What destabilizes the protagonist's philosophy in this regard is the revelation, delayed until midpoint in the story, of her recoil from carnality since early adolescence. Predating her sickness, that revulsion at *all* flesh prompted multiple acts of self-mortification: "rezala pal'tsy tupym nozhom, tushila o ladoni zazhennye spichki, kolola veny tupymi, rzhavymi bulavkami, prizhgla kak-to ruku raskalennym dokrasna nozhom" ([she cut her fingers on a blunt knife, extinguished burning matches on her palms, pricked her veins with blunt, rusty safety-pins, and burned her hand with a red-hot knife], 202). Although this stage anticipates the visible onset of her disease, Tarasova purposely leaves hazy whether it actually symptomatizes the initial psychological effects of the mysterious syndrome. Even as the protagonist attributes her sudden plunge into spiritual vacuity and indifference ("polnaia bezdukhovnost', kruglyi vnutrennii nol' . . . chernaia dyra" [complete lack of spirituality, a perfect inner zero . . . emptiness, a black hole], 197) to her medical condition, she pointedly notes that her retrospective version of events may be dictated by psychological expediency. In the final analysis Tarasova remains noncommittal about origins. Whether the protagonist's spiritual malaise and her abhorrence of the flesh transformed her body into its current hideous state or whether physical decay corroded her psyche remains a question that Tarasova purposely leaves open. Her interest lies not in providing answers but, rather, in meeting the challenge of exploring in a *novel* fictional form an *immemorial* metaphysical problem: the opposition of soul/body and spirit/matter—an antimony gendered in Western culture and thus of paramount importance to feminists (to which I shall return). The freshness of Tarasova's treatment springs partly from her disregard for institutionalized literary inscriptions of gender.

A particularly striking aspect of the two stories under analysis is that their intensive focus on the female body is not sexualized. If the physical body here functions as a symbolic medium, as Mary Douglas contends it inevitably must (122), that symbolism operates within an emphatically philosophical system.[40] Although both authors convey the palpability of the flesh, unlike Petrushevskaia, Vaneeva, Gorlanova, and Vasilenko—all writers who likewise register its vulnerability and anguish—Ulitskaia and Tarasova write as though literary conventions have not overdetermined women's bodies as the stimulus to male sexual desire. Instead of embracing or polemicizing against that tradition, they simply ignore it.[41] Furthermore, by crossing gender boundaries in their appropriation of Christ's crucified flesh as precedent and homologue, they culturally redefine the possibilities for inscribing women's bodies. Neither icons of probity nor idols of perversity,[42] those bodies as trope and legible testament of suffering mortality reorient the metanarrative of women's fiction from romantic passions to the singular Passion.[43] Whatever its redemptive powers (null in Tarasova's godless universe, infinitesimal in Ulitskaia's less tragic scheme of things), regendered Passion marks a watershed in contemporary Russian women's writing.

The Pleasures of Lipped Subjectivity or the Hormoned Heroine

> How can I tell you that there is no possible evil in your sexual pleasure—you who are a stranger to good(s).
>
> —Luce Irigaray, "When Our Lips Speak Together"

In addition to enriching discursive strategies, the rediscovery of physicality, as well as the elimination of a puritanical censorship in Russia,[44] has facilitated (or coincided with, if one does not wish to beg causality) a revival of sexuality that no longer requires neutralizing mediation in contemporary fiction. In this atmosphere of receptivity to what was previously anathemized, readers of current women's prose have witnessed the emergence of the Tom Jonesian post-Soviet heroine—Tomasina Jones, as it were—hard on the heels of the sexless Soviet Shamela. Whether in the variant of the pigtailed Komsomolka, the kasha-stirring mother, or the homey and homely helpmate, this hormoneless paragon belonged to the gendered images fabricated by the ideological state machinery that logically drove a woman on national Soviet television to the absurd, and by now notorious, assertion: "We have no sex."

The fictional rehabilitation of female sexuality is dramatized through the newly hormoned heroine who dominates a series of works from the 1980s and 1990s that recast women's desire. Formerly domesticated and desexualized into the civic zeal of communal Soviet maternity, that desire is now foregrounded as individual bodily pleasure conveyed through female subjectivity. A far from exhaustive list of pertinent texts might include Tolstaya's "Ogon' i pyl'" (Fire and Dust, 1986); Galina Shcherbakova's "Tri 'liubvi' Mashi Peredreevoi" (The Three "Loves" of Masha Peredreeva, 1990), written in 1985; and "Dochki, materi, ptitsy i ostrova" (Daughters, Mothers, Birds, and Islands, 1991); Vasilenko's "Za saigakami" (Going after Goat Antelopes, 1982) and "Shamara" (1990); Palei's *Kabiriia s Obvodnogo Kanala* (Cabiria from the Bypass, 1991); and Ulitskaia's "Gulia" and "Lialin dom" (Lialia's House, *Bednye rodstvenniki,* 1990).[45]

With few exceptions, mainstream Russian literary tradition punished women's unsublimated sexual pleasure through death or diminished and trivialized its importance through ridicule. Active female sexuality symptomatized flaw, anomaly, or excess—something to be overcome or extirpated, certainly not indulged. Sexual women were figures of fun (to be derided, like Zamiatin's fishy U in his novel *My* [We]) or doom (to be eliminated, like Tolstoi's Anna Karenina, Leskov's Lady Macbeth, and Zamiatin's I-330). Moreover, the tradition packaged woman's pleasure as an outgrowth or corollary to romantic love, restricted its experience to young women in tragic cases (to older women in comic ones), alluded to it in periphrastic euphemism, and filtered it through a male perspective.

By contrast, new women's prose fully and unjudgmentally

acknowledges female pleasure as physical appetite; refers to it and to various other bodily processes, such as menstruation and birthing, with calm explicitness; and allows that pleasure either to speak directly or through the mediation of another woman's vantage point. The specific mode and significance of that pleasure are remarkable for their diversity as well as their departure from canonical inscriptions.[46]

In these narratives decades-old concepts of female modesty, propriety, monogamy, and "dignity in old age" operate chiefly as categories to be overturned. Vasilenko's Shamara, for instance, guiltlessly enjoys getting drunk with a female friend, loudly articulates her desire for a "man" (not the italicized One and Only but the lower-case generic man), and readily has intercourse with "the enemy" to purchase the release of her lover from jail. Shcherbakova's Masha matter-of-factly decides to experiment with selling her body on the market of informal prostitution, only to come away with no money and a pregnancy, which she parlays into a safe berth with the family of a boyfriend who did *not* father her child. Ulitskaia's sixty-something-year-old Gulia (whom Soviet social and literary conventions would automatically relegate to "babushkadom") with glee and gusto sets out to seduce her closest friend's son and later relishes bragging about her success to her fellow pensioners. Moreover, Shcherbakova, Tolstaya, Palei, and Ulitskaia manage to inscribe female lust as a healthy drive that they nevertheless treat with irreverent, demythologizing humor. Without embracing Fay Weldon's mordant bleakness, they share her sardonic skepticism regarding the relationship between love and sex.

One of this fiction's boldest innovations is its readiness to push to its sexualized "logical" conclusion the perception of fundamental sameness across generations: "My Mother, Myself." Translated into plot, this chronological mirroring entails a young man's sexually servicing both mother and daughter, an emotionally freighted triangulation more common in Western film (e.g., Pasolini's *Teorema* and Peter Greenaway's *The Draughtsman's Contract*) than in Russian literature. That scenario is played out (with humor) in Shcherbakova's "Daughters, Mothers, Birds, and Islands" and in Ulitskaia's "Chosen People" and (with complex implications to which I shall return later) "Lialia's House." As an inevitable consequence of such triangulation, maternity undergoes far-reaching metamorphoses, with a middle-aged mother no longer relegated to a self-effacing psychological bulwark at home but now reconfigured as a "heroine" in her own right, active instead of acted upon, capable of generating narrative.

The equation of narrative momentum with sexual energy, as noted earlier, finds most colorful exemplification in Tolstaya's "Fire and Dust," whose intriguing protagonist, Pipka (Cunty or Pussy) instantiates the punning promise of Luce Irigaray's lips "speaking together," whereby mouth and labia dovetail. Pipka's flair for spinning outrageous and seductive stories (analogized with the *Thousand and One Nights*) is inseparable from her sexual allure; indeed, her narrative talent not only magically attracts males who appear blind to her physical defects but is also the major if indirect impetus for Tolstaya's own narrative.

Sex and storytelling similarly rub together in Marina Palei's *Cabiria from the Bypass,* whose *siuzhet* (plot development) hinges almost entirely upon the sexual adventures of its lusty heroine, Raimonda (or Mon'ka) Rybnaia. Like Tolstaya's Pipka, Mon'ka is a spatially marked heroine who self-confidently arrogates to herself the male prerogative of bold movement through space in search of multiple *physical* encounters of the unmistakable kind. Both she and Pipka are, unsurprisingly, associated with liquids, nakedness, and bodily marks. And both are presented through the ironic, ambivalent reporting discourse of their antipode: the conventional Soviet woman with both feet (and the rest of the body) firmly planted in domesticity and what America now rather nauseatingly calls "family values." The skillfully deployed double-voicedness of that discourse enables Tolstaya and Palei to convey simultaneously their narrators' envious opprobrium and the seductiveness of their protagonists' irrepressible sexual verve.

What is particularly striking about some of these narratives is their deconstruction of a double binarism: not sexual aggressors but themselves objects of sexual desire, men now serve various enabling but *secondary* purposes in women's lives. But, more interesting, women's unfettered sexual activity here, contrary to custom, does *not* pull the reader back into the ancient binary opposition between body and soul that automatically feminizes materiality and masculinizes spirit. And it is worth examining how Tolstaya, Palei, and Ulitskaia—in "Fire and

Dust," *Cabiria,* and "Lialia's House"—achieve a tentative reconciliation, a negotiable route, between body and soul in their portrayal of the hormoned heroine.

Tolstaya, characteristically, seeks a solution in language, specifically, in the associative powers of metaphor. From the outset she populates her narrative with beings and objects whose names point to philosophical concepts and carry culturally loaded associations. The very title of "Fire and Dust" adverts to life and passion, on the one hand, and death and desuetude, on the other; Pipka, whose nakedness, sexual escapades, states of heat and cold, along with her name of Cunty/Pussy, evoke the physical pole of the body-soul antinomy, is consistently described in terms of her *inner* traits: her madness (i.e., rich imagination), her *gaping* mouth, from which cascades one fabulous tale after another, and her broken teeth, which become replaced with radiant whiteness ("blazing mouth filled with sparkling white teeth" [109]). Moreover, her mysterious residence of Perlovka not only irrevocably transforms whoever visits there but in its name conjures up the ancient Greek symbol of the pearl for the soul liberated from the dying body. And finally, her death, whose ambiguity suggests the nonfinality of her departure, is metaphorized as an unquenchable flame extending heavenward ("a pillar reaching to the skies" [115]). By narrative's end Pipka the fornicator becomes transubstantiated, suggesting that transcendent spirit may be part of, rather than antithetical to, sexual gourmandism.

Palei's "Cabiria" likewise leans heavily on language for destabilizing polarization. Mon'ka's disease—a defect of the heart—ultimately kills the heroine through cancer but keeps the ambiguity of her significance alive throughout the narrative. *Porok serdtsa* means not only "heart defect" but also "vice of the heart." That paronomasia leaves open the door for a moralistic view of her antics and a moralistic reading of the text. It also draws on the immemorial rhetorical tradition of troping the heart as the sanctuary of the emotions, the citadel of love. While allowing those possibilities, Palei dwells above all on the physical nature of Mon'ka's frailty and, in so doing, rescues the most overworked and overdetermined human organ in literature from an exclusively tropological status. Mon'ka's polysemous heart becomes the locus of intersection between body and soul, between a literal and a metaphorical reading of the text, just as the Bypass Canal of the title adverts both to her address and to her sexual/emotional life's path.

Among contemporary women prosaists perhaps only Petrushevskaia rivals Ulitskaia in range as regards the exploration of myriad—and normally taboo-ridden—forms of sexuality. Yet nothing could be more remote from Petrushevskaia's toughly wounded litany of horrors than Ulitskaia's restrained and extraordinarily humanized treatment of what Russian tradition would surely condemn as perverse. "Lialia's House," included in her collection titled *Bednye rodstvenniki* (Poor Relatives), explores how an unconventional wordless coupling impinges on the psyche of its protagonist.

Unlike Tolstaya and Palei, Ulitskaia does not interpose a mediating center of consciousness between Lialia and the reader, for the immediacy of Lialia's vision is critical to the story's turning point. A middle-aged, married academic with two adult children, Lialia enjoys a series of light, casual affairs until she becomes sexually hypnotized by her son's young friend Kazia. In a scene reminiscent of an analogously decisive moment between an "aggressive" female and a male "patient" in Tolstaya's "Poet i muza" (The Poet and the Muse), but much more boldly sexualized here, Lialia visits Kazia as he lies sick in bed. Baring his supine, aroused body, at his invitation she mounts him and rides her way to climax. Vowing that each time is the last, she repeatedly reprises that experience, in complete silence, until the day she arrives unnoticed, to discover her daughter Lena impaled on Kazia, engaged in the identical exertion. Until this juncture Kazia has been portrayed in overwhelmingly physical (if passive) terms: Ulitskaia emphasizes his beauty, the impressive size of his erection, his dream of disciplining his body so as to fly through space (he is the acrobat son of circus performers), and so forth. In vulgar parlance Kazia could be called the Stakhanovite "hot stud" more than capable of satisfying both mother and daughter, yet one endowed with the clichéd cultural markings of femininity (beauty, passivity, nurture).

The episode leads first to Lialia's prostration and ultimately to her spiritual awakening: after two related visions—one of Kazia in self-propelled flight, the other of a tenuous paradise—she consistently suffers from an uncontrollable sense of compassion for all the beings and objects in her orbit. In short she penetrates into the inner meaning of Virgil's phrase "*lacrimae rerum*" (*The Aeneid*) and remains irremediably, tearfully, attuned to the potential vulnerability of all matter, the fragility of the world.

While fully acknowledging woman's sexual pleasure, then, Ulitskaia collapses the binarism of body and soul without resorting to the kind of purple prose that D. H. Lawrence, the chief male apostle of programmatic fornication, favored in his philosophizing about the "metaphysical fuck." Moreover, in the figure of Lialia she erases the age-old gendered nature-culture dichotomy by making Lialia a teacher of French literature, hence presumably not only a sophisticated product, but also a professional analyst, of culture. Indeed, the tenor of the narrative implies that Lialia's acculturated side enables her receptivity to varied aspects of "nature." However cryptic the story's conclusion, even a resistant reader cannot mistake Ulitskaia's steadfast refusal to moralize or diminish her middle-aged heroine's sexual drive. Like Tolstaya and Palei, Ulitskaia entertains a more complex and richer apprehension of the human body and of female sexuality than posited by Soviet ideology and much of Western philosophy.

Without vulgarizing or idealizing the hormoned heroine, new women's prose, then, continues the process of wresting gender from a geriatric blueprint of femininity composed of pre- and proscriptions based on a politicized but hypothetical norm. This fiction encourages feminists to contemplate a utopian future in which that pseudonorm has become as much a relic of a bygone era as the busts, statues, and medals designed to immortalize the father and protofather of the Soviet Union, Stalin and Lenin.

Notes

1. See such classics of romantic exaltation as Hoffmann's "Der Goldene Topf," Shelley's "Endymion," Lermontov's "Demon," and Odoevskii's "Sil'fida," which all cast woman as the conduit to the divine.
2. On the role of Lavater's physiology and Gall's phrenology in Russian literature, see Helena Goscilo, "Lermontov's Debt to Lavater and Gall," *Slavonic and East European Review* 59, no. 4 (October 1981): 500–515. See also the series of articles by Edmund Heier: "'The Literary Portrait' as a Device of Characterization," *Neophilologus* (Amsterdam) 60, no. 2 (April 1976): 321–33; "Lavater's System of Physiognomy as a Mode of Characterization in Lermontov's Prose," *Arcadia* 6, no. 3 (1971): 267–82; "Elements of Physiognomy and Pathognomy in the Works of I. S. Turgenev (Turgenev and Lavater)," *Slavistische Beiträge* (Munich) 8 (1977). On Lavater's importance for eighteenth- and nineteenth-century fiction, see Graeme Tytler, *Physiognomy in the European Novel* (Princeton: Princeton University Press, 1982).
3. On the standard female ideal constructed in the nineteenth century, see

Martha Vicinus, *Suffer and Be Still* (Bloomington: Indiana University Press, 1972).

4. Descriptive formulas recall Heine's summary of Bellini's appearance as a "sigh in pumps." Sof'ia, the heroine of Elena Gan's "Medallion" (1839), "kazalas' vozdushhnym sushchestvom, sporkhnuvshim ne khotia na zemliu" (seemed an aerial being, who'd flitted unwillingly down to earth) (*Biblioteka dlia chteniia* 34 [1839]: 31). Elena, in Durova's *Igra sud'by* (The Play of Fate), is "devushka . . . v semnadtsat' let, sozdannaia telom i dushoi dlia ukrasheniia obshchestva" (a girl of seventeen, created in body and soul for the adornment of society) (*Biblioteka dlia chteniia* 38 [1840]: 22). The unbroken continuity posited between women's physical and spiritual/emotional selves provides a contrastive background for the hero's more complex and discontinuous identity.

   Even the independent Karolina Pavlova, in her tentatively feminist novel *Dvoinaia zhizn'* (A Double Life, 1848), teetered on the brink of purplish patches when describing her virginal heroine as "brave and beautiful"—hair thick, eyes lively, and figure especially slender in her riding habit (chap. 4).

5. For Turgenev's debt to Romanticism, see Marina Ledkovsky, *The Other Turgenev: From Romanticism to Symbolism* (Würzburg: Colloquium Slavicum /Jal-Verlag, 1973); and, more recently, Jane T. Costlow, *Worlds within Worlds* (Princeton: Princeton University Press, 1990). Although Tolstoi programmatically stressed the discrepancy between physical beauty and moral rectitude (e.g., in Mariia Bolkonskaia, on one hand, and Anatolii and Hélène Kuragin, on the other), he nonetheless espoused the seemingly deathless Romantic precept of innocent eyes as a reflection of moral purity (e.g., Mariia Bolkonskaia and Kitty).

   This binarism generated entire series of associative, value-laden nature (hence, misperceived as "natural") imagery: woman as flower, star, butterfly, deer, etc., versus woman as fire, snake, and bird of prey.

6. As Vladimir Sorokin pointed out in a recent interview, however, Russian literature lacked a palpable sense of flesh. See Vladimir Sorokin, "Provintsial'nyi 'Roman' Vladimira Sorokina," *Moskovskie novosti* 64 (18–25 December 1994): 19.

7. The 1890s and 1900s ushered in the Decadent period of Russian culture, during which permissiveness in bodily and sexual matters accommodated an unprecedented range of pseudoscientific and artistic investigations of an erotic and explicit nature—for example, by Artsybashev, Kuzmin, Rozanov, and Somov, among others. For a discussion of this transgressive phase in Russian letters as instantiated by Remizov's erotic tales, see Greta N. Slobin, "Remizov's Erotic Tales: Stylisation and Subversion," *The Short Story in Russia: 1900–1917*, ed. Nicholas Luker (Nottingham: Astra Press, 1991) 53–72.

8. Reviewers of, and authors represented in, the collection *Ne pomniashchaia*

zla (The Woman Who Remembers No Evil) have remarked on the frequency with which titles and texts resort to the image: Tatyana Tolstaya's "Krug" (The Circle), Liudmila Petrushevskaia's "Svoi krug" (Our Crowd), and T. Gorbulina's "Krug" (Circle). As the introduction to the anthology states, "nado pomnit', chto dlia zhenshchiny zamknutyi bytovoi krug, krug ada,—eto eshche i krug zhizni, predpolagaiushchii neskonchaemost' puti, ego vysokoe postoianstvo" (one should remember that for a woman the closed circle of everyday life, the circle of hell, is also the circle of life, which presupposes the endlessness of the road, its elevated constancy, 4). Lidiia Ginzburg, in "Zapiski blokadnogo cheloveka" (Notes of a Siege Survivor), conceives of the circle as the "siege's symbol of a consciousness locked within itself" that can break out of the circle through an active deed. Hence, "to write about the circle is to break out of the circle" (Decter 48–49).

9. Victor Hugo, for instance, achieved his strongest effects by regularly exploiting through violation the universal equation between angelic looks and an angelic temperament.
10. On this, see Amy Mandelker, *Framing* Anna Karenina (Columbus: Ohio State University Press, 1993).
11. As Solomea Pavlychko argues, in Ukraine, too, sex, "which appeared on the pages of literary texts for the first time several years ago, is often there merely to give the artist an excuse for exercising new vocabulary" (Solomea Pavlychko, "A Catfish for Your Thoughts: Ukrainian Literature at the Turning Point," *Agni* 39 [1991]: 194).
12. She does, however, reconcile that opposition in at least one story, as I discuss later in this chapter.
13. In *Iz kuba*, 71–89; translated in Decter 317–32.
14. A truncated translation of "Shamara" was published in *Women's View* (*Glas* 3 [1992]: 26–50).
15. Bakhtin's concept of the carnivalized body as a form riddled with activated orifices would seem particularly apt for characterizing women's physicality in recent prose, were it not for the absence of the communal spirit that Bakhtin deems critical to carnival. Less Rabelaisian than existential, the physiological dimension in current women's fiction issues from a desolate sense of "lost illusions" rather than lending itself to the robust joys of subversive celebration.
16. For good measure Petrushevskaia also includes dismemberment, in her earlier play entitled "Liubov'" (Love) and in her cycle of brilliantly grisly stories, "Pesni vostochnykh slavian" (Songs of the Eastern Slavs).
17. As Mary Douglas has remarked, tears are a special category, for they are "naturally preempted by the symbolism of washing" and, more important, are not related to the bodily functions of digestion or procreation (125).
18. For an analysis of Petrushevskaia's discursive practices, see Helena Goscilo, "Body Talk in Current Fiction: Speaking Parts and (W)holes," *Stanford Slavic Studies* 7 (1993): 145–77.

19. See, for instance, the censorious dismay of Evgeniia Shcheglova's "V svoem krugu (polemicheskie zametki o 'zhenskoi proze')," *Literaturnoe obozrenie* 3 (1990): 19–26; and the hysterical indignation of Pavel Basinskii's "Pozabyvshie dobro?" *Literaturnaia gazeta* (10 February 1991): 10. For a translation of and commentary on these articles, see the introduction to Helena Goscilo, ed., *Skirted Issues: The Discreteness and Indiscretions of Russian Women's Prose. Russian Studies in Literature* 28, no. 2 (Spring 1992); and chapter 3 of this volume. Galina Belaia, Konstantin Kustanovich, and Andrei Zorin have presented talks at conferences on the recent upsurge of physiological explicitness (which they refer to as naturalism, or "chernukha") within fiction of the last decade.
20. Catherine Clément's irresponsibly exaggerated claim that "all the women in opera die a death prepared for them by a slow plot" contains a kernel of truth, and the identification of the dying, singing "feminine figure" might account in part for the success of the rock opera *Jesus Christ Superstar* (Clément, *Opera, or the Undoing of Women* [Minneapolis: University of Minnesota Press, 1988], 45).
21. For a discussion of how in turn-of-the-century England the gender-specific iconography of the Passion became androgynous, particularly in the art of the Pre-Raphaelites, see Nina Auerbach, *Woman and the Demon* (Cambridge, Mass.: Harvard University Press, 1982). Her study offers useful commentary on the Victorian cult of sublime domesticity distilled in Coventry Patmore's "Angel in the House" (1855–56) (see Auerbach 63–109).
22. The art critic Robert Hughes emphasizes Holbein's gift for intense detail and for capturing precisely the human face and form (Hughes, *Nothing if Not Critical* [New York: Alfred A. Knopf, 1990], 31–33).
23. The occasion in question was a conference arranged around Tolstaya's visit to the University of Texas at Austin in 1990. A session devoted to contemporary women writers stimulated an exchange in which Tolstaya participated and volunteered the remark in question.
24. The felicitous phrase is Susan Sontag's, as is the aperçu that the cult of love in the West is an aspect of the cult of suffering, the latter being the supreme token of seriousness (Sontag, "The Artist as Exemplary Sufferer," *Against Interpretation* [1961; reprint, New York: Dell, 1966]). Self-sacrifice in love has become sanctified as women's true "womanly" role in Russian culture.
25. Warner's study is excellent for establishing the unchanging features in the image of the Virgin, while simultaneously tracing the permutations it underwent throughout history. Although Russian Orthodoxy traditionally has emphasized the Virgin's role of intercessor more than do other religious groups, it nonetheless venerates her for roughly the same qualities: chastity, compassion, and (maternal) love. As Warner rightly notes, the legends of the Virgin have held real women to impossible and inhuman standards of perfection.
26. For the significance of agoraphobia and various eating disorders as merely the hyperbolization of desiderata for women's conduct, see Susan R. Bordo,

"The Body and Reproduction of Femininity," *Gender/Body/Knowledge: Feminist Reconstructions of Being and Knowing,* ed. Alison M. Jaggar and Susan R. Bordo (1989; reprint, New Brunswick and London: Rutgers University Press, 1990): 13–33. Bordo partly endorses Helena Michie's thesis that female hunger "figures unspeakable desires for sexuality and power" (13), according to which gluttony would image an insatiable appetite for sex and power. Yet, in much contemporary Russian women's fiction, food is clearly compensation for impotent frustration, and its consumption lacks the joyous celebratory indulgence that Michie attributes to recent feminist inversions of Victorian values. See Helena Michie, *The Flesh Made Word: Female Figures and Women's Bodies* (New York: Oxford University Press, 1987), 12–29.

27. Katia's apostrophe to God echoes Ivan Karamazov's rejection of God's creation on account of innocents' suffering. Ivan's spiritual rebellion prompts him to "return his ticket," to refuse a world governed by the inexplicable workings of divine will. Like Ivan, Katia demands justice "here and now," not in the Heavenly Kingdom.
28. That polemic surfaces at irregular intervals: for example, when the protagonist mocks such cinematic formulas as a failed suicide that triggers an awareness of love and leads to a happy ending ("traditsionnyi triuk melodramy" [the traditional trick of melodrama, 189]).
29. As the editors of the volume, which borrowed the story's title, observe, reaction to the then twenty-two-year-old author's writing split into those who "accepted" it and those who found it unendurable. The only contemporary woman writer whose sense of terminal desolation matches Tarasova's uncompromisingly dark vision of the world is Liudmila Petrushevskaia.
30. This ironic hyperbolic installation of the standard notion that the kitchen is "woman's place," the home her sphere, provides an eloquent illustration of Bordo's thesis (see n. 25).
31. Whether such an illness actually exists is unclear. Tarasova seems to have transformed an empirical relation in physics concerning the compression and expansion of a gas at constant temperature into a disease metaphor. Called Boyle's Law or Mariotte's Law, the relationship was discovered by the British physicist Robert Boyle (1662) and the French physicist Edme Mariotte (1676).
32. These may be read as stages on her road to Calvary.
33. This constitutes but one of Tarasova's many anti-Platonist maneuvers.
34. In that existentialist sense, then, she epitomizes Womanhood according to John Berger's gendered concept of visual contemplation: men watch, while women watch themselves being watched—that is, internalize male subjectivity. See John Berger's *Ways of Seeing* (1972; reprint, London: BBC and Penguin Books, 1977). Several factors in the story, however, qualify such a reading of the protagonist's self-definition: her analogy with Christ, her attitude toward corporeality before the onset of her sickness, and her knack

for cool-headed analysis. In other words, her vision of the world and self is bifocal.

35. Consciously or otherwise, Tarasova borrows the patients' response to the storm from Bulgakov's *Master and Margarita.*
36. Loss of memory, in fact, is a symptom of the protagonist's illness.
37. Such a concept of mankind belongs to naturalist thought, solidly grounded in materialism, as evident in the writings of Emile Zola, Mikhail Saltykov-Shchedrin, Theodore Dreiser, and Frank Norris.
38. Such a hierarchy, of course, presided over artistic depictions of religious themes, illustrations to works on chivalry, and philosophical paintings, all of which rely on the vertical axis for their symbolic ordering of materials—for example, the knight on a horse beneath the open skies.
39. In Dostoevskii's last novel the episode in which Zosima's lifeless body starts to smell as it "prematurely" decays deals precisely with the psychological difficulty of reconciling the less appealing aspects of nature's laws with faith in divine transcendence.
40. The philosophical cast to Tarasova's story, in fact, prompted Pavel Basinskii, in his waspish review, to dub the narrative "Existentialism in skirts" (Goscilo, *Skirted Issues,* 89).

    Although Tarasova incorporates what may be considered the female subgenres of recipe and list into her texts, the genre in which she works is close to philosophical meditation. In addition to "Ne pomniashchaia zla," see "Ty khorosho nauchilsia est', Adam," which, with the aid of dense physiological detail and accreted lists, ruminates on humankind as arch despoiler and consumer of a world it neither knows nor comprehends (*Novye Amazonki,* ed. S. Vasilenko [Moscow: Moskovskii rabochii, 1991], 277–301).
41. Both stories relegate men to the status of hearsay characters. Even in that capacity they play a tangential role. In Ulitskaia's narrative Katia responds more strongly to her mother's betrayal than to her husband's. The two men who figure in the life of Tarasova's protagonist are her father and a Jewish fellow patient at the asylum. The only trait that distinguishes her father is his habit of beating her, presented as no different from or more significant than any other abuse she suffers. Her relations with the Jew—a much older, witty raconteur—are completely devoid of eroticism and romance. Thus, while not omitting all mention of males, both narratives take for granted their peripheral relevance to the protagonists' lives.
42. I borrow the phrase from Bram Dijkstra's study of "fantasies of feminine evil in fin-de-siècle culture," *Idols of Perversity* (New York and Oxford: Oxford University Press, 1986).
43. In this regard it is instructive to compare these texts with Turgenev's "Zhivye moshchi" (Live Relics), whose heroine Lukeriia's similarly stunted body results from a romantic rendezvous (Passion from passion) and leads to a lyricized suffering haloed by pantheistic *caritas.* See I. S. Turgenev, *Zapiski okhotnika* (Huntman's Notes).
44. A study that argues for the unforeseen benefits that accrue from censoring

literature is Lev Loseff, *On the Beneficence of Censorship* (Munich: Otto Sagner, 1984).

45. Ulitskaia's first anthology of stories, titled *Bednye rodstvenniki,* appeared in Russia in 1994, after translations had been published in France and Germany. All citations from "Gulia" and "Lialin dom" rely on the pagination of the author's manuscript.
46. For an analysis of a kindred evolution in anglophone fiction, see Gayle Greene's *Changing the Story* (Bloomington: Indiana University Press, 1991).

5

Women's Space and Women's Place

> Space is always suddenly bethinking itself: I am here, and here, and over there! It is forever cropping up somewhere at the back of your head. Not in front, but behind: sneaking up on you from the rear.
>
> —Abram Tertz, *A Voice from the Chorus*

Time and Space: Opposition Versus Union

In a recent issue of *New Left Review* an article by a geographer named Doreen Massey deplores the tendency among current sociologists and cultural commentators to privilege time over space. Surveying the most influential publications that engage the time/space issue, Massey chides Ernesto Laclau and Fredric Jameson for opposing spatiality to temporality in a characteristic maneuver of reductionist binarism and depoliticizing the realm of the spatial by equating it with stasis. Massey's critique of these related conceptualizations derives in large measure from her gender consciousness, specifically her awareness that a dichotomous dualism formulated as presence and absence (A/not-A) has come under most articulate and sustained attack from feminists, whose efforts to dismantle gendered binarism are too well-known to warrant exposition here.[1]

Dichotomous conceptualization of the A/not-A variety (exemplified in the polarized gender distinctions ingrained in most Western thought) militates against change and, Massey correctly argues, inevitably not only prioritizes the first term of the dualism over the other but also defines only the first positively.[2] Accordingly, time is conceived in terms of "change, movement, history, dynamism" ("male" categories), while "space, rather lamely by comparison, is simply the absence of these things" (Massey 72) (i.e., the lack that Western thought, with Freud's aid, has identified as "female").[3] For Jameson, as for Laclau, the temporal (i.e., dislocated, changing history) carries connotative associations with transcendence, while the spatial (i.e., the cyclical rhythm of simple reproduction) evokes immanence. In this "system of interconnected dualisms" dynamism, dislocation, History, and transcendence are coded as male (Father Time), thereby predicating stasis, cyclical reproduction, and immanence as female (Mother Earth) (74).

Rather than upgrading the status of space within the dualistic configuration, Massey concentrates on exposing the anachronistic assailability of the scientific assumptions fueling the space-time opposition (Massey 75). She legitimately contends that, by conceptualizing space as a passive arena in which objects interact—as posited in Newtonian physics—one overlooks a major principle of modern physics, which maintains that "the underlying reality consists of a four-dimensional space-time," with the identity of things *constituted through interactions* that in turn *create or define* space and time (76, 79). While Massey's refutation hits the mark, a richer, more concise, and appealing alternative to explicitly dismissing Newton in favor of Einstein is Bakhtin's chronotope theory,[4] which Massey's otherwise informed and thoroughly reasoned article utterly overlooks, perhaps out of ignorance.

The indissoluble link between time and space, as Bakhtin sensibly noted, is a prearranged marriage of true convenience, for each category unavoidably charges and is charged by the other. Today's psychobabble would label the relationship one of codependency. A divorce signals the end of narrative, which, in a sense, means the end of existence (a nod to Kant).[5] For the purposes of this essay, however, I shall impose a temporary and incomplete separation of that genuinely "dynamic duo," downplaying temporality (without bypassing it, however), so as to focus on space. Instead of subscribing to the ludicrous notion of space as an *innately* gendered phenomenon, I examine how contemporary Russian women's fiction genders space.

Throughout history the sociopolitical circumstances specific to a given culture have bred associations, which subsequently became sedimented in that culture's collective psyche, between certain locales and gender, while leaving other areas negotiable, neutered, or neglected. If one may generalize, somewhat sweepingly, that conventional gender disposition has allied women with domestic or private space (the home, the kitchen, and the nursery) and men with public or open space (be it the bank, the courtroom, or the great outdoors), as a preliminary step that broad claim needs refinement: at a minimum the male study or workshop belongs to domestic space, even if it produces items for public consumption. Furthermore, class plays a decisive role in such a comprehensive mapping, for female farm laborers inhabit a radically different space from, say, aristocratic salon hostesses, such as Mariia Volkonskaia and Evdokiia Rostopchina. So Coventry Patmore's "Angel in the House" (1855–56)—that icon of Victorian segregation—cannot blind us to the Floosie or Fiend in the Field, the temptress of Tolstoi, threshers, and tractor drivers in rural areas, as prefigured by Thomas Hardy's Tess of the d'Urbervilles.

Gendered Space: Hospitality and Hospitalization

The distinctive chronotope of the prison in nineteenth-century poetry and fiction (by Byron, Hugo, Stendhal, Dickens, and Dostoevskii) evolved into its modern variant in the camp literature authored by Aleksandr Solzhenitsyn, Varlam Shalamov, and Georgii Vladimov. Although the prison memoirs of Evgeniia Ginzburg and Irina Ratushinskaia suggest that the genre is not totally alien to women writers, the literary tradition is nonetheless male.[6] Drawing on a stable gendered tradition, the masculinized prison camp chronotope has its feminized counterpart in the chronotope of the hospital, which figures prominently in recent Russian women's prose yet lacks comparable antecedents. History and cultural convention partly account for that absence: those of the privileged classes in Russia, who during the privacy-oriented era of tsardom dominated literature as both subject and source, summoned doctors to their homes whenever they required medical attention. Patients were treated and women delivered in the familiar, personal comfort of their own beds. Thus, hospitalization, as a relatively late cultural phenomenon, occurs infrequently in literature of the nineteenth and early twentieth centuries. Moreover, whether out of squeamishness or ignorance, authors approach it obliquely, gingerly reporting it as an event occurring "behind the scenes," instead of launching into protracted descriptions of a hospital routine or patients' sufferings.[7] Exceptions occur principally in fiction concerned with war, such as Tolstoi's *Sevastopol'skie rasskazy* (Sevastopol Sketches) and *Voina i mir* (War and Peace), and countless Soviet war novels, in which the hospital mirrors the battlefield, inasmuch as it tests masculine fortitude in the face of mortal combat with a quieter version of the same dread enemy: death itself.[8]

By contrast, the civilian hospital functions as a major chronotope in numerous female texts of the last two decades, which conceptualize it primarily as carceral space. In Irina Velembovskaia's story "V trudnuiu minutu" (Through Hard Times), a male patient in a district hospital tellingly confides to the female protagonist held there overnight: "Bol'nitsa—vtoroia tiur'ma. Khot' pogovorish' s chelovekom, i to veselee" (A hospital is just another prison. At least if you talk to someone it's cheerier [193; 264]).[9] Similarly, the heroine of Inna Varlamova's novel *Mnimaia zhizn'* (A Counterfeit Life) calls the women in her cancer ward "prikovannye k tachke svoei bolezni katorzhnitsy" (branded prisoners, chained to the wheelbarrows of their disease [37; 40]).

The prison analogy operates in a number of ways. Hospitalization means confinement (if not enforced incarceration), a spatial restriction that, in narrative terms, places a special burden on time. Given the relative stasis instrinsic to a hospital or prison setting, which imposes varying degrees of constraint on customary movement, time necessarily alters its contours and significance. It swells and decelerates, permitting the epistemological and narrative luxury of perceiving things close up and in slow motion. As regimen acquires inordinate ascendancy over the lives of patients and personnel, time undergoes domestication through regular repetition that in the context of near immobility formalizes activities into ritual. On the surface this imposition of pattern dictated by the clock creates the illusion of meaningful order and control over circumstances that humans fundamentally cannot govern: the creation and cessation of life. In short the hospital chronotope structures an existentialist condition along domestic lines. It conventionalizes the shocking juxtaposition of birth and death by organizing them into kindred activities differentiated merely according to the micro-space they occupy within the larger macro-unit of the hospital.

Moreover, the systematized codes of behavior constructed by hospital personnel, along with their medical skill, enable them to exercise power over the patient. The latter, conversely, upon entering this highly regulated environment, abrogates virtually all power—over her own body, her schedule, her social milieu, and, ultimately, her fate. Rendered helpless by virtue of signing or being signed into an institution administered according to what often seem arbitrary rules, the patient typically learns to subordinate her desires to the group imperative. In her passive role of dependency upon the presumed skill of strangers, she is less active than acted upon. Hence, the unlimited potential for the transformation of the patient into a victim (e.g., in Liudmila Petrushevskaia's "Svoi krug" [Our Crowd].

Since physical incapacity or weakness limits external mobility, the "action" that transpires in narratives with a hospital setting tends, from the patient's perspective, to become interiorized. Thus, the preponderance, in this brand of fiction, of philosophical exchanges and psychological analysis and discovery (e.g., in Tat'iana Nabatnikova's "Na pamiat'" [In Memoriam]. Inasmuch as ultimate questions of existence—literally, those of life and death—are decided in a hospital, it affords an ideal venue for psychological revelations, critical turning points, and opportunities for access to self-knowledge (e.g., in Varlamova's *A Counterfeit Life*). And, from a purely practical standpoint, a hospital stay provides the contemporary Russian woman respite from the endless round of professional and domestic duties that keep her running, like Alice in Wonderland, so as to stay in the same place. In that sense *hospital* may be synonymous with *haven*, as in Petrushevskaia's "Skripka" (Violin).

In addition to closed space and a highly regularized external time that liberates an internal, reflective narrative time, a hospital setting entails division along gender lines. That differentiation accurately reflects real-life conditions in Russia and elsewhere, for medical decorum prescribes the segregation of men from women. In a broader sense, too, medicine is a gender-marked field, for nursing and orderly work ("protsedury, ot kotorykh muzhchiny obychno ukloniaiutsia, ostavliaia zhenshchinam vse nechistoe, otvratitel'noe" [the performance of the 'dirty and disgusting things that men usually disdain' 160; 139]), as I. Grekova puts it, remain female professions in Russia. Since the majority of Russian doctors are also women, the hospital ward in most women's fiction appears as an emphatically female sphere.

Within this context each patient interacts with two overlapping social groups: the chiefly female hospital personnel, stratified roughly according to principles informing any social hierarchy, and the fellow patients, brought to a common human level through the democratizing forces of medical need. A third group, normally the only one containing male members, consists of family, friends, or associates from the outside world. These visitors either open up the perimeters of the ward onto a wider social environment of which they serve as a reminder or themselves become assimilated into the narrower self-contained community at least for the duration of their visit. They remain largely alien and "Other," "outsiders" figuratively as well as literally, despite their intimacy or blood ties with the patients. Their primary narrative function—as catalysts to emotional crises or occasional passive observers on the sidelines—precludes their substantial input in sustaining the work's temporal-spatial center. In Varlamova's novel, for instance, the protagonist's "dom i vse prezhnee . . . bezvozvratno otstalo, otorvalos'" (home and all her past . . . had been left far behind, had receded into the distance [39; 42]).

Hospital conventions force representatives of all walks of life—of various political, intellectual, religious, and moral convictions, of different class, background, race, and age—to coexist, if only temporarily, side by side. Hence, the equation of a woman's hospital ward with a microcosm of the female segment of society. Moreover, a more encompassing social picture characteristically emerges indirectly from patients' conversations, which supply the more comprehensive purview in which to contextualize women's individual and collective fates. Paradoxically, a hospital ward, precisely by virtue of its spatial circumscription, automatically implies the larger context that it ostensibly excludes.

Among the numerous contemporary Russian women's narratives relying on the hospital chronotope, the most memorable are Velembovskaia's "Through Hard Times" (1965), Petrushevskaia's "The Violin" (1973) and "Bednoe serdtse Pani" (Pania's Poor Heart, 1988), Varlamova's *Counterfeit Life* (1978), Viktoriia Tokareva's "Nichego osobennogo" (Nothing Special, 1981), Grekova's *Vdovii parokhod* (Ship of Widows, 1981) and "Perelom" (The Break/Crisis, 1987), Iuliia Voznesenskaia's *Zhenskii Dekameron* (The Women's Decameron, 1985), Natal'ia Sukhanova's "Delos" (1988), Elena Makarova's "Na sokhranenii" (Carried through to Term, 1976), Nabatnikova's "In Memoriam" (1984), and Marina Palei's "Otdelenie propashchikh" (The Losers'

Division, 1980s). The commonality unduly emphasized by the juxtaposition within such a listing should not blur the appreciable differences among these texts or their authors. Some, such as Varlamova, Voznesenskaia, Petrushevskaia, and Makarova, exploit the potential of the chronotope more fully than others (e.g., Velembovskaia). Furthermore, works dealing with sickness or injury (Tokareva, Nabatnikova) must be distinguished from those focusing on pregnancy (Sukhanova, Makarova, Palei), for by definition the assumptions, expectations, and norms of the two diverge. United, nonetheless, through the shared element of the hospital chronotope, the narratives all offer a critique of the appalling conditions prevailing in Russian hospitals: outmoded equipment, ramshackle maintenance of buildings, understaffing, lack of essential medicines, insufficiently trained or outright incompetent personnel, unsanitary conditions, widespread bribery, indifference to patients, and indigestible food. In Grekova's "Break/Crisis" the immobilized doctor, like the other patients, has to bribe the nurses for practically every service they perform; a husband in *A Counterfeit Life* quite openly pays a nurse to take care of his wife, and her response of "That's too much money" confirms that receipt of funds for fulfilling standard nursely duties is standard procedure; in *Ship of Widows* the victim of a stroke is tended not by the staff but, rather, by her son, who takes up temporary residence in the hospital so as to provide her with the attention normally identified with a nurse's or orderly's responsibilities; in "Nothing Special," "The Violin," and "Through Hard Times" food brought by patients' friends and family supplements the meager or inappropriate diet supplied by the hospital facilities.

In "Pania's Poor Heart" doctors misdiagnose pregnancy as a tumor, and the mistake goes undetected for months. Varlamova observes in *A Counterfeit Life,* in which liver cancer causes the death of a patient treated for stomach cancer, that "v subbotu i voskresen'e vrachei dnem s ognem ne naidesh', ne bol'nitsa, a gostinitsa" (on Saturdays and Sundays you couldn't possibly find any doctors—it was more like a hostel than a hospital [37; 39]). In "Nothing Special" Tokareva notes:

> Medsestra ushla obizhennaia, potomu chto ee unizili pri bol'noi. A bol'nye schitalis' v bol'nitse bolee nizhnim chinom, chem medsestra i dazhe sanitarki. . . . V bol'nitse zhili svoi poriadki, po kotorym

> ne nakhodilos' togo, chto nuzhno, a bylo to, chto ne nuzhno. (*BA* 78; 562–63)
>
> [The nurse went off in a huff because she'd been humiliated in front of a patient. And patients ranked lower in the hospital than did nurses and even orderlies. . . . The hospital observed its own procedures, according to which what was needed could never be found, and what wasn't, could.]

Of one surgeon Tokareva says: "Ee bol'nye vyzhivali sovershenno sluchaino, ne blagodaria, a vopreki Paisinomu vmeshatel'stvu" (Her patients survived purely by chance, not owing to, but in spite of, Raisa's intervention. It was said that Raisa had got her job through some high connection, and to remove her was impossible [84–85; 567]). Sukhanova's story, in which an assistant's dilatoriness during an operation costs a newborn baby's life, exposes universal administrative indifference to problems of the most basic sort: "Kazhdyi den' chto-nibud' otkazyvalo: vodoprovod, kanalizatsiia, elektroprovodka. Khodil v gorzdrav, v ispolkom, v gorkom—ushi zatykali" (Every day something stopped working: water pipes, plumbing, electrical wiring. I'd go to the public health department, the executive council, the local Party branch—no one would listen [148; 69–70]).[10] These flaws in the microcosm of the hospital may be generalized into the pervasive deficiencies, the perennial shortages, and the staggering inefficiency that blight Soviet-Russian society at large, and particularly its service sector.

Owing, no doubt, to the deplorable standards of hygiene maintained in public facilities as well as to prudishness, entrenched practices that would strike most Western cultures as irrational or outmoded isolate expectant mothers from friends and family—including the expectant father—before, during, and after delivery. As a highly revealing section of Sukhanova's "Delos" argues, despite official Soviet glorification of motherhood, male-dominated society and literature find it expedient to ignore the actual process of birthing:

> Rody, beremennost'—o nikh i voobshche pisat' neprilichno: u muzhchin, pozhalui, tak i strast' pritupit'sia mozhet. . . . Nash muzhskoi razum podskazyvaet nam, chto rody ne tema dlia liter-

> atury. No imenno zhenshchiny vot v etikh rodzalakh platiat za razum. (153; 73)
>
> [In general it's considered improper to write about such things as labor and pregnancy: that could put a damper on male passion. . . . Our masculine reasoning tells us that labor is not an appropriate subject for literature. But it's the women who pay for this reasoning in the delivery rooms.]

In effect, Russian women give birth in complete isolation, often without sedatives and anesthetics, and are prevented from sharing their experience with anyone close to them. Neither doctors nor personnel evince any sensitivity to the psychological effects of such separation, for by and large the hospital cultivates not a bedside but, rather, a broadside manner. For example, in *Ship of Widows* the personnel examining Anfisa Gromova, who anticipates going into imminent labor, comment: "U etoi skoro. Ne zhenshchina, slon" (This one'll be quick—she's an elephant, not a woman! [50; 86]), and her vocal anxiety about the baby withheld from her after delivery elicits the rebuke: "Tishe, tut ne bazar. Sto vas lezhit, ni odna ne pozvoliaet, chto ty. . . . My rabotaem, a ty oresh' kak porosia?" (Hush! This isn't a market-place! There are a hundred of you in here, and you're the only one making a fuss. . . . We're all working here and you howl like a pig! [51; 88]). Gossiping nurses in "Nothing Special" carelessly allow a patient to overhear a conversation about how the doctor operating on her made a gross error in his incision. Razmetal'skii, the head of ob-gyn in Palei's "Losers' Division," routinely ridicules and insults the peasant women on whom he cold-bloodedly performs abortions.

This official indifference to female psychology contrasts dramatically with the support and affirmation women generally find among their wardmates, even if the latter also prove a source of conflict and tension. Female bonding results in part from the extent to which life within a ward is laid bare for group consumption. Few, if any, secrets remain unguessed or unrevealed. Furthermore, the leisurely, externally uneventful pace of hospital existence permits the exchange of biographies and confidences, which unites women through the revelation of hardships that seem less individual than endemic to their gender. The same configuration of unimaginable, brutal sufferings repeats itself in the histories of women from the most diverse backgrounds, as witnessed in *The Women's Decameron,* in which a shipyard worker, a doctor of biology, an engineer, a music teacher, an airline stewardess, a "dissident wife," a Party functionary, and a "tramp" have no difficulty arriving at a common understanding as they share and evaluate one another's life stories. A parallel cross-section of female society appears in *A Counterfeit Life,* "The Break/Crisis," and "Carried through to Term," in which empathy also forges relations among representatives of widely divergent allegiances and temperaments, particularly regarding the highly problematized, gendered issue of abortion.

Although contemporary Russian women's fiction identifies birthing, abortion, and sickness as essentially female problems, their solution, however spurious, seems to reside in the hands of men. Despite the feminization of the medical profession in empirical reality, masculine figures of authority rule the world depicted in the narratives under analysis. The so-called good doctor Volodia in "Pania's Poor Heart" takes it upon himself to deliver Pania's baby, contrary to her request for an abortion on the grounds of ill health, advanced years, and an overburdened domestic situation; the ultimate decision about when the homeless, pregnant, single young woman in "The Violin" should leave the ward apparently belongs to the "paternal" head physician; the strongly opinionated pronatalist chief of the maternity hospital who performs the complex operations in "Delos" is a bachelor, and the best surgeon entrusted with the most complicated operations in Tokareva's "Nothing Special" is also male. In Grekova's *Ship of Widows* nurses cannot curb the protagonist's agitation without appeal to a higher guardian of discipline: the male doctor who instantly silences her by accusing her of hooliganism. Although his female assistant arranges the abortions that Dr. Razmetal'skii in Palei's "Losers' Division" cannot or refuses to handle, his decisions and status in the hospital override hers. And Grekova's "Break/Crisis" boasts two powerful male personae who determine the middle-aged heroine's life: the hospital chief and the omniscient "eaglelike" Dr. Chagin, who neatly resolves all of her personal and medical dilemmas.

Among the many insights emerging from the hospital chronotope the most dispiriting from a feminist standpoint is that Russian men wield power, while women by force of habit subordinate self-fulfillment to the series of gendered moral imperatives pragmatically elided with countless aspects of Soviet institutions and officially promulgated for the presumed well-being of the entire society. By exploring the conditions of women as patients (and eternally patient), the feminized chronotope of the hospital in women's prose materializes the gender-specific dynamics of policy-sanctioned victimization. If within the masculine prison/camp chronotope a paradoxical access to spiritual enrichment and independence rescues malehood from the dehumanizing processes that accompany loss of liberty (e.g., in Solzhenitsyn's *V kruge pervom* [First Circle] and Abram Tertz's *Golos iz khora* [A Voice from the Chorus]),[11] hospitalization seems to vouchsafe women primarily physical "rewards" of an ambiguous kind—recovery of health, the vaunted delights of maternity, the termination of "unwanted" pregnancies. Moreover, the psychological cost of these "benefits," in the form of moral anguish, humiliation by medical staff, and complete loss of privacy in the midst of existential isolation, belongs to the commonplace realm of *byt,* the everyday world of humdrum existence, and therefore lacks the moral "grandeur" of men's philosophical struggle against the more blatantly repressive constraints of a time/space structure officially acknowledged as totalitarian.

Whereas the prevalence of the hospital chronotope may be generalized across the full spectrum of recent Russian women's fiction, no other categories of gendered space are shared by the vast majority of contemporary female writers. Accordingly, hereafter I abjure universalizing statements that erase distinctions, to focus on space in the works of Liudmila Petrushevskaia, Tatyana Tolstaya, and several representatives of new women's prose.

Petrushevskaia's "Home": Illusion, Liminality, and Incarceration

While given to dissolving temporal markers, Petrushevskaia's drama and prose not only meticulously particularize but also densely psychologize space. As her ur-text, "Cherez polia" (Through the Fields, 1983), makes clear, for Petrushevskaia the Home (*teplyi dom*) represents the irresistible illusion of existential security—a retreat from the perils of nature and history.[12] Her works teem with two-way traffic, as desperate loners seek sanctuary in a family domicile from the impersonal horrors of the outside world, while those suffocated by the emotional traumas of betrayal and indifference from their "loved ones" flee in desperation from the imprisonment of a putative "home." Hence, the prominence of the threshold as a locus of spiritual liminality in Petrushevskaia's works (emphasized in the pointedly titled "Lestnichnaia kletka" [The Stairwell] and in the universal search for a "place to stay" in numerous stories and plays, in which the spiritually dispossessed hope is to be "taken in": "Rasskazchitsa" [The Story Teller], "The Violin," "Our Crowd," and *Vremia noch'* [Night Time, 1992]). These unfortunates do, indeed, get "taken in"—metaphorically, inasmuch as they mistake the armies of Genghis Khan for the Salvation Army.

In a sense the impulse to entrust one's soul to a healing environment (always illusory) merely plays a dephysiologizing variation on the hospital motif in Petrushevskaia, who obsessively checks all of her hearsay mothers (unwanted complications) into hospitals. Characteristically, mothers either remain in their wards or die, just as the spiritually wounded never recover from their malaise. In that regard the "Izilirovannyi boks" (Isolation Box) for terminally ill cancer patients in her one-act play is a matrix metaphor for Petrushevskaia's worldview. The inhabitants are "prigovorennaia k smerti" (sentenced to death [*Cinzano,* 318; *Pesni,* 234]), utterly alone, with all hopes reduced to fantastic delusions.

Isolation or defensive immurement within the domestic domain is a related Petrushevskaian topos. As characters barricade themselves in locked rooms to escape from or defy their abusive cohabitants, home becomes carceral, or punitive, space—a prison that punishes those on both sides of the door, as in "Gigiena" (Hygiene) and *Night Time.* In the latter, for example, the protagonist-narrator attempts to wreak subtle psychological revenge on her family by conspicuously isolating herself in her tiny room, while suspecting her mother, who, in turn, holes herself up in her bedroom, of attempting suicide behind her blocked door:

> dver' babushki priperta s toi storony, ia s trudom priotkryla shchel', dver' byla priperta pis'mennym stolom. . . . zachem ona zabarrikadirovalas'? . . . Ia vvalilas' v ee komnatu, ona sidela bessil'no na svoem divanchike (teper' on moi). Veshat'sia sobiralas'? (101)

> [grandmother's door was blocked from inside, I had had difficulty opening it just a crack, the door was blocked by the desk. . . . why had she barricaded herself in? . . . I tumbled into her room, she was sitting listlessly on her sofa (it's mine now). Had she been planning to hang herself?]

Petrushevskaia transforms the fabled refuge of home into a claustrophobic environment of spiritual laceration, sadistic exposure, and ceaseless emotional vampirism. She revises the genre of the family romance into a horror story.

Similarly, Petrushevskaia adroitly travesties the communal domestic feast (fundamental to the genres of the symposium and the idyll, with their harmonious gathering), degrading it into a grotesque anticommunion. So-called friends and family members assemble at table to enact Dostoevskian scandals, with hysteria, physical violence, seedy revelations, and exposés of nasty or criminal deeds that erode and sunder relationships instead of reaffirming them. As "Our Crowd" and "Syraia noga" (A Raw Leg) illustrate, Petrushevskaian groups convene on pseudofestive occasions not to celebrate but to annihilate. The final Easter feast in "Our Crowd," rather than culminating in a resurrection, ends with the heroine's beating her son until he bleeds, while the party in "A Raw Leg" disintegrates when the host smashes his wife into bloody unconsciousness in the bathroom (*Tri*, 101–2).

Anyone seeking an antidote to the cloying sentimentality of Victorians' idealization of domestic space as a tranquil haven from the push-and-slash of competitive public energies can do no better than to read Petrushevskaia's fiction or drama. For she envisions home as the quintessential site of psychic warfare and emotional evisceration, materialized in multiple forms of physical violence.

Tolstaya: Space as Biography and Creative Freedom

Tolstaya's treatment of space is more varied and differentiated according to age and character type. Within Tolstaya's associative construction of locale older women tend to inhabit cramped apartments that document their lives via the objects amassed in them: outmoded furniture, kitschy bibelots, photographs, and various mementos that infuse space with subjective history and catalyze narrative (e.g., "Milaia Shura" [Sweet Shura]). In cinematic terms these overloaded, enclosed spaces exemplify "closed form," intimating the inward turn of the dweller's life as she retreats increasingly into the rich holdings of memory. Protagonists like Shura are the curators of their own biographies, displayed in confined quarters that recall antiquated museums. A variant on this subjectivized historical space is the attic (so central to "'Na zolotom kryl'tse sideli . . .'" [On the Golden Porch . . .]), overrun by the fantastic bric-a-brac that holds magical allure for the young but for the adult represents inertness and somnolent desuetude.

Of all Tolstayan narratives underscoring the identification of domestic space and old women, "Samaia liubimaia" (Most Beloved) makes that connection most explicit: as the dacha in which Zhenechka thrived sags and grows dilapidated with time's passage, so does Zhenechka; each, in Tolstaya's words, "*tikho stareet*" (quietly ages [*Sleepwalker*, 106, 110; "'*Na*,'" 102, 105]). This Usher-like synonymity emerges in such passages as the following, in which Zhenechka's spirit (i.e., voice) blends into, and becomes indistinguishable from, the dacha's atmosphere:

> Uiutno lezhal na skaterti golos Zhenechki, netoroplivo povestvuia telefonnomu spravochniku, pepel'nitse, iablochnomu ogryzku o svoikh radostiakh i volneniiakh. . . . rovnym potokom tekla ee dusha iz telefonnykh dyrochek, rastekalas' po skaterti, isparialas' dymkom (106)
>
> [Zhenechka's voice lies cozily on the tablecloth, unhurriedly telling the telephone book, ashtray, and apple core about its joys and worries. . . . her soul flows from the telephone receiver in an even stream, spills over the tablecloth, evaporates like smoke.] (111)

In the same story Tolstaya extends "feminine space" to include the garden as a symbolic gauge of nurturing capacities, or the ability to raise the next generation along with healthy blooms. Space in such instances is emphatically temporalized, for Tolstaya suffuses it with temporal markers in the form of objects that stimulate elegiac memories of a past valorized largely through its transitoriness. Hence the prevalence of the Edenic garden in her earliest stories.[13]

Curiously, whereas the association between old women and apartments offers poignant occasion for poetic/lyrical reflections on the part of Tolstaya's narrators, young women's devotion to domestic space, its contents and embellishment, tends to connote philistinism, an acquisitiveness that Tolstaya satirizes with implacable hostility: for example, in "Ogon' i pyl'" (Fire and Dust), "Spi spokoino, synok" (Sweet Dreams, Son), and "Poet i muza" (The Poet and the Muse). What accounts for her ironic treatment of that attachment is the absence of historical significance. With no profound personal experience animating rooms and their contents into valued participants in an individual life, the desire to possess and expand that ahistorical space inevitably acquires negative moral overtones.

In contrast to this apparently conventional conflation of woman and home is Tolstaya's colorful countergendering of a space traditionally coded as male: that is, the adventure space of open seas, unchartered peregrinations unconstrained by teleology (what Bakhtin calls "adventure-time" [87]). That expansiveness of movement, unsurprisingly, accompanies sexual freedom, most notably in "Fire and Dust," in which the audaciously named Pipka happily embarks not only on involuntary voyages to exotic lands but also on casual congress with strangers. A comparably magical and unfettered female character, Tamila, in "Svidanie s ptitsei" (Rendezvous with a Bird), occupies the fairytale space of mythic mountain, dragon kingdom, etc., that entertains all possibilities. Both Pipka and Tamila, significantly, are associated with imagination, with the "creative space" that is synonymous with a no-woman's-land of original narration (a temporal artistic form). Through the chronotope of creativity (i.e., storytelling) Tolstaya empowers both Pipka and Tamila with movement through boundless time and space. And that creativity, as in Lewis Carroll's *Alice in Wonderland,* entails a self-metamorphosis articulated through richly elaborated spatial categories that more often than not take precedence over the temporal.[14] In other words, Tolstaya's perspectivism cannot accommodate a space devoid of temporality and a time untethered to space.

New Women's Prose: Moving Out

If new women's prose may claim to have ushered in any innovations regarding gendered space, it probably would be by analogy with the movement of painters called "Peredvizhniki" (Itinerants). As did Repin and other of its representatives with their canvases, the younger generation of writers has brought women's prose outdoors. Bella Ulanovskaia in the minutely detailed topographies of her hunting sketches, Larisa Vaneeva in her ecologically conscious rhapsodies on the wonders of nature, Valeriia Narbikova in her flights to the liberating stretches of the seashore, and Svetlana Vasilenko in her vivid renditions of traumatized landscape all transfer their female protagonists from bounded interiors into outdoor environments that interact with or mirror their psyches. This extension of female space functions as a kind of prophylactic against the automatic elision of womanhood with the domestic sphere. Ulanovskaia, in fact, tends to situate her female protagonists amid untamed nature (e.g., in the autobiographically coded novella *Albinos* [1984]), in scenarios evoking typically masculine confrontations with the "great unknown" as a rite of passage, while Vasilenko frames her heroines' intensely sensual self-awareness in public settings contaminated by the apocalyptic aura of a postnuclear world.[15] Above all, unpredictable mobility, a restless movement that signals psychological displacement—accentuated, moreover, by abrupt narrative shifts—marks such otherwise diverse texts as Narbikova's *Ravnovesie sveta dnevnykh i nochnykh zvezd* (The Equilibrium of Light of Diurnal and Nocturnal Stars), Vaneeva's "Antigrekh" (Antisin), and Vasilenko's "Za saigakami" (Going After Goat-Antelopes). By amplifying female space, the new prose has reconstituted woman's perspective as subject and object: her purview is not confined to domestic and professional matters nor her existence reduced to that of a stock character in the stale tragicomedy of contemporary *byt*. Her week is *not* like any other.

One might say that, when women "knew their place," they occupied a circumscribed, convention-bound space; contemporary Russian women's fiction has remapped that territory along imperialistic lines, so as to encompass a broader range of possibilities for women's being. By so doing, it has wrested womanhood from the stasis and immanence of gendered not-A status, thereby qualifying as one of the few glasnost phenomena to effect an authentic perestroika.

Notes

1. The earliest, most original, and thought-provoking attempts belong to Mary Ellmann (1968) and Hélène Cixous (1975).

2. In deconstructionist parlance the second term becomes the repressed, or the "unsaid."
3. A woman, in Freud's theory of penis envy, may be minimally defined as a man lacking a penis. On Freud's views on women and femininity, see the introduction in Young-Bruehl 3–47.
4. Entitled "Forms of Time and the Chronotope in the Novel," the essay is contained in Bakhtin 84–258.
5. As Bakhtin notes, Kant in the "Transcendental Aesthetics" of his *Critique of Pure Reason* defines space and time as "indispensable forms of any cognition" (ibid., 85).
6. Perhaps one can draw a limited analogy between the risks undertaken by men in political and military crises with those that women face in the more everyday circumstances of birthing. That parallel is implicitly drawn in Ernest Hemingway's *A Farewell to Arms,* in which Frederic Henry's life is under constant threat in battle (the arms of war), yet Catherine succumbs to death during childbirth ("love's arms").
7. Mental hospitals, however, proliferate in earlier fiction, probably because they signal intellectual malaise and invite symbolic interpretation, just as certain physical sicknesses lend themselves to metaphoric usage (see Foucault, *Madness and Civilization,* and Sontag, *Illness as Metaphor*).
8. Amid the plethora of military medical settings, Solzhenitsyn's *Rakovyi korpus* (Cancer Ward) and Boris P'etsukh's recent "Anamnez i Epikriz" (1989) stand out as rare exceptions in male prose.
9. The pages refer to *Balancing Acts* and Velembovskaia, respectively. Hereafter, for the sake of brevity, the former will be identified as *BA*. Whenever an English translation is available, I cite from the English source first, then from the Russian. The page numbers in parentheses follow the same sequence.
10. In Goscilo and Lindsey, *Wild Beach* (hereafter *WB*).
11. Solzhenitsyn's *First Circle* consistently develops the paradox of prison as the ideal venue for attaining spiritual freedom. See statements to that effect volunteered by Nerzhin, Prianchikov, Adamson, and Sologdin. Comparable passages may be found in Tertz, such as the following:

> I like the slow tempo of our existence here compared with the usual rhythm of life which people outside willy-nilly adopt in order to be in time for the bus, the office or the cinema. The mind, therefore, works somehow more naturally in camp—it doesn't have to calculate all the time how to get ahead of somebody else. . . . And existence opens its blue eyes all the wider. (234; *Golos iz khora,* 668)

12. On this, see Ivanova; see also Goscilo, "Petrushevskaia's Vision: No Ray of Light in the Kingdom of Darkness," (paper delivered at AAASS Conference in Arizona, 1992).
13. On Tolstaya's evocation of Eden, see Goscilo, "Paradise."

14. Pipka, for instance, appears in many shifting guises, all inseparable from precisely delineated locales: pathetic orphan at Rimma's house, irresistible seductress in her own Perlovka dwelling, victim, prize, and adventuress on the ship and remote islands, where she has sexual relations with a series of different men, a smiling beauty in Australia, or a bright-burning flame turned to coal on the Iaroslavl Highway. Tamila's changing identity likewise depends on the nature of the space she occupies, whether it be magic mountain, semi-enchanted garden, or rumpled bed. On the role of movement through space and its relevance to gender and potential for change, see Auerbach.
15. For samples of these writers' prose, see *Ne pomniashchaia zla* as well as the three anthologies of translations titled *Soviet Women Writing, Women's View,* and *Lives in Transit.*

6

New Members and Organs: The Politics of Porn

> Pornographers are the secret police of male supremacy.
>
> —Andrea Dworkin, *Pornography*

> [T]he wenches don't do anything for my prong, . . . but when I get ready to really put the screws hard to a man, with all the authority vested in me by the state . . . it looks up at the sky, and sometimes I get so worked up that I spatter my britches all over.
>
> —Viktor Erofeev, "The Parakeet"

Until perestroika finding pornography in Moscow was less likely than encountering a singing nun at a bazaar. Yet by 1990 *Moskovskie novosti* (Moscow News) reported a lively trade in girlie magazines at newsstands, an adolescent complained to *Vecherniaia Moskva* (Moscow at Night) about the pornographic videos inundating the city, and metro stations and dashboards of taxis routinely displayed pictures of women wearing only a pout or a smile.[1] Public reactions to the relentless omnipresence of naked flesh pressured Gorbachev, in fact, to establish a commission, on 5 December 1990, charged with elaborating measures to safeguard the country's morality. Anyone curious about the effectiveness of that official body may consult reflections on the topic by one of its members, published in the glossy *Playboy* clone *Andrei*.[2] By mid-1992 pornography was thriving as a mainstay of the novelties introduced, along with kiwis and deodorants, into Russia's capital.

Amid the all-pervasive renewed Petrine drive to "catch up" with the West, such an influx of ostensibly liberating, uncensored materials might appear as an exercise in freedom according to the modern Western model. As the editors of *Andrei* announced in their second issue:

"We're certain that *Andrei* and its battle helped strengthen democratic tendencies in the area of social awareness and rights" (*Andrei*, 2:3). Their certainty is, I contend, misguided. It originates in the fallacy of phallic "freedom," which merely exchanges one form of political enslavement for another. What purportedly furthers the cause of democracy is a publication that specifically targets only the male half of the population, presumably justifying its abusive exploitation of the other (female) half via body instrumentalization on the following grotesque grounds: "The first Russian journal for men . . . is essential today, for it is precisely men who more than anything need liberation from stressful aggressiveness and lack of satisfaction."[3] As the apostle of a new, true Word, the editor vows to combat the psychology of "'a slavish sexuality'—rigid, crude, hypocritical, and blind," thus unwittingly delineating the profile of his own journal. What, after decades of censorship and regimented puritanism, impresses Russians as hard-won delivery from restraints merely enacts a substitution: the sexual Stallion replaces Stalin, institutionalizing a kindred mode of ritualized repression.

What potential repercussions does the tidal wave of porn inundating Moscow in the early 1990s have for women's status in Russian society? On what grounds can one legitimately designate pornography a gendered issue? Russians increasingly speak of the widespread current unemployment as a dilemma predominantly affecting women.[4] May the same be said of pornography? Since the materials energetically hawked in Russia's capital and elsewhere rely on Western models or originate in the West, a brief glance at the Western sociocultural framework of porn production and consumption provides a useful point of reference.

Born to Porn in the West

In England, Canada, and the United States pornography automatically raises several interrelated issues that fuel impassioned controversy on a recurrent basis: those of definition (porn vs. erotica), legality (constitutional freedom of expression), and morality (motivation and effects of porn). Feminist scholarship (especially by Andrea Dworkin and Catharine MacKinnon)[5] and concerted political action have decisively shifted the focus of discussion in recent years by radically gendering the debate on pornography. That debate shows little sign of slackening, for the voluminous official reports and scholarly studies intended to curb or understand the production, dissemination, and consumption of pornography (as well as extensive press coverage of incidents such as the Mapplethorpe case and scandal-creating rock videos by Madonna and Michael Jackson) have unwittingly contributed to its publicity.[6] Moreover, since the mid-1980s not only specialists in cultural studies but also political groups defending pornography on First Amendment grounds (e.g., the Feminist Anti-Censorship Taskforce [FACT]) have kept that debate alive while also producing a steadily expanding scholarship on the topic.

The profits of the current U.S. pornography industry reportedly exceed those of the conventional film and record industries combined (Dworkin).[7] And, although Denmark may boast of being the first country, in 1967, to legalize all pornography (Hughes xiv), the United States holds pride of place as the modern muck Mecca.

Astute in identifying and exploiting new markets, the porn industry has expanded from a low-yield, covert business to a "highly visible multi-billion dollar industry,"[8] branching out into multiple categories of products and services, including film, videos, books and magazines, mail-order sales, under-the-counter materials, sexually explicit computer communications (e.g., SEXTEX), "Dial-a-Porn" recordings, and "sexual devices" and paraphernalia—such as artificial vaginas and penises, lotions, potions, elixirs, whips, and chains—usually stocked in "adult" bookstores and sex or S/M shops.[9] Analyses of porn that confine themselves to written texts of the *Fanny Hill* and *Story of O* variety smack of an earlier, monolithic era predating the New Age porn boom. Their purview does not take into account "water sports," rectal inflation, and the administration of enemas, for example, as techniques for sexual arousal. Resorting to esoteric models from high culture, these earlier studies theorize titillation,[10] whereas the ultimate aphrodisiac in today's porn is, patently, annihilation.[11] Yet even commentators who have waded through the entire range of pornographic genres—both "soft-core" and "hard-core"[12]—have confessed defeat in pinpointing the constitutive features of porn.

Definition

As Catharine MacKinnon has remarked, the dilemma of definition disturbs only those who attempt to legislate or combat pornography: "No pornographer has any trouble knowing what to make; no adult bookstore or theatre has any trouble knowing what to stock; no consumer has any trouble knowing what to buy."[13] Clearly, like Justice Potter Stewart, they "know it when they see it." Yet scholars, critics, journalists, and various government commissions appointed to investigate the nature and consequences of pornography have struggled unavailingly to arrive at an uncontested definition. For instance, David Loth's monograph *The Erotic in Literature* uses the term *pornography* interchangeably with "obscenity, erotica, smut, filth, etc.," as encompassing "those writings about sex or eliminative functions which past or present officials or influential groups have suppressed or tried to on the ground that they were morally corrupting or degrading" (Loth 10). Such a simplistic ahistorical blend of randomness with comprehensiveness would place Ovid's *Ars Amatoria,* Flaubert's *Madame Bovary,* Joyce's *Ulysses,* Lawrence's *Lady Chatterley's Lover,* and Henry Miller's novels alongside sadomasochistic items advertised in *Last Gasp.*[14] Anthony Burgess views a pornographic work as a substitute for a sexual partner, a means of achieving sexual catharsis without an "act of erotic congress"—that is, as a "harmless" onanistic device within an Aristotelian sexual drama (Burgess 5).[15] Stanley Edgar Hyman and the majority of educated liberals essentially share Burgess's position (Hyman 35–41).[16]

Problems of definition likewise have plagued the official commissions on pornography and censorship—constituted in part to clarify precisely *what* needs to be censored—which have not reached a terminological consensus. The Johnson Commission (1970) denied *pornography* all legal significance, opting for *explicit sexual materials* as the key term, sometimes alternating with *erotica.* The Williams Committee (1979) differentiated between *pornography* and *erotica,* interpreting the latter as anything that "expresses sexual excitement rather than causes it" and *pornography* as combining two features: the function or intention of arousing an audience and a content that explicitly represents "sexual materials (organs, postures, activity, etc.)." The Meese Commission sweepingly dismissed both terms as labels for subjective disapproval (*pornography*) or approval (*erotica*) of explicit depiction of sex, pleonastically substituting *obscenity* to characterize material that "has been or would likely be found obscene in the context of a judicial proceeding."[17]

For the most part, scholarly works, the press, and everyday usage have tended to treat *erotica* and *pornography* as synonymous.[18] Among those who draw a distinction the criteria for differentiating between the two vary significantly. Informal conversations reveal that, for many, the degree of explicitness draws the (inevitably blurred) dividing line between erotica and porn. By contrast, those trained in high culture studies credit erotica (especially in written form) with artistic skill, often teasing out of a text a philosophy of principled rebellion or tragic "thanatic sexuality" that "redeems" it from the ignominy of the "unartistic"—porn.[19] For feminists making the distinction, egalitarianism and mutuality between sexual partners are the decisive factors. The widespread acceptance of a purely stylistic hierarchy, which equates erotica with sophistication (a "higher-class," less crude presentation of the same materials) may explain the preference in recent Russian porn for subtitling any narrative devoted exclusively to graphic copulation, tireless fellatio, and comparable acts an "erotic story" and to adopt such coy titles as *Kupidon* (Cupid), the Roman Eros, for its pricier porn magazines. (As a guide to contents, the labeling on both is superfluous, for the naked women on the covers and their porn-coded stance instantly signal the genre.) Alain Robbe-Grillet wittily summed up the psychology governing nomenclature in the aphorism: "La pornographie, c'est l'érotisme des autres."[20]

Legality

Whereas most detractors of pornography (e.g., George Steiner, Ernest van der Haag, George P. Elliott) base their objections on moral grounds, opponents of censorship (e.g., Harry Levin, Peter Michelson, Paul Goodman) advance the civil liberties argument.[21] The latter camp posits an all-or-nothing scenario, whereby limiting a pornographer's freedom of expression sets the society on the "slippery slope" leading to fascism (Cole 162). The texts regularly invoked to buttress this apocalyptic prediction are novels by Joyce, Lawrence, and Miller, not *Playboy, Hustler, OUI,* and *On Our Backs* or films like *Deep Throat* and *Snuff*.[22] Transferred into Russian culture, the tactic would entail justifying the publication of, say, "Shvedskaia troika" (Three-Way), a fictional mini-odyssey of ejaculations, on the basis of Pushkin's *Gavriliada.* In any event, the commonplace that censorship of phenomena offensive to some violates the First Amendment may be countered by the argument that dissemination of material abusive to women constitutes a form of defamation and warrants injunction against "group libel."[23] Whether such a restraint is feasible remains moot, while the nature of materials currently accessible to practically anyone interested in porn suggests the impotence of censorship in overseeing its publication.

Marketing Psychology and Morality

The motivation for pornography, on the one hand, and its effects, on the other, have been the subjects of countless discussions. Although one need not share the Marxist concept of porn as intrinsic to the commodity culture of capitalism, few would dispute that the capitalist system of supply and demand regulates the porn market. A desire for sexual stimulation prompts the purchase of porn, while the reward of financial profit drives its production. For that dynamic to operate, sex must be accorded the primacy it enjoys in the United States. Yet anyone who attributes Americans' obsession with sex and porn to their inherently greater sexuality overlooks the commodification of (1) sexual desire and (2) its promised fulfillment via advertising. Both are mythical products promoted by the very same forces that satisfy the needs they artfully create: big business.

As various studies of subliminal seduction have demonstrated, finely tuned strategies of "consumer engineering"[24] have enabled manufacturers to sell everything from cars and furniture to clothes, cosmetics, and alcohol by projecting flattering, illusory self-images onto the potential buyer—as someone subject to that special sexual hunger that, not coincidentally, will be appeased through the acquisition of whatever product is being featured.[25] All media, with varying degrees of sophistry and sophistication, convey the message that sexual desire and desirability (of a visible, marketable sort) are critical to a full life, to popularity, happiness, etc. Cleverly packaged, manipulative ads that play and prey upon "illicit" wish-fulfillment fantasies have sold the public, in fact, on a pseudonormative sexuality shared by those marked for success. That sexuality has become naturalized, in other words, through techniques of psychological suggestion. To consolidate, verify, and propagate national standards of sexual taste (originally codified and propagated by the media), publications like *People* sponsor surveys that elect, for example, "The Sexiest Man of the Year." These processes (of collusion between power and pleasure and the institutionalization of the resultant identities) instantiate what Michel Foucault has called "implantation of perversions" (Foucault, *History of Sexuality,* 1:36–49). Although psychologists, anthropologists, and sociologists increasingly recognize that sexuality is subject to shifting social constructions (its configuration and dynamics reinforced through interest groups operating behind the scenes), diehard skeptics continue to lyricize sex as the "spontaneous surge" of "natural impulses"—a perception carefully cultivated by the very ads that belie it.[26] Of all forms of mass culture, advertising most clearly testifies to the mainstreaming of pornographic values (Cole 41). The symbiosis between them, as John Ellis has noted, has stirred few objections, "other than from feminists" (Ellis 93).[27] Yet, given advertising's attested manipulative power, the relationship surely complicates (if not undermines) the notion that pornography enhances and flourishes amid liberty, civil or any other.

While few dispute the incentives for the sale and purchase of porn, opinions diverge dramatically about its effects, both on participants and consumers. By and large, partisans of porn endorse it as innocuous, even culturally enriching ("it extends the boundaries of the permissible") or therapeutic (enabling a healthy release of "tension" that otherwise might erupt in physical violence). The antipornography contingent maintains exactly the reverse, adducing if not causal then at least correlational links between porn and violent crime. Hearings investigating male violence against women or children have been unable to establish causality (in the legal or the scholarly sense) between the two and are unlikely to do so in the future. Officials, moreover, have shown reluctance to recognize even a connection between the defendant's attested habitual use of pornography, which eroticizes beatings, mutilations, rape, and murder, and the imitative acts of abuse he perpetrates on his victim. Whereas findings strike some (e.g., Linda Williams)[28] as inconclusive, others (e.g., Dworkin and MacKinnon)[29] firmly believe that porn conduces to violence or, at the very least, desensitizes men, intensifies their callousness to women, increases rape myths, and entrenches misogynistic stereotyping. Indeed, some sociologists (e.g., Harry Brod) maintain that porn, with its hyperbolized penile performances, alienates men from their own bodies and increases male impotence, while decreasing their capacity for satisfaction (Brod 197).

Such notions have been challenged as prescribing an artless "realist" aesthetic to pornography that posits no disjunction or area of negotiability between screen and text, on the one hand, and everyday life, on the other—essentially the same grounds on which the West traditionally has faulted the aesthetic of socialist realism (SR). Yet the genre of porn itself adopts realism as its guiding principle, even as it caters to fantasy.[30] And, just as countless Russian readers "identified" with SR heroes, so do many Americans extrapolate real-life scenarios from screen and page. To completely abstract the transaction between viewer/reader and his porn materials is to divorce arousal from everyday reality. If porn sets out to excite the imagination, it does so not because the latter dwells in sublime isolation but, rather, because it can trigger inspiration in the groin that *may* take to the streets instead of being "safely" localized between the sheets. To assert that porn relates just to fantasy is no less naive than to draw a straight, narrow line between the consumption of porn and real-life acts of violence. Consumers of porn, unlike those who theorize about them, do not approach their materials subtly, with Byzantine complexity. Theorists may invoke Kant,[31] but most porn users want "cunt."

Feminist Perspectives

Feminists have fundamentally revised the pornography debate by spotlighting what until the advent of feminism seemed to have escaped everyone else's attention: the gendered nature of porn. The fact that film, videos, magazines, "fiction," and other categories of porn typically depict naked women as disposable instruments of male pleasure, ready and eager to perform *any* kind of sexual service, led feminists to reassess the genre in terms of political power. Accordingly, antiporn feminists define porn as a *practice* and *presentation* of sexual subordination, whereby female submission to male dominance (and violence) is played out in sexually explicit terms degrading to women, for the purpose of arousing a (preponderantly male) audience.[32] Reduced to a passive object of male subjectivity, the woman in porn fulfills the depersonalized function of stimulating and gratifying men's desires (both within and outside the form). Enlisted to serve the cause of male orgasm, she endures or performs whatever act will ensure that climax, from submitting to anal penetration to being whipped or snuffed out. She supplies what the male demands, for pornography mandates that women be whores. The feminist critique of porn, then, not only defines it as sexist in content but also deplores its production as exploitative, its effects as misogyny fostering, and its consumption as destructive to men (Soble 150).

Inasmuch as I examine Russian porn from the standpoint of gender, my discussion allies itself with and operates within this feminist definition of pornography.[33] On the question of censorship I find myself located squarely between the feminists who demand that all porn be eliminated through censorship, on the one hand, and those who, on the other, oppose any censorship of the pornographic materials (presumably including violent child pornography) they claim to abhor, on the questionable grounds that following their convictions would align them with the fundamentalist Right. In short, they choose the political camp of big business—hardly a bastion of liberal values, despite its profitable dissemination of pornographic elements in advertising—so as to avoid a "contaminating association" with more obviously, self-avowedly conservative forces.[34]

Quasi-Excursus: The Etymological Variant and "Intergirl"

The etymology of *pornography* points to the debasement of women that inheres in the genre. Derived from the Greek, the term combines *graphos,* depiction or writing, with *porne,* prostitute or whore (normally the lowest of slaves in Greece),[35] with the important proviso that the material of "literary" Greek pornography concentrated on aspects of the prostitute's life other than her professional exertions. Otto Brendel defines these early treatments as "novelistic written biographies of celebrated courtesans" (Brendel 64).[36] In modern times, in fact, the amateur, unofficial status of women's prostitution is crucial to pornography, which rarely concerns itself with paid professionals.

In this respect Vladimir Kunin's *Interdevochka* (Intergirl, 1988)[37] is a curious case of hybridization, whereby a text that is pornographic *only* according to the etymological definition (we learn mainly about Tania's nonprofessional activities) relies on the titillation attaching to prostitution and sexually transmitted diseases to preach high culture myths about Russia, while sounding the social alarm about the dangers of AIDS. *Intergirl* is Valentin Rasputin's *Pozhar* (Fire) transplanted to Leningrad's sexual market during extensive Russian emigration. Its implications fully accord with the Marxist view that pornography represents the commodification of sexuality under capitalism.

Issued by the establishment publishing house of Molodaia Gvardiia (Young Guard) in 100,000 copies, *Intergirl* contains two forewords: a brief endorsement by the influential sexologist Igor' Kon, who correctly singles out for emphasis the work's admonitory function; and an essay by a journalist from *Literaturnaia gazeta* (Literary Gazette), which itself fulfills that function, as indicated in his title, "V gruppe riska" (In the Risk Group), referring to AIDS. Tellingly, the text of the novel proper contains no explicit descriptions of sexual acts (a must for porn) and, whenever it incorporates expletives or vulgarisms, it opts for such largely desexed terms as *svoloch', mraz',* and *podonok* over sexually derived "obscenities" of the *okhuet'* and *pizdet'* type. While asexual, the text nonetheless is vulgar in the manner once ridiculed by Tatyana Tolstaya in an interview: in its preoccupation with various brands and names of commodities, which relentlessly repeat themselves whenever clothes, cars, makeup, perfumes, etc., are mentioned. Needless to say, these are all Western imports, weapons with which the corrupt materialist West invades innocent Russia to tempt and degrade it.

The dominant lexicon of *Intergirl* is that of *economics* (not sex), of *capital* (we learn varieties of slang for money in general, for foreign currency, etc.), which makes sense in light of the work's agenda—to propagate traditional Russian/Soviet (i.e., anticapitalist) myths: (1) the moral superiority of Russians' vaunted generosity, spirituality, and emotional intensity to Western materialist values (the heroine's, the truckdriver Vitia's, the reformed schoolboy Kozlov's); (2) the sacrosanct nature of motherhood—a mother's love, like love *for* one's mother, transcends all other ties (exemplified in Tania and her mother, Alla Sergeevna); (3) the sacrosanct nature of the Motherland, which proselytizes the unique inseparability of Russians from their native land (note the sentimental nationalism of Tania, her mother, and Verka, the former Moscow prostitute living in Stockholm); and (4) the apparently deathless stereotypes of "whore with a heart of gold" and "woman as nurse," which converge in the person of Tania, who simultaneously is a "warm-hearted" prostitute and an efficient, compassionate, nurturing nurse. A tender, loving daughter, she will go to any lengths to vouchsafe her mother's comfort and happiness; she cares about her patients, loves animals, quotes Pasternak from memory, etc. In short, Kunin revives Karamzin's bathetic scenario, "Poor Tania," showing that "ibo i prostitutki liubit' umeiut!" (prostitutes, too, know how to love!).

Kunin operates both sides of the street, so to speak: he treats such provocative topics as prostitution, rape, AIDS, and suicide, in the process dropping an endless trail of brand names of products calculated to stimulate cupidity (not arousal). Yet he wraps everything in a moralistic tract on the level of comic book complexity. As a solution to Russia's highly complex dilemmas, the work delivers simplistic homilies: "death over dishonor," "happiness cannot be found in wealth/possessions," "home [i.e., mother and Russia] is best," etc. It would be difficult to find a less erotic text than this clutch of recipes for safe and sanctioned conduct founded primarily on a rejection of the reductively perceived values of the West. In fact, the porn and pornographic transactions overrunning Moscow in 1991–92 seemed to instantiate the very dangers that Kunin's premonitory parable tried to avert.

The First Gasp: Meat Comes to Moscow

Strange Bedfellows

By a masterstroke of associated pseudocoincidences, Russia has lacked not only effective condoms[38] but also a developed national tradition of porn. During the early 1990s it imported the bulk of its pornography from Latvia (Riga) and "borrowed" from Western sources for its own (re)products, as well as modeling its "original" creations on foreign paradigms.[39] Probably the most subversive aspect of these semipirated publications was their infraction of copyright law. In all other respects they conformed faithfully to the stringent rules of the genre.

The suddenness of porn's acceptability in Russia forced its production and circulation into patterns that were simultaneously centripetal and centrifugal. Owing to the scarcity of available materials, the same shots were reproduced randomly on various covers of translated and original fiction (e.g., the identical picture graced the covers of *Fortuna,* no. 2 [1991], published in Riga, and of the story "Kanikuly v Kalifornii" (Holidays in California); the same nude women reappeared thoughout entire issues of a magazine (e.g., nos. 3 and 6 of *Cupid,* published in Riga); the same item surfaced in several different packages (e.g., the story "Meteostantsiia" (Weather Station), printed separately and also in *Sex-Hit,* no. 2). Concurrent with this frugality was a profligacy that presupposed readers' voraciousness for anything vaguely related to sex or the body: certain publications offered a potpourri of wildly heterogeneous items, some of which acquired a risqué coloration or alteration of status by virtue of arbitrary juxtaposition with radically different pieces. How "neutrally" does a reader absorb "scientific" information about biological processes or dictionary definitions of such basic terms as *deviancy* and *frigidity* in a column printed alongside a bared pudendum or pneumatic breast clutched in a male hand? Such chaotic inclusiveness especially prevailed in papers such as *Eshche* (More), published in Riga; *Sex-Hit,* published in Riga; *Sovershenno intimno* (Entirely Intimate), published in Riga; *Spid-info* (Aids-Info), published in Moscow; and sex digests. These threw together a dizzyingly mixed assortment of standard porn shots; reports on sexual diseases; illustrations of possible positions for sexual play; personal ads (incomparably more down-to-earth and practical than in the United States);[40] letters from readers seeking advice or sharing their "sexual" experiences (the naïveté of some is extraterrestrial); purely pedagogical, or how-to, items; "scandals" gleaned from the Western press; and much more.[41] Particularly jarring for proponents of high culture was the lack of differentiation between comic book nudes in suggestive poses and reproductions of famous paintings by Rubens and other representatives of Art. Within Russian porn, then, the Venus de Milo was likely to rub elbows (*only* metaphorically speaking) with a *Playboy* centerfold, their sole common denominator being their gendered nudity. For the purposes of the genre, however, both were merely undressed female bodies, artfully "presented."

To acquire a sizable enough collection of porn so as to arrive at some fruitful generalizations about "representative" texts, I purchased everything pertinent I could locate throughout Moscow. In every instance I was the only female buyer. Westerners who query why women numbered quite high among the porn peddlers on the streets apparently forget that hunger applies powerful pressure even on the most passionate convictions. As unemployment soared, for some of the women, the "opportunity" to sell porn was not only their sole option but a "stroke of good luck." As several of them noted, they never even examined what they were hawking and were indifferent to the publications' contents.

Apart from films and videos (which I exclude from my discussion), the categories of porn that flooded Moscow in the early 1990s[42] may be broken down into (1) "static" visual, that is, pinups of individual women on posters or within magazines and newspapers; (2) "dynamic" visual or narrative visual, that is, "action" shots of a couple or series of such, grouped so as to suggest narrative development within a temporal flow; (3) verbal narrative, that is, texts that elaborate a plot (the covers of these normally designate the genre of the contents, via one or more nude bodies, sometimes accompanied by the tautological classification "erotic story" and the revelatory declaration of caution cum exclusion, "for men only"); and (4) *anekdoty* (anecdotes) about "sex." The first three categories both recycle Western forms and slavishly imitate their conventions, which are strictly coded to suggest a single overdetermined scenario.

Static Visual: The Hole as Whole

Pinups by definition are of woman, offered up according to a number of time-tested formulas calculated to commodify her as a generalized object for male use. Completely undressed or with breasts, bottom, and/or vagina exposed and highlighted, she becomes reduced to parts, in what Alan Soble and other Marxists have called the "dismemberment syndrome" that ensures women's alienation.[43] She invariably assumes a position that emanates passivity, submission, languor or insatiability and invites sexual possession or violation (e.g., on her knees; crouching, with buttocks thrust out at the camera; supine, with thighs spread wide). Boots pulled up to her naked thighs may be used to evoke the standard sexualized image of horseback riding (Tolstoi lives), while the leather/suede conjures up bondage or other S/M paraphernalia.

Though static in form, the pinup anticipates narration by imaging woman as a hole waiting to be filled, for porn tells and sells the timeless "story of *O.*" Hence, the highlighting of her anus, vagina, and mouth—the last, inevitably pouting and moist, sometimes licking, sucking, or encircling a surrogate penis (fruit, bottle, etc). If her face is visible (not mandatory for a genre that works to erase identity), her eyes are either closed in anticipated ecstasy or fixed directly on the viewer, "soliciting" him.

In accordance with porn's privileging of size, pinups favor generous breasts (with nipples darkened and perky—like Lenin, always "na postu" [on watch])—and lush pubic hair,[44] which intimate comparable proportions in sexual appetite and apertures that promise a pornucopia of orgasmic delights. If healthy and robust, the woman exudes a capacity for insatiability and epic exertions (the Amazonian "sex machines" fantasized as "*zhenshchiny roboty, nakachannye dikarki*" [women robots, inflated savages] [*Andrei,* 2:89]). If delicate or frail, she is sooner coded for S/M pain, accentuated by smudged, dark eye makeup that connotes a bruised sexuality (Cole 41).[45]

The genre carefully orchestrates appurtenances and setting: animals—especially dogs, cats, and horses—hint at the woman's animal nature (evident in the synonyms of *pussy* and *beaver* for a woman's pudendum) and have specific cultural associations with sex. Dogs, as is well-known, have been (ab)used for intercourse with women in porn films. Cats are ambulatory realized metaphors (or hyperbolized metonyms) for a woman's "pussy" (a visual rhetoric exploited in the first issue of *Andrei,* in which the centerfold nestles a cat between her legs, her face rapt with pleasure). The horse, especially the stallion, is a traditional symbol of male potency (*proizvoditel'* or the obsolete *al'fons*), hence the shot of Katia Volkova, the centerfold in *Andrei* (2:42), on horseback, arranged so that the neck of the horse resembles an enormous phallus emerging from between her gripping thighs. The purple prose explicating the sexual narrative, however, is transposed to a less obvious visual representation, of Katia straddling a chair:

> Ei khochetsia szhat' goriachego skakuna nogami, podat' emu shpor, oshchutit' shchekochushchii barkhat korichnevoi shkury. Ona chuvstvuet sebia i vsadnikom, i sil'noi gibkoi loshad'iu, i iznezhennoi damoi sveta. Toi, k komu oni skachut po opasnoi doroge. (2:43)

> [She wants to squeeze the hot racer with her legs, give him the spur, feel the ticklish velvet of his brown coat. She feels that she is both a rider and a strong, flexible mare, and a spoiled woman of the world—the one to whom they race along a dangerous road.]

The *they*, of course, encompasses the entire male readership of the magazine.

Settings likewise are carefully selected for their associative qualities. Accordingly, the showcased "goods" are sprawled on luxurious sheets, stretched out on the floor, or lolling in abandonment out in the "natural, untamed" outdoors, often beside water (the promise of other liquids). Their pose and environment all advert to the woman's readiness for "no holds barred" intercourse. Unlike the wife reluctantly performing her uxorial duty, such a woman has (as the title of an American film eloquently puts it) "gotta have it."

The meticulous choreography that organizes the components of pornography transforms women's nakedness into highly self-conscious nudity, according to John Berger's insightful distinction:

> To be naked is to be oneself.
>
> To be nude is to be seen naked by others and yet not recognized for oneself. A naked body has to be seen as an object in order to become a nude. (The sight of it as an object stimulates use of it as an object.) Nakedness reveals itself. Nudity is placed on display.
>
> To be on display is to have the surface of one's own skin, the hairs of one's own body, turned into a disguise which, in that situation, can never be discarded. The nude is condemned to never being naked. Nudity is a form of dress. (Berger 54)

Indeed, given the rote repetition of the "dress" regulations, in pornography nudity has become women's uniform.

Pornography "dresses" women this way so that man may perceive himself as the complementary opposite, the invading conqueror of this coded territory ("woman as land"), equipped "to penetrate the mystery within." Submission implies assertion (or violation); passivity invites activity (or violence); "large holes" can be filled only by large penises, etc. These aggrandizing devices generate an ego-stroking, cock-inflating image of the implied (omni)potent man that facilitates the male consumer's projection of himself into the picture, so to speak, as the active participant in the scenario automatically implied by the genre.

His alternative of voyeurism is built into the cultural disposition of gender roles. According to *Penthouse* publisher Bob Guccione, women are "natural" exhibitionists, whereas men are natural voyeurs (Cole 36–37). Berger's formulation echoes Guccione's but in a context that denaturalizes the role assignment and illuminates the origins of female self-voyeurism:

> Men look at women. Women watch themselves being looked at. This determines not only most relations between men and women but also the relation of women to themselves. The surveyor of woman in herself is male; the surveyed female. Thus she turns herself into an object—and most particularly an object of vision. (47)

Hence the profusion of mirrors for women's alienating, voyeuristic self-examination in pornographic art, film, and writing. Although pinups literally feature only women, in a more meaningful sense women are ontologically absent, while the dominant presence is male. The male buyer and his desires determine not only the manufacture of the product but also the "layout" of the "parts" that collectively constitute the object—that is, "woman."

Dynamic Visual: The Metaphysics of Absence

In visual pornographic scenarios with two or more players the male viewer may exercise essentially the same options: identification with the actual male portrayed, voyeurism, or a combination of the two. While this category may appear more evenhanded insofar as it incorporates men alongside women into the representation, that impression of gender parity is quickly dispelled. The balance of power between the heterosexual couple (or group members) engaged in intercourse, preliminary fondling, or exchange of meaningful looks, etc., duplicates the gender conventions that regulate pinup aesthetics.

Since women are the user-friendly disposables, multiple-participant groupings constellate several women around one male for, as Cole remarks, "the dynamic between pin-up and consumers is that of a gang bang" (Cole 36). Shots of couples contrast the woman's nudity or her exposure of one or more "key areas" (breasts, buttocks, vagina) with the man's fully or partly dressed state. Like the godhead,[46] the male penis in heterosexual pornography tends to be invisible—underlit, so that its contours remain shrouded in darkness, hidden by the man's careful posture, or strategically shielded by the woman's body, which, of course, is fully revealed. As the symbol of male identity ("manhood"), the Alpha and Omega in whose cause pornography has come into being, the penis remains largely "unpresentable."[47] Its mode is action (the active male subject), not contemplation (the passive female object).[48] Canadian law prohibits as obscene and mainstream American custom discourages as unsettling any shot of an erect penis. In like fashion, among the publications sold in Russia during 1990–92 the ratio of exposed (flaccid) male organs to bared pudenda was approximately 1:100.[49]

The rigid conventions of porn militate against turning men into objects for display, as Bob Guccione discovered when he experimented with *Viva* magazine (1972). Reversing gender roles, *Viva* featured explicit accounts of women's sexual adventures, punctuated with photos of nude men (penises at rest). To emphasize the men's virility the magazine placed them in forest settings ("man in control of wide expanses"), on ski slopes (the "intrepid sportsman"), and on horseback (the "Marlboro cowboy"). Readers' objections that the men "looked like homosexuals" (which presumably explained the poor sales) forced the magazine to close down. The lesson in lower mathematics? Boobs + butt = quintessentially a woman; pecs + penis = less than a man (Cole 37–38). Hence, their respective bodies appeared in postures and at levels emblematic of their unequal image and power: the woman was photographed prone, supine, or in some recognizably supplicating position, whereas the man, as the ringmaster in control, sat or stood. Since then both the boom in the gay porn industry and the increasing tendency in late-1980s' and early-1990s' advertising to display young male bodies as sexual objects has modified that earlier polar binarism (which, however, still prevails in Russia). The overwhelming majority of porn in the West still operates upon the principle of women's utter subordination to male desire.

A photograph published in the second issue of *Andrei* condenses a host of genre topoi that beg for closer analysis along these lines. The carefully arranged tableau shows a white (possibly marble) statue of Napoleon on a red tablecloth (coded to suggest blood and passion), standing, arms folded, between a seated woman's spread thighs. The military figure of Napoleon, instantly recognizable through his uniform, universalizes malehood as arrogant conqueror. As a monument (literally and figuratively) to boundless power, Napoleon for Russians is the violent invader who confidently enters unknown terrain and by whatever methods necessary imposes sovereignty over it. An unstoppable force, on the one hand, Napoleon nonetheless exudes an aura of olympian calm, on the other, because he is immobilized (and desexed) through the cool, "tamed" medium of marble or stone that immortalizes him and his historical role. Strategically stationed at the picture's center, he instantly dominates the viewer's attention as the man of action whose garb and pose suffice to establish his unique identity. The land to be forcibly entered and subdued looms behind him as the "field of his activity," where he can "prove himself."[50] It is the anonymous expectant vagina, bared but blocked off from the viewer, who sees only the pubic hair surrounding Napoleon as background. Thus, while physically reduced by compositional proportions to modest (unaroused) penis size, Napoleon is symbolically inflated to cosmic proportions as historical referent (a cultural monument celebrated by the Western world). In the "parry and thrust" of phallic battle he will invade between the woman's thighs that flank him, eager to submit to the sword.

Woman here is fragmented, genre-coded as "every-man's-land," nothing more than spread legs. A black lacy garter on her otherwise nude right thigh and her black-gloved left hand, resting "protectively" against the left groin and pubic hair, signal both frivolity and helplessness in the face of aggression, respectively. Faceless, lacking all identity, woman is generalized into "cunt," the fetishized body part that defines her role in the universe of male activity and values. The "hole" of her vagina (i.e., zero of her being), obstructed by Napoleon's figure, is transposed onto the enormous ring decorating the gloved finger of her hand (a convention borrowed from striptease routines),[51] playing on the immemorial association between jewels and women's genitals.[52] The picture, then, erases the live woman photographed and dismembered in it, while installing the presence of the man via inert facsimile. *Both* function as cultural objects—invested, however, with unequal political power.

Verbal Narrative: Hype, Hyperbole, and Taboo

If, as Linda Williams contends, visual pornography strives to make the invisible (i.e., Pleasure) visible, then the goal of its Gutenberg counterpart is to print the unprintable. Critics have emphasized the more visceral appeal of the visual, which tends not only to elicit stronger and more immediate audience reactions but also can function more economically, as acknowledged by the cliché "A picture's worth a thousand words."[53] This may especially obtain when the nude body and its acts are represented, for verbal mediation tends to dilute the instant impact normally attributed to a directly apprehended visual image. Victor Erofeyev, in an interview on eroticism, declared: "sila gologo tela takova, chto [,] uvidev ego, mozhno zabyt' o tom, chto chelovek govorit" (the power of bare flesh is such that once you've seen it you can forget about what a person is saying [Erofeev 2]). Yet words may strongly affect our perception of the visible nude (the difference between silent and sound film), just as the ability of the written word to conjure up visual images is crucial to published texts. In fact, printed pornography appropriates a number of authentication techniques from film as well as sharing the gender stereotyping that reinforces unequal distribution of power in visual genres.

Porn fiction sold as a separate item in Moscow of the early 1990s had a specific look: a compilation of twelve to fifty-odd pages folded in half and stapled together to form a slim booklet, it usually had a randomly selected cover sporting a naked or near-naked woman in a suggestive pose or couples positioned in some form of sexual readiness or beyond. Runs of the computer-typed texts varied from five hundred to fifty thousand copies, offered most frequently for a negotiable price (*tsena dogovornaia*)—a pimp eager to make a deal. Barter and exchangeability ruled the packaging, in fact, for the identical cover could appear on several different texts, or, conversely, the same story could have several different covers, just as it could bear various titles (e.g., "Rodovoe okonchanie" [Family Completion][54] by S. Khalyi surfaces elsewhere as simply "Okonchanie" [Completion]). The narratives belonged to one of three categories, not always easy to distinguish because of hurried, sloppy production:

1. Translations from Western sources bearing authors' names: (e.g., Jeanette Rich-Paterson's "Letnie kanikuly" [Summer

Vacation], Michelle D'Clercq's "Iuzhnyi roman" [Southern Romance]).[55] Intentionally marketed by its purveyors as a Western commodity for the status that attaches to foreign goods, this category dominated the porn market.

2. Anonymous texts, in which the only clue to the country of origin was the characters' names (e.g., Iolanthe de St. Ives in "Prikliucheniia v otele 'Svetlaia luna'" [Adventures in the "Bright Moon" Hotel]), which may not have been completely reliable evidence, since American and English names often mixed with Russian ones, without explanation.
3. Original Russian creations, with author's name attached. The likelihood of a market-oriented adoption of pseudonyms seemed strong, however, particularly in such cases as "Shvedskaia troika" (Three-Way). Although an indisputably Russian text, it purported to be the inspiration of O. Konner (American or Irish O'Connor?), which not only has a Western ring (a significant selling point) but also evokes the French *con* (not for its current primary meaning of "dumb bastard" but for its earlier one of "cunt" [Mercier 27]).

Both translated and domestic Russian pornography adhered fairly closely to standard precepts of the genre. Action in pornography is the *act* of sex (the single indispensable element), presented in such a way as to stimulate readers' arousal. In a sense the genre presupposes an impotent as its most "difficult" or resistant reader (a view shared by Soble), for its choices rest on the premise that "regular" sex alone is "insufficient cause" for excitement. To elicit the necessary frisson, what is prohibited must be *ex*hibited. Interdictions depend on a hypothetical norm validated by a social community. Thus, porn necessarily violates taboos and breaches boundaries in those areas of sexual activity that, according to communal standards, symptomatize deviation from normalcy: (1) location and frequency of act, and (2) number, age, and position of participants.[56] In other words, nonstop, non–missionary-style sex, outside of bed, with adolescents and pensioners, preferably in groups. Hence, in "Three-Way" Sasha and Vitia have three-way sex with Liliia, a woman in her sixties devoted to masturbating men to orgasm; Viktor in "S golodu" (Out of Hunger) performs cunnilingus on Lin [Lynn?] during her menstruation, extracts her tampon for intensification of pleasure, and finally climaxes together with her son's girlfriend, Kim, when she urinates on his testicles as they both straddle a toilet seat. D. Harber's "Desiat' let vo sne" (A Ten-Year Sleep) (elsewhere called "Vospominaniia molodoi zhenshchiny" [A Young Woman's Recollections]) condenses perhaps the greatest number of generic topoi: mutual onanism (hetero and homo), group sex with the aid of aphrodisiacs, fellatio, voyeurism, sodomy, and incest (between father and daughter).

"Sex" is the masterplot of porn, with orgasm as its "natural" culminating point. The importance of quantity in porn's economics of pleasure builds repetition into the genre, which is why those who decry porn on other than moral grounds typically complain of boredom at witnessing "one sex act after another." Yet, while the experience of pleasure is iterated, the means of achieving it must vary, which explains why the principle of escalation structures the genre. If the first orgasm is attained through conventional sex, the second must involve either an increased number of partners or some less orthodox route to climax. How the rule of escalation operates is nicely (and nastily) illustrated by Jeanette Rich-Paterson's "Summer Vacation," a classic text of sexual initiation. The fifteen-year-old virgin Ania enjoys her first sexual discharge in the woods when her twenty-five-year-old distant relative Robert manually brings her to orgasm, her second when he actually deflowers her. She then progresses to intercourse with a thirty-five-year-old monk, "Brother" Petr, inside a room on church grounds. If at first blush her next coupling—with twenty-eight-year-old "Brother" Klement—seems to contradict the imperative of augmentation, the formidable dimensions of his instrument ("23–25 centimeters," she notes in appreciative awe) and the confessional as his Sadean choice of setting dispel that impression. Size and site compensate for reduction of age. Ania next succumbs to forty-five-year-old "Uncle" Jim, before moving on to three-way sex and fellatio with both uncle and brother (the pseudofamilial mode of reference capitalizing on the incest taboo).

The auditory accompaniment is also subject to escalation: heavy, irregular breathing and gasps expand to moans and groans and reach a crescendo of shrieks and shouts that would put the Hallelujah Chorus to shame, even as the female voice continues to plead for "harder, faster, more." What this text artlessly exposes, then, is the mathematical organization of unappeasable appetite. Not development but increment extends the narrative, which ends only when the author's imagination (masquerading as the protagonists' sexual energy) runs out of steam.

Of course, the performance principle that informs the construction of male sexuality demands tangible evidence of capacity. Consequently, a mainstay of porn is the mathematical formulas invoked regarding size (in which male organs are concerned, biggest is still best), frequency (males seem capable of epically heroic reprisals, which correspond to women's constant voracity), and quantity (people virtually bathe in each other's sexual emissions—in a convention doubtless appropriated from the "money shot" in film [authentication via a close-up of external ejaculation]). In short, hyperbole is porn's privileged trope.

What most eloquently testifies to the formulaic nature of porn, like that of the Harlequin Romance, are the how-to manuals in the West that catalog the genre's essential ingredients and the recipes for mixing them.[57] Yet, for all their mechanical predictability, over the last decade both genres have pushed back the limits of acceptability. That is why one reads Stephen Ziplow's *Film Maker's Guide to Pornography* (1977) with a certain nostalgia for the "kinder, gentler" brand of porn whose definitive features his checklist inventories. Stressing the supremacy of the "money shot," Ziplow also includes masturbation, conventional sex (heterosexual, penis in vagina), lesbianism, oral sex (cunnilingus and fellatio), orgies, three-way sex (heterosexual), and anal sex (the recipient presumed to be female). Sadomasochistic rituals (affectionately called "sadie-max") and thanatic sex, now a commonplace in all categories of porn,[58] are conspicuously absent from Ziplow's list. The rule of escalation, then, affects not only the internal structure of the genre but also the evolution of the genre itself, which inevitably responds to changes in social values. Yet one constant persists, whatever the permutations: male supremacy.

Although the dynamic of male dominance and female submission so blatant in visual materials seems weakened in pornographic writings marketed in Russia, most texts nonetheless propagate gender stereotypes. In the realm of sex the male organ rules: men are authoritative figures of initiation, endowed with skill, creativity, and persistence, whereas women, as receptacles, "take in" the male lessons, penises, hands, fingers, and various objects of choice thrust into them.

Hard Lessons and Softening Devices

Not unlike socialist realism and the Bildungsroman, some of the porn fiction sold in Moscow had a pedagogical cast, most pronounced in narratives of initiation, which trace the induction of a naïf into the mysteries of "forbidden" sex acts by a seasoned specialist. Curiously, the lesson seems also directed at the reader, for many texts resort to a terminology for bodily equipment and (re)actions more likely to inform the ignorant than inflame the excitable. "Western" words with Greek or Latin roots, instead of a purely Slavic lexicon, preponderate in what I would call a purely functional naming: *fallos, vagina, sperma, klitor, orgazm.* The dearth of a rich Russian vocabulary for body parts and sexual activities partly accounts for this reliance on "dictionary" nomenclature, which effectively distances the reader.

Even more curious is the slippage into euphemism and periphrasis—canonical rhetoric within soft porn. Michelle D'Clercq's [*sic*] "Southern Romance" offers a fascinating instance of periphrasis that, nonetheless, installs the paradigm of visual porn. In describing his sexual congress with a woman he meets at the beach, the narrator (a married father and experienced sexual athlete) conjures up the image of sex as warfare by repeatedly referring to his penis as *oruzhie* (weapon) and *orudie* (instrument), while words applied to the woman advert to her animal nature: she is a *naezdnitsa* (rider), her vagina a *zavetnaia iama-norka* (secret burrow-hole), her clitoris a *dovol'no strannyi zverek* (rather strange little animal); when she performs fellatio, he analogizes her licking motions with a cat's. The invocation of two distinct sets of associations (military vs. zoological) underscores the author's inscription of other gendered differences. The male as controlled and controlling pragmatist (an adulterer seeking short-term impersonal gratification, lying so as to pacify the woman who represents merely one of numerous *x*-night stands) contrasts with the accommodating, vulnerable female (ready to abandon job and home for his sake and to satisfy his every desire). Their encounter emotionally enslaves *her* but certifies *his* virility as an emblem of power.

If in "Southern Romance" porn's reputed liberating function is belied by gender stereotyping, in "Weather Station" and elsewhere the conformist aspects of the genre manifest themselves in self-censorship.

Although this "erotic" novella brims with such generic commonplaces as three-way sex, lesbianism, rape, fellatio, and implement-aided onanism, it either employs coy euphemisms for sexual parts and acts (e.g., "kholmik" [mound], "vvesti 'druga' v 'domik' " [introduces the "friend" into the "little house"]) or replaces them with ellipses (e.g., "Alesha podoshel, razdvinul rukami iagoditsy i vvel svoi chlen v moiu . . ." [Alesha came up, spread my buttocks and introduced his member into my . . .], "ia snova nachal . . . Natashu" [I started . . . Natasha anew], "delai posle etogo so mnoi vse, chto khochesh', tol'ko . . . menia" [after this, do with me what you will, only . . . me]). Prudery wreaks havoc on narrative continuity when, for instance, a series of question marks and ellipses substitutes for the description of Liia's rape, occasioning a bewildering shift in point of view that makes the ensuing passage incomprehensible. Such devices signal not license but, in fact, suppression in a genre touted as promoting and betokening freedom.

Anecdotes: Loss of Oral Potency

Subversive license, by contrast, inheres in the genre of the joke (*anekdot*), which Andrei Siniavskii has conceptualized as a peculiarly Russian form of contemporary folklore (Terts 77–95). In a remarkable operation that evokes the transsexuality motif in pornography (e.g., "Family Completion"), the logic of the current popular culture market has transplanted the *anekdot* onto the pages of porn and sex publications. In so doing, it has transformed an authentic oral art form whose success depends on the individual "teller's" skill in delivery—on a live performance in which timing, tone, accent, and emphasis play a crucial role—into an inert item, mechanically reproducible and reproduced.[59]

Anekdoty not only appear (then and now) alongside other materials in magazines and papers devoted to sex (e.g., SEX-*bespredel* [no-holds-barred SEX]) but also constitute the entire contents of slim digests (e.g., *Daidzhest* SEX *anekdotov* [Digest of SEX *Anekdoty*]) and more substantial collections (e.g., SEX *Anekdoty*), invariably featuring a nude and/or suggestively posed woman on the cover. If Siniavskii's notion that the genre lives *by* suppression has any legitimacy, this sudden rash of "anecdotitis" may well prove fatal to its survival. For, as Siniavskii maintains:

> What lies at the basis of the genre [of the *anekdot*] and the conditions in which it works, develops, and exists is a violation of certain conventional norms of behavior and speech. It's as if the *anekdot* wants to be prohibited, liquidated on the spot, and it lives on just this supposition and expectation. Give it freedom, remove the prohibition, and it will die. (78)

It would be myopic to deduce publishers' awareness of the transgressive nature of *anekdoty* from such titles as "Smekh i grekh: 72 anekdota" (Grin and Sin: 72 *Anekdoty*) published in Kiev, for these compilers patently locate transgression not in the genre per se but, rather, in the theme of sex. This much is evident from such packaging techniques as highlighting the *a, k,* and *t* in *anekdot* to stress the sexual "act" implicitly offered by the nudes scattered throughout the paper's pages.

Most collections group *anekdoty* according to a familiar situational typology (e.g., a gynecological appointment; a spouse's unexpected return home; a visit to a brothel; a trip abroad) that explores sexually related themes, usually cast in a problematic mode: fears of impotence, anxieties about performance, sexual incompatibility, adultery, and the like. While such topics and their treatment might reveal something about prevailing attitudes and mores in Russian society, the specifics of the genre hardly conduce to reader arousal. The climax to which the *anekdot* moves is the *pointe* that brings a release of plot tension through laughter prompted by the witty closure. That is why, as Siniavskii correctly argues, "as an authentically folkloric, oral form of poetry, it fades on paper, losing the live voice, mimicry and gestures that accompany it, and sometimes practically reifies it completely, like pantomime" (91). To present this quintessentially oral genre in written form, then, is to castrate it (the Greek word *anekdotos,* in fact, means "unpublished"). Without the performance component that is inseparable from its subversive gesture, the *anekdot* becomes reaccented, drawing attention to its thematic concerns, its significance as social document. Read (as opposed to heard) from this shifted perspective, *anekdoty* reveal the ubiquity of adultery, mistrust between the sexes, and the currency of the rape myth—at least among the male population. But anyone seeking "porn pleasure" from these pseudoliterary eunuchs is doomed to disappointment.

The Porn of Politics: Airbrushing a Myth

If Western pornography is the political product of the capitalist economic system, in Soviet Russia politics has been the pornographic product of a utopian imagination unrestrained by ethics. Whereas Western billboards typically advertise commodities by implicating them in a sexual mystique, Soviet Russian slogans and signs invariably advertised ideology through promises of a future paradise. According to the "wish-fulfillment" scripts of the politicosocioeconomic structures that have produced them, the larger-than-life symbolic ideals of both advertising campaigns capture (indeed, master) the public imagination. For these carefully elaborated figures suggest the tangible realization of their societies' dominant dreams. Through their *visible* example, they validate the possibility of formidable achievements in those arenas that collective fantasy invests with significance. If the pinup (or her "tamed" relative, the model) represents the "ideal" of the Western billboard, her Russian analogue is, unquestionably, Stalin.[60]

With the early 1990s Russian scholarship began examining the "selling strategies" used to fashion the image of Stalin along semidivine lines (a procedure earlier mapped out by the prototyrant Nero).[61] Under Stalin's own supervision film, fiction, and the press orchestrated a comprehensive drive that enabled Stalin to emerge (like the pinup) as "all things to all men." Stalin's omnipotence, according to this script, derived not from his readiness to murder when expedient (the reality) but, instead, from his omniscience in all spheres: his prophetic vision, military prowess, artistic genius, democratic convictions, compassion, and self-abnegation (the illusion). It is undoubtedly the irreconcilable discrepancy between the claims and the reality of Stalinism that prompted Liudmila Petrushevskaia to adduce the following passage from P. Proskurin's *Imia tvoe* (Your Name) as a sample of Russian pornography:

> This evening, to his annoyance, Stalin, who loved this very opera with a . . . morbid passion, . . . didn't feel the satisfaction he always anticipated. . . . Briukhanov privately registered Stalin's barely noticeable movement as he abandoned himself with his whole body to what was happening on stage, and Briukhanov realized that he'd been waiting for precisely that moment . . . From very

> close Briukhanov saw Stalin's eyes and he was startled at their youthful brilliance. (Petrushevskaia 238)

The perfect congruence between this account and the voyeuristic strain of porn derives from their common transparent deceit: a prearranged scene, with every detail calculated in advance, is presented as the viewer's chance intrusion upon an individual during a moment of private self-oblivion. In porn the unwary woman might be undressing, bathing, or masturbating; in Proskurin, Stalin is anticipating a "total" pleasure enabled by his musical sensitivity. Both versions of purportedly unwitting self-exposure rely on illusion (the woman's "innocent" sexuality, Stalin's passionate love of the arts) that may be manipulated through lies. Both exact a high price from their consumers, who seek one thing, pay for another, and receive a third. Both mask brutality of sorts through aestheticizing myths.

The homology emerges most clearly in the iconography of sexuality and political power as regards dress, pose, proportion or perspective, setting, props, and facial expression of the subject (i.e., object "on sale"). Shots of the pinup coordinate all details so as to convey sexuality: her mandatory nudity and suggestive pose (often supine or prone) of intimate invitation, often accentuated by "frivolous" items such as see-through lingerie, lacy garter, even toys, and often photographed from above so as to seem powerless. By inverse contrast Stalin wears his perennial military uniform (even during peacetime), always buttoned up to the throat, so as to project simultaneously his "eagle eye" for detail and his readiness to defend "Mother Russia" and her/his "children." To emphasize his imperturbable control and inspired leadership, he either stands upright above the "teeming masses"[62] or is seated over a map, both variants implying that he controls all he surveys (people, territory, and nature). In group pictures he holds center stage, his "presence" conveyed by the reactions of those surrounding him, its force augmented by the angle of the camera, which captures him from below. Gerasimov's cult painting of him with Voroshilov shows Stalin towering symbolically over the country's capital; in the Stalin statue at the Paris World Fair (1937) the Napoleonic placement of his right hand and the forward movement of his body project Stalin's "cosmic" power. If the pinup's setting and props evoke "naughty" pleasures, Stalin's emblematize power, duty, and competence; hence, he is depicted in a battlefield or beside tanks, sporting military boots and reassuringly puffing on a pipe (the Father of all Russia as phallic authority). The centerfold's bushy mound as a promise of sexual bounty has its desexed equivalent in the luxurious fullness of Stalin's mustache, which connotes a military rather than sexual virility. And finally, because both pinup and Stalin, as visual incarnations of an ideal, must transcend their physical reality, photographers obligingly airbrush their portraits so as to erase all imperfections.[63] In short, although the power relations they construct for the beholder are polar opposites, the (desexed) *Kul't* image and the (sexed) pinup image are structured by the same pornographic aesthetic.

To posit such a convergence between pornography and Stalin may strike skeptics as perverse. Yet Moscow's truck drivers subliminally recognized and celebrated their commonality during glasnost by displacing the portraits of Stalin on their dashboards with pinups. Those who welcome pornography as a long-delayed access to freedom of expression, then, would benefit from reading J. S. Mill's essay "On Liberty," which cautions against freedoms that impinge upon the liberty and selfhood of others. Readers of Russian pornography might ask themselves why, if pornography sings freedom's song, it does so only in male chorus. Why, if scopophilic pleasures are so natural and liberating, they are limited to only half of the country's population and constructed according to musty formulas from the West. Meanwhile, from the vantage point of a Westerner trained in dismantling self-serving constructs, the porn revolution in Moscow has merely ushered in yet another Party, with different organs and members but an all-too-familiar agenda of domination.

Postscript

By spring 1994 the porn that had flooded *lotki* (bookstalls) throughout Moscow in 1991–92 had virtually disappeared from the streets. *Andrei* was defunct, and the only porn items readily available in all sections of the city were the three issues of the Russian edition of *Penthouse*. Ironically, owing to recent market forces, the fate of "Russian" porn now coincides with that of Russian literature. The dynamics of supply and demand determining the sale of printed matter have relegated both to specialty stores. Volumes of such venerated classics as Dostoevskii,

Tolstoi, and Mandel'shtam prove as rare finds at street stalls as "Three-Way" or "Summer Vacation."

Just as dozens of scholarly books result from joint ventures between Russian specialists and their subsidizing Western counterparts, so the Russian purveyors of porn have negotiated contracts with Western experts, enabling Russians to purchase the Russian edition, for example, of *Penthouse* or *Playboy*. Moreover, hopes of improved sales encourage publishers of diverse convictions and quality to include items that embrace or verge on pornography in their magazines and newspapers, from *Ogonyok* to *Zhenskie dela* (Women's Affairs). For instance, the latter monthly has expanded phenomenally since its inception in 1994. Under the editorship of Liubov' Panova, the paper, with its logo of a nude woman on the cover, now boasts a run of 450,000 copies, even though by Moscow standards the price for its twenty-four pages runs high. Its November 1994 issue (no. 11) carried a "report," typical for the paper, on "Miss Sis'-94" (Miss Tit-94), the two accompanying photographs of Zena Fulsom(e?) exploiting the camera's versatility to inflate fantastically her already quite remarkable bared breasts to a size about four times her head. Moreover, nightclubs and stage performances in Moscow routinely include nude women. With the steady assimilation of pornographic features into everyday life in the capital, the future of porn in Russia depends on the pleasures and perils sought by its consumer populace and the patterns of a culture and economy that still await stabilization.[64]

Notes

1. On the market in pornography, see Sidorov and Demidov 38. For the letter of complaint by a fifteen-year-old male student, see *Vecherniaia Moskva* (25 April 1990): 2. By 1990 pinups of nude women decorated virtually all taxicabs in Moscow. When an American male passenger sharing a cab with me ironically asked one cabdriver whether the "nudie" shot displayed on his windshield was of his wife, the man laughed, and to the query "So, who is she?" revealingly replied, "No one."
2. The article, in the form of a diary, is by Leonid Konovalov, "Narod trebuet reshitel'nykh mer," *Andrei* 2 (1991): 16–18.
3. This *profession de foi* launched the inaugural issue of *Andrei* in 1991. By 1994 *Andrei* was defunct, much of its staff having transferred to the Russian edition of *Penthouse*.

4. By early 1993 women constituted approximately 80 percent of the unemployed in Moscow and St. Petersburg. See chapter 1.
5. Dworkin, who has researched pornography for many years and written copiously on the topic, and MacKinnon, then a professor of law at the University of Minnesota, both had contracts with the City Council in Minneapolis to develop an ordinance relating the violation of women's rights in regard to pornography to civil rights. Since U.S. publishers refused to publish the record of the public hearings that took place in December 1983, the transcript came out in England in a volume entitled *Pornography and Sexual Violence: Evidence of the Links* (London: Everywoman Ltd., 1988); hereafter cited in the text as *PaSV*.

   For documentation of Dworkin and MacKinnon's activities, see Donald Alexander Downs, *The New Politics of Pornography* (Chicago: University of Chicago Press, 1989).
6. The brouhaha around Robert Mapplethorpe's photograph exhibition in Cincinnati (1990) revived a host of questions normally triggered by the appearance of works considered pornographic by some segments of society: freedom of artistic expression, the rights and obligations of sponsoring agencies such as the National Endowment for the Arts, the distinction between art and pornography. On this, see Cembalest, 136; and "Body Politics," editorial in *Commonwealth* (November 1990): 627. For the implications of the Mapplethorpe phenomenon, see Mercer, "Just Looking for Trouble: Robert Mapplethorpe and the Fantasies of Race," in Segal 92–110.

   Although explicit sexuality and sadomasochism in rock lyrics and videos, on record jackets, and during concert performances have become standard fare, occasionally a particularly extreme version of such materials will elicit public outrage. Witness the scandals around the group 2 Live Crew's recording of "As Nasty as They Wanna Be" and videos by Madonna and Michael Jackson.
7. Unnumbered page of preface, following xl. At the Minneapolis hearings Dworkin cited an article claiming that pornography annually accrues about seven billion dollars, which would place it fortieth in the list of Fortune 500 largest companies in terms of profit (*PaSV*, 10–11). She has come under fire from partisans of pornography for making unsubstantiated assertions. Given her most recent claim that sexual intercourse between men and women by definition is a form of rape, Dworkin qualifies as the most radical "feminist" on issues of sex and gender.
8. U.S. Department of Justice (1986), *Attorney General's Commission on Pornography Final Report*, 1353.
9. For a rundown on the various categories, see Hawkins and Zimring 30–52.
10. See, for instance, the influential essay by Sontag, "The Pornographic Imagination" (131–69). To viewers of such porn classics as *Deep Throat* and purchasers of "under the counter" publications, Sontag's ruminations on aesthetics, philosophical speculation, Henry James, and Georges Bataille must have an intergalactic ring.

11. As Ed Donnerstein (a psychologist at the Center for Communications Research at the University of Wisconsin) testified, porn material "has changed quite drastically" since 1968 (*PaSV*, 22). See also Donnerstein; Gubar and Hoff.
12. *Hard-core* originally referred to the actual perpetration of the acts represented in the porn materials as part of their production, whereas *soft-core* simulated them. Nowadays *soft-core* tends to designate less explicit treatments of sexual acts, often euphemized through a romantic haze. This designation has led to analyses of Harlequin romances, for example, as "soft porn." Indeed, that genre polarizes gender along lines of dominance, control, power, and violence for men and submission, helplessness, disempowerment, and acceptance of brutalization by women. On the genre, see Faust; Modleski; Radway; and Snitow 35–58; 141–61. For additional sources, see Soble 21 n. 41.
13. Comment at the Women Law Conference in New York, 1986, quoted in Cole 170 n. 18.
14. *Last Gasp*, a mail order catalog published in San Francisco, advertises comics, art books, cards, records, body art, videos, games, magazines, T-shirts, drugs, and children books. It caters to the broadest possible audience: gay, straight, and bisexual; fetishists, sadists, masochists, pedophiles, etc. I thank Peter Scotto for acquainting me with its marvels.
15. Susan Cole has objected that to accept the so-called cathartic value of pornography is difficult "when murder victims' bodies are strewn with pornographs, or when the dresser drawers of child-killers like Clifford Olson are crammed with pornographic magazines" (Cole 45).
16. "The true defense of pornography and obscenity, as they encourage sexuality, is that they are harmless or beneficial" (40).
17. These three official bodies were, respectively, the Commission on Pornography and Obscenity constituted by the U.S. Congress in 1967; the Home Office Departmental Committee on Obscenity and Film Censorship; and the Attorney General's Commission on Pornography. See Hawkins and Zimring 20–29. On the *Final Report* of the Attorney General's Commission on Pornography (1986), see Bloom 9–25. Bloom's assessment of the Meese Commission's efforts slights its receptivity to feminist ideas and formulations. The report not only directly asserts that pornography is degrading to women and used to generate male "lustful pleasure" but also echoes Robin Morgan's famous maxim, "Pornography is the theory; rape is the practice" (*Attorney General's Commission on Pornography* 1 [1986]: 78).
18. That point is made about the Russian public by Leonid Konovalov in his piece on the Russian commission. See *Andrei* 2 (1991): 16.
19. Works by the Marquis de Sade, Henry Miller, John Cleland (*Fanny Hill* [1749]), Pauline Réage (*The Story of O* [1954]), and Erica Jong belong to the conventional corpus of "erotic" texts. Commentators such as Susan Sontag, for example, often with the aid of Georges Bataille (*Death and Sensuality: A Study of Eroticism and the Taboo* [1969]), analyze these texts in terms of "artis-

tic superiority." Sontag, whose essay brims with subtle and thought-provoking insights, approvingly quotes Paul Goodman's maxim "The question is not *whether* pornography, but the quality of pornography," assuming that quality is an unproblematic universal measure (Sontag 131–69, esp. 169).

20. Cited in Charney 1. Charney himself avoids the problem of definition by referring to the works he investigates as "sexual fiction."
21. See their essays in the collection edited by Hughes, *Perspectives on Pornography.*
22. A milestone in porn film, Gerard Damiano's *Deep Throat* (1972) brought instant notoriety to Linda Marciano, who, as Linda Lovelace, portrayed a woman with a unique physiological displacement: her clitoris was located in her throat. At the Minneapolis hearings on pornography Marciano testified that throughout the filming of *Deep Throat* its agent, Charles Traynor, imprisoned her, physically brutalized her, and forced her at gunpoint to have sex with animals. She describes these experiences in her autobiography *Ordeal.* See Crabbe 44–68.

    An entire subgenre of hard-core porn derives its name from the feature-length commercial film by the husband and wife team of Michael and Roberta Findlay titled *Snuff* (1976). It popularized evisceration of women and their death (they are "snuffed out") as a "turn-on." In her book on porn film Linda Williams argues, with unpersuasive logic, that the film is not pornographic but, rather, a variant on the slasher film. Yet the capacity of porn to assimilate elements from the slasher genre, which also favors female victims, is self-evident (on this, see Clover 187–228). What Williams calls the "replacement of orgasm's 'little death' by real death" *conflates* the two (Williams 189–95).
23. That has been proposed by Tong 1–18, esp. 10–12.
24. This is the title of the definitive guide by Roy Sheldon and Egmont Arens (1932) to the economic control of a mass audience through psychological manipulation grounded in the insights of Freud, Jung, Adler, and Pavlov. On this and other aspects of subliminal seduction, see Ewen.
25. See, for instance, Ewen and Ewen; and Sobel. For an incisive early study that pioneered both the key term and the sociopsychological approach to media material see Key.
26. See, for example, the unsigned article in *Sex-Hit,* which makes the "natural" argument for pornography: "Pornography simply shows people as they're made, including their sexual organs" ("Chto takoe khorosho i chto takoe plokho?" *Sex-Hit* 2:3).
27. Which, in the context of Ellis's values, means "no one who matters."
28. See Williams 184–228.
29. "To show how the concept of pornography conditions and determines the way in which men actually treat women" is how MacKinnon formulated the agenda at the Minneapolis hearing (*PaSV,* 9).

30. On this and the formative role of André Bazin in the realist theory of film, see Williams 184–96.
31. Indeed, as Suzanne Kappeler justly points out, Kant's theory of aesthetics, which lists women among the "soulless" products of fine art, makes woman an object of aesthetic perception awaiting "animation" by the perceiver's genius (Kappeler 45–46).
32. Susan Cole stresses the importance of viewing porn not as a concept or a representation but, rather, as a practice (Cole 7–12, 24–25). For a more extended, particularized definition, see Dworkin xxxiii.

    One might object that gay male porn does not represent women, but such an objection ignores the widely recognized fact that in gay male relationships the "passive" or less "macho" partner plays out the female role in a heterosexual relationship. In such cases "woman" functions as sign.

    Since the pornography that reached Russia during the early 1990s presupposed a heterosexual male audience, the issue of gay and lesbian porn lies outside the concerns of this survey.
33. Although feminists largely agree on the definition of *pornography*, they are divided about the means of combatting it. Whereas radicals such as Dworkin and MacKinnon unwaveringly opt for strict censorship with a view to elimination, feminists advocating liberal values hesitate to agitate for a solution that would compromise their broader political allegiances by aligning them with a stance traditionally identified with political conservatives (the New Right). Yet another group of feminists is reluctant to adopt a position that would imperil erotica produced by and for women. In short, the pornography controversy continues to divide feminists.
34. For a sampling of stances by women who agitate against censoring pornography, see the fascinating essays in Burstyn.
35. In the ancient world *pornographos* reportedly referred to inspiring depictions of varieties of sexual intercourse that decorated the walls of a house of prostitution in Pompeii, for instance (Tong 2).
36. What puzzles me about this statement is that a "celebrated courtesan" would most probably belong to the higher class of prostitute, called the hetaira.
37. The Russian original, simply called *Interdevochka,* is available in English translation, *Intergirl: A Hard Currency Hooker,* trans. Antonina W. Bouis (New York: Bergh Publishers, 1991).
38. The 1990s may go down in Russian history as the Popular Culture Re/naissance (or Pregnancy Era), as uncoordinated "quickie" reproduction (Unplanned Parenthood) overpopulated streets and markets with commodities that the economy had difficulty absorbing.
39. According to Red Stripe Books, however, several "erotic" texts have merely been suppressed. The publisher, housed in New Jersey, so far has released two novel-length books in English translation: (1) the purported *Memoirs of a Russian Princess: Gleaned From her Secret Diary,* anonymous and, according

to the editor's conjecture, "penned about the year 1796"; and (2) from the mid-eighteenth century, *The Russian Serf Girl: The Story of Grushenka,* based on a 1933 Paris edition. The latter supposedly tells the story of a serf girl who resembled and so could substitute for Princess Nelidova Sokolova (in bed and elsewhere) when the princess engaged in extramarital frolics. Grushenka reportedly later became the madam (Grushenka Pavlovsk) of "one of the most notorious brothels in all of Russia," in which capacity she became implicated in the sudden death of one Iurii Rybin. See the introduction and preface to *The Russian Serf Girl.*

40. If the costs cited for such ads are accurate, they, by contrast, are prohibitive for certain segments of society (no hope for pensioners). *Cupid,* for instance, charged forty rubles per ad, a price archly specified "dlia ddzentel'menov" (for gentlemen) and at that time equivalent to a week's pension.

 The ads supply information not usually found in their Western counterparts: references to men's excessive drinking, assurances of economic health, frank admissions of having children who will have to be reckoned with in any relationship that might eventuate, and the like. They also imply certain trends—for example, young men's eagerness to meet older women and, in the case of gays, older men; a concern with physical fitness; men's expressed conviction of their ability to bring any woman full satisfaction.

41. Of course, publications of a serious informational nature have also proliferated in recent years: Igor' Kon's articles, reporting on Western trends and offering data à la Kinsey; Aleksandr Nezhdanov's sexological primer, *Populiarnaia seksologiia* (Popular Sexology [Riga], 1990); a book-length examination by various sexologists of typical sexual-emotional problems between heterosexual couples, based on scores of received letters, *Mysteries of a Twosome* (Moscow: Tainy dvoikh, 1990); translations from the *Kamasutra,* etc.

 The third issue of *Cupid* advertised a forthcoming sex encyclopedia by Sergei Mamulov, from which it extracted a rundown of various "authorities'" recommended normative doses of sexual activity (the frequencies stipulated indicate that people prefer watching and talking about sex to engaging in it). See *Cupid* 3:14.

42. Through lack of information about what kind of porn circulated in other Russian cities, my comments pertain to Moscow, since I do not wish to generalize on the basis of materials sold there (and in some cases, Petersburg) but possibly unavailable elsewhere.

43. As Soble justly observes, the images of woman perpetuated through porn subject her to alienation through the "dismemberment syndrome" that manifests itself in physical, linguistic, and photographic modes: through the separation of limbs from the trunk of her body during violent sexual or nonsexual assault (and, in the East, through clitoridectomy); through the practice of depersonalizing women by referring to them via "lower" body parts ("cunt," "twat," "piece of ass"); through advertisements that anato-

mize women's bodies by picturing only their hands, feet, and especially breasts, hips, and buttocks. Pornography merely carries the last a step further by spotlighting their breasts, legs, rears, and genitals (Soble 56–58).

44. Women coded for specialists in "woman as child," however, are apt to have small breasts and shaved mounds. According to Florence Rush, the woman-child is fast becoming the sexual ideal in the States. In the second issue of *Andrei*, among the comic book images of women drawn by Svetlana Borisova is that of Zosia, lush of body (if emphatically weak of mind), with hair in girlish pigtails, white socks, and a teddy bear beside her (91).
45. See Kwinter.
46. Cole points out that the law (e.g., in Canada) treats the penis as "sacred, scary or profane," to be "hidden at all costs" (32).
47. On the undisplayability of the penis in the United States, see Segal's essay "Sweet Sorrows, Painful Pleasures" (Segal 63–64).
48. The grammatical usage of the vulgar Russian equivalent for *to fuck* makes the distinction between the two modes crystal clear. When used transitively (and not reflexively), *ebat'* and *trakhat'* may only have a female object (men "fuck" women, who may only "be fucked"). My thanks to Aleksandr Zholkovskii for his helpful explanation of this and related verb usages.
49. These figures represent a rough estimate of the number of exposed vaginas, as opposed to the precise count of the five uncovered male penises (four at rest, one at attention).
50. There is an ambivalence, however, in the photograph, which simultaneously expresses the male fear of losing the self in the vastness of the overwhelming mother (in Napoleon's case, Mother Russia), of "falling through the crack." My thanks to Kolia Padunov and Bozenna Goscilo for their insights in this area.
51. On striptease as a ritual that establishes the woman as an object in disguise and on the role of jewels in this process, see Barthes 84–87.
52. On the connection between the two, and Diderot's play with that link in his *Les Bijoux indiscrets*, see Williams 1.
53. For the validity and limitations of this view, see ibid.
54. The polysemous title is difficult to render into English, for the adjective *rodovoe* means "birth-related," "ancestral," and "family," while *okonchanie* has the meaning of "completion" and "termination"—which, in this context, suggests sexual "coming." The playful text does not help in arriving at a satisfactory word choice that would yield a "natural-sounding" English title.
55. Contained in an issue of the paper *Sex-Hit*, printed in Riga, where, judging by the number of publications, the porn industry must keep the city's entire population employed.
56. None of the Russian materials consulted challenged the interdiction against crossing race boundaries and species, although in Villi Konn's science fiction narrative "Pokhozhdeniia kosmicheskoi prostitutki" (The

Adventures of a Cosmic Prostitute) the protagonist falls in love with an insect who assumes female form.

57. For Harlequins, see *Harlequin Romance and Harlequin Presents Editorial Guidelines* (Ontario: Harlequin Books, 1984).

58. These aspects of pornography particularly disturb feminists, who have been reprimanded by "liberals" for generalizing about all porn on their basis. Yet the (largely legitimate, though not unproblematic) point feminists try to make is that sadomasochism and "thanatic" porn only make explicit and carry to a violent extreme what in implicit and more restrained form makes up "regular" pornography. On this, see Cole; and Dworkin.

59. On the effects of such processes, see Benjamin 219–53. Of course, without modern technology Russia's recent pirating of masses of Western materials, in violation of copyright, would be impossible.

60. Lenin fulfilled a similar function, but, for the sake of their contemporaneity, I shall focus on the modern pinup and the Strong Hand.

61. For an intelligent survey of the methods used and the image cultivated in these efforts, see Dobrenko 3–34.

62. For instance, in Toidze's painting of Stalin with the railway workers (1926) or in Finogenov's of Stalin at the front (1941). See Hingley, pages of illustrations between 106–7.

63. For the permutations in the literary portrait of Stalin over time, see Dobrenko.

64. For an analysis of the current market in cultural production and distribution, see Condee and Padunov.

Works Cited

Agonito, Rosemary. *History of Ideas on Women*. New York: Perigee Books, G. P. Putnam's Sons, 1977.

Anonymous. *Memoirs of a Russian Princess: Gleaned from her Secret Diary*. Secaucus, N.J.: Red Stripe Books/Lyle Stuart, 1989.

———. *The Russian Serf Girl: The Story of Grushenka*. Secaucus, N.J.: Red Stripe Books/Lyle Stuart, 1989.

Attwood, Lynne. *The New Soviet Man and Woman: Sex Role Socialization in the USSR*. Bloomington: Indiana University Press, 1990.

Auerbach, Nina. *Woman and the Demon*. Cambridge, Mass. and London: Harvard University Press, 1982.

Azhgihina, Nadezhda. "Razrushiteli v poiskakh very (Novye cherty sovremennoi molodoi prozy)." *Znamia* 9 (1990): 223–24.

Bakhtin, M. M. *The Dialogic Imagination*. Trans. Caryl Emerson and Michael Holquist. Austin: University of Texas Press, 1981.

Barta, Peter I. "The Author, the Cultural Tradition, and Glasnost: An Interview with Tatyana Tolstaya." *Russian Language Journal* 147–49 (1990).

Barthes, Roland. "Striptease," *Mythologies*. New York: Hill and Wang, 1972.

Basinskii, Pavel. "Pozabyvshie dobro?" *Literaturnaia gazeta* 7 (20 February 1991).

Beauvoir, Simone de. *The Second Sex*. Paris: Gallimard, 1949. Trans. H. M. Parshley. New York: Alfred A. Knopf, 1952.

Beer, Gillian. "Representing Women: Representing the Past." In *The Feminist Reader*, ed. Catherine Belsey and Jane Moore. New York: Basil Blackwell, 1989.

Belyaeva, Nina. "Feminism in the USSR." *Canadian Woman Studies* 10, no. 4 (Winter 1989): 17–19.

Benjamin, Walter. "The Work of Art in the Age of Mechanical Reproduction."

Illuminations. 1955. Reprint. New York: Harcourt, Brace and World, 1968, 219–53.

Berger, John. *Ways of Seeing.* 1972. Reprint. London: BBC and Penguin Books, 1977.

Bitov, Andrei. *Pushkin House.* 1987. Reprint. Ann Arbor: Ardis, 1990.

Blake, Patricia, and Max Hayward. *Half-way to the Moon: New Writing in Russia.* Garden City, N.Y.: Anchor/Doubleday, 1965.

Bloom, Clive. "Grinding with the Bachelors: Pornography in the Machine Age." In Day and Bloom, *Perspectives on Pornography.*

Bordo, Susan R. "The Body and Reproduction of Femininity." In *Gender/Body/Knowledge: Feminist Reconstructions of Being and Knowing,* ed. Alison M. Jaggar and Susan R. Bordo. 1989. Reprint. New Brunswick: Rutgers University Press, 1990: 13–33.

Brendel, Otto. "The Scope and Temperament of Erotic Art in the Greco-Roman World." *Studies in Erotic Art.* New York: Basic Books, 1970.

Brod, Harry. "Eros Thanatized: Pornography and Male Sexuality." In Kimmel, *Men Confront Pornography.*

Brownmiller, Susan. *Against Our Will: Men, Women and Rape.* New York: Simon and Schuster, 1975.

Buckley, Mary. *Women and Ideology in the Soviet Union.* Ann Arbor: University of Michigan Press, 1989.

———, ed. *Perestroika and Soviet Women.* Cambridge: Cambridge University Press, 1992.

Burgess, Anthony. "What Is Pornography?" In Hughes, *Perspectives on Pornography.*

Burstyn, Varda. *Women Against Censorship.* Vancouver and Toronto: Douglas and McIntyre, 1985.

Campbell, Beatrix. "Writer's Room with a View." *Guardian* (21 February 1989): 35.

Cembalest, Robin. "The Obscenity Trial: How They Voted to Acquit." *Art News* (December 1990): 136.

Charney, Maurice. *Sexual Fiction.* London and New York: Methuen, 1981.

Chuprinin, Sergei. "Drugaia proza." *Literaturnaia gazeta* 6 (8 February 1989): 4–5.

Chuprinin, Sergei, and Dmitrii Urnov. "Plokhaia proza." *Literaturnaia gazeta* 6 (8 February 1989): 4–5.

Cixous, Hélène, and Catherine Clément. *The Newly Born Woman.* Trans. Betsy Wing. 1986. Reprint. Minneapolis: University of Minnesota Press, 1988.

Clark, Katerina. "Not for Sale." *Stanford Slavic Studies* 7 (1993): 189–205.

Clément, Catherine. *Opera, or the Undoing of Women.* Minneapolis: University of Minnesota Press, 1988.

Clover, Carol J. "Her Body, Himself: Gender in the Slasher Film." *Representations* 20 (Fall 1987): 187–228.

Cole, Susan. *Pornography and the Sex Crisis.* Toronto: Amanta Publishers, 1989.

Condee, Nancy, and Vladimir Padunov. "*Makulakul'tura*: Reprocessing Culture." *October* 59 (Summer 1991): 79–103.

———. "The ABC of Russian Consumer Culture: Readings, Ratings, and Real Estate." In *Soviet Hieroglyphics,* ed. Nancy Condee. Bloomington: Indiana University Press/BFI, 1995, 130–72.

Costlow, Jane T. *Worlds within Worlds.* Princeton: Princeton University Press, 1990.

Crabbe, Anthony. "Feature-Length Sex Films." In Day and Bloom, *Perspectives on Pornography.*

Daly, Mary. *Beyond the Father.* Boston: Beacon Press, 1973.

———. *Gyn/Ecology.* Boston: Beacon Press, 1978.

Day, Clive, and Clive Bloom, eds. *Perspectives on Pornography.* New York: St. Martin's Press, 1988.

Debreczeny, Paul. "'*Zhitie Aleksandra Boldinskogo*': Pushkin's Elevation to Sainthood in Soviet Culture." *South Atlantic Quarterly* 90, no. 2 (Spring 1991): 269–92.

Decter, Jacqueline, ed. *Soviet Women Writing.* New York: Abbeville Press, 1990.

de Man, Paul. *Allegories of Reading.* New Haven and London: Yale University Press, 1979.

———. *Critical Writings, 1953–1978.* Minneapolis: University of Minnesota Press, 1989.

Dobrenko, E. "Sdelat' by zhizn' s kogo? (Obraz vozhdia v sovetskoi literature)." *Voprosy Literatury* 9 (1990): 3–34.

Donnerstein, Ed. *The Question of Pornography: Research Findings and Policy Implications.* New York: Free Press, 1987.

Douglas, Mary. *Purity and Danger.* 1966. Reprint. London and New York, 1991.

Draine, Betsy. "Refusing the Wisdom of Solomon: Some Recent Feminist Literary Theory." *Signs* (Autumn 1989): 144–70.

Drozdova, Marina. "Sublimation from Socialism." In *Red Women on the Silver Screen,* ed. Lynne Attwood. London: Pandora Press, 1993.

Dworkin, Andrea. *Pornography: Men Possessing Women.* New York: E. P. Dutton, 1989.

Ellis, John. "Photography/Pornography/Art/Pornography." *Screen* 21, no. 1 (1980): 81–108.

Ellmann, Mary. *Thinking about Women.* San Diego, New York, and London: Harcourt Brace, 1968.

Erofeev, Viktor. "Konsul'tatsiia dlia GF." *Gymanitarnyi fond* 12 [115] (1992): 2.

Erofeyev, Victor. *Russian Beauty.* London: Hamish Hamilton, 1992.

Evtushenko, Evgenii. *Literaturnaia gazeta* (3 May 1989): 11.

Ewen, Stuart. *Consuming Images: The Politics of Style in Contemporary Culture.* New York: Harper Collins/Basic Books, 1988.

Ewen, Stuart and Elizabeth. *Channels of Desire: Mass Images and the Shaping of American Consciousness.* New York, 1982.

Faust, Beatrice. *Women, Sex, and Pornography.* New York: Macmillan, 1980.

Fein, Esther B. "'Adam's Rib' Finds Hope Amid Pain." *New York Times* (3 May 1992).

Feinstein, Elaine. "Poetry and Conscience: Russian Women Poets of the Twentieth Century." In *Women Writing and Writing about Women,* ed. Mary Jacobus, 136–37. London: Croom Helm, 1979.

Foucault, Michel. *The History of Sexuality.* Vol. 1. Trans. Robert Hurley. New York: Vintage Books, 1990.

———. *Madness and Civilization: A History of Insanity in the Age of Reason.* Trans. Richard Howard. New York: Random House, 1965.

Freeman, John, and Kathleen Berton. *Moscow Revealed.* New York: Abbeville Press, 1991.

Friedman, Susan. "Modernism of the 'Scattered Remnant.'" In *Feminist Issues in Literary Scholarship,* ed. Shari Benstock. Bloomington: Indiana University Press, 1987.

Gorbachev, Mikhail. *Perestroika: New Thinking for Our Country and the World.* New York: Harper and Row, 1987.

Gorky, Maxim. *Mother.* 1947. Reprint. Secaucus, N.J.: Citadel Press, 1974.

Gorlanova, Nina. "Novella." *Eros, syn Afrodity.* Comp. S. Markov. Moscow: Moskovskii rabochii, 1991.

Goscilo, Helena. "Body Talk in Current Fiction: Speaking Parts and (W)holes." *Stanford Slavic Studies* 7 (1993): 145–77.

———. "Lermontov's Debt to Lavater and Gall," *Slavonic and East European Review* 59, no. 4 (October 1981): 500–515.

———. "Monsters Monomaniacal, Marital, and Medical: Tolstaia's Regenerative Use of Gender Stereotypes." In *Sexuality and the Body in Russian Culture,* ed. Jane Costlow, Stephanie Sandler, and Judith Vowles. Stanford: Stanford University Press, 1993, 204–22.

———. "Paradise, Purgatory, and Post-Mortems in the World of Tat'jana Tolstaja." *Indiana Slavic Studies* 5 (1990): 97–114.

———. "Petrushevskaia's Vision: No Ray of Light in the Kingdom of Darkness." Paper delivered at the American Association for the Advancement of Slavic Studies Conference in Tucson, Ariz., 1992; published in Russian translation by Ural Pedagogical University in Ekaterinburg, 1996.

———. "Speaking Bodies: Erotic Zones Rhetoricized." *Fruits of Her Plume: Essays in Contemporary Russian Women's Culture.* Armonk, N.Y.: M. E. Sharpe, 1993.

———. "Women's Wards and Wardens: The Hospital in Contemporary Russian Women's Fiction." *Canadian Woman Studies* 10, no. 4 (Winter 1989): 83–86.

Goscilo, Helena, ed. *Balancing Acts.* 1989. Reprint. New York: Dell Publishers, 1991.

———, ed. *Skirted Issues: The Discreteness and Indiscretions of Russian Women's Prose. Russian Studies in Literature* 28, no. 2 (Spring 1992).

Goscilo, Helena, and Byron Lindsey, eds. *Glasnost: An Anthology of Literature under Gorbachev.* Ann Arbor: Ardis, 1990.

———. *Wild Beach and Other Stories.* Ann Arbor: Ardis, 1992.

Graff, Gerald. "The Pseudo-Politics of Interpretation." *Critical Inquiry* 9, no. 3 (1983): 597–610.

Gray, Francine du Plessix. *Soviet Women: Walking the Tightrope.* New York: Doubleday, 1989.

Greene, Gayle. *Changing the Story.* Bloomington and Indianapolis: Indiana University Press, 1991.

Grekova, I. *Ship of Widows.* Trans. Cathy Porter. Evanston, Ill.: Northwestern University Press, 1994.

———. *Vdovii parokhod. Novyi mir* 5 (1981): 66–147.

Gubar, Susan, and Joan Hoff, eds. *For Adult Users Only: The Dilemma of Violent Pornography.* Bloomington: Indiana University Press, 1989.

Haraway, Donna. *Signs* 4, no. 1 (1978): 21–60.

Hawkins, Gordon, and Franklin E. Zimring. *Pornography in a Free Society.* Cambridge: Cambridge University Press, 1988.

Heier, Edmund. "Elements of Physiognomy and Pathognomy in the Works of I. S. Turgenev (Turgenev and Lavater)," *Slavistische Beiträge* (Munich) 8 (1977).

———. "Lavater's System of Physiognomy as a Mode of Characterization in Lermontov's Prose," *Arcadia* 6, no. 3 (1971): 267–82.

———. " 'The Literary Portrait' as a Device of Characterization." *Neophilologus* (Amsterdam) 60, no. 2 (April 1976): 321–33.

Heilbrun, Carolyn G. *Toward a Recognition of Androgyny.* 1964. Reprint. New York: W. W. Norton, 1982.

Hingley, Ronald. *Joseph Stalin: Man and Legend.* New York: McGraw-Hill, 1974.

Hubbs, Joanna. *Mother Russia.* Bloomington: Indiana University Press, 1988.

Hughes, Douglas A., ed. *Perspectives on Pornography.* New York: St. Martin's Press, 1970.

Hutcheon, Linda. *A Poetics of Postmodernism: History, Theory, Fiction.* New York and London: Routledge, 1988.

Hyman, Stanley Edgar. "In Defense of Pornography." In Hughes, *Perspectives on Pornography.*

Iampol'skii, Mikhail. "V poiskakh utrachennogo naslazhdeniia" (Erotika v russkom kino). Video supplement to *Ogonek* 5 (1990).

Il'ina, Natal'ia. "K voprosu o traditsii i novatorstve v zhanre 'damskoi povesti.' " *Novyi mir* 3 (1963): 224–30.

Index on Censorship 3 (1989).

Irigaray, Luce. *Spéculum de l'autre femme.* Paris: Minuit, 1974.

———. *This Sex Which Is Not One.* Trans. Catherine Porter. Ithaca: Cornell University Press, 1985.

Isaak, Jo Anna. "Reflections of Resistance: Women Artists on Both Sides of the *Mir.*" *Heresies/IdiomA* 7, no. 2 (1992): 26.

Ivanits, Linda. *Russian Folk Belief.* Armonk, N.Y.: M. E. Sharpe, 1989.

Ivanova, Natal'ia. "Bakhtin's Concept of the Grotesque and the Art of Petrushevskaia and Tolstaia." In *Fruits of Her Plume: Essays in Contemporary*

Russian Women's Culture, ed. Helena Goscilo, 21–32. Armonk, N.Y.: M. E. Sharpe, 1993.
———. "'Kogda by zhizn' domashnim drugom . . .'." *Literaturnaia gazeta* 4 (1986): 72–74.
Jackson, Robert Louis. "'Matryona's Home': The Making of a Russian Icon." In *Solzhenitsyn*, ed. Kathryn Feuer, 60–70. Englewood Cliffs, N.J.: Prentice-Hall, 1976.
Jacobus, Mary. "Is There a Woman in This Text?" *New Literary History* 14 (Fall 1982): 117–41.
Kappeler, Susanne. *The Pornography of Representation*. Minneapolis: University of Minnesota Press, 1986.
Katerli, Nina. "Polina." *Neva* 1 (1984): 11–60.
Kay, Susan. "A Woman's Work." *Irish Slavonic Studies* 8 (1987): 115–26.
Keller, Evelyn Fox. "Feminism and Science." *Signs* 7, no. 3 (1982): 589–602. Reprinted in *Women, Knowledge and Reality*, ed. Ann Garry and Marilyn Rearsall. Boston: Unwin Hyman, 1989, 175–88.
Kelley, Mary. "The Sentimentalists: Promise and Betrayal in the Home." *Signs* 4, no. 3 (1979): 434–46.
Key, Wilson Bryan. *Subliminal Seduction: Ad Media's Manipulation of a Not So Innocent America*. New York: Signet, 1973.
Kimmel, Michael, ed. *Men Confront Pornography*. New York: Crown, 1989.
Konets veka 4 (1992): 146–48.
Konovalov, Leonid. "Narod trebuet reshitel'nykh mer." *Andrei* 2 (1991): 16–18.
Koppel, Ted. Broadcast of "Sex in the Soviet Union." January 1991.
Korotaev, V., ed. *Mat': Stikhotvoreniia russkikh i sovetskikh poetov o materi*. Moscow, 1979.
Kristeva, Julia. "Signifying Practice and Means of Production." *Edinburgh '76 Magazine: Psychoanalysis, Cinema and the Avant-Garde*. Edinburgh, 1976.
Kundera, Milan. *Life Is Elsewhere*. New York: Alfred A. Knopf, 1974.
Kunin, Aleksandr. *Interdevochka*. Moscow: Molodaia gvardiia, 1988.
———. *Intergirl: A Hard Currency Hooker*. New York: Bergh Publishers, 1991.
Kwinter, Kerri. "The Fashioned Face." *Fuse* (March 1980).
Lapidus, Gail. *Women in Soviet Society*. Berkeley and Los Angeles: University of California Press, 1976.
Lawton, Anna. *Kinoglasnost: Soviet Cinema in Our Time*. Cambridge: Cambridge University Press, 1992.
Ledkovsky, Marina. *The Other Turgenev: From Romanticism to Symbolism*. Würzburg: Colloquium Slavicum/Jal-Verlag, 1973.
Lermontov, Mikhail Iu. *Sobranie sochinenii* in 4 vols. Moscow: Khudlit, 1957.
Levitt, Marcus C. *Russian Literary Politics and the Pushkin Celebration of 1880*. Ithaca: Cornell University Press, 1989.
"The Life of Alexander Pushkin." *Golden Legacy* Illustrated History Magazine. Vol. 14. Dix Hills, N.Y.: Fitzgerald Publishers, 1972.
Literaturnaia gazeta (20 December 1989).
Literaturnaia Rossiia (4 December 1992).

Longino, Helen E. "Can There Be a Feminist Science?" In *Women, Knowledge, and Reality: Explorations in Feminist Philosophy*, ed. Ann Garry and Marilyn Pearsall. Boston: Unwin Hyman, 1985, 203–16.

Loth, David. *The Erotic in Literature*. New York: Julian Messner, 1961.

MacKinnon, Catharine A. *Feminism Unmodified*. Cambridge, Mass.: Harvard University Press, 1987.

Mandelker, Amy. *Framing* Anna Karenina. Columbus: Ohio State University Press, 1993.

Martin, Emily. "The Egg and the Sperm: How Science Has Constructed a Romance Based on Stereotypical Male-Female Roles." *Signs* 16, no. 3 (1991): 485–501.

Massey, Doreen. "Politics and Space/Time," *New Left Review* 196 (November–December 1992): 65–84.

McCuaig, Kerry. "Effects of Perestroika and Glasnost on Women." *Canadian Woman Studies* 10, no. 4 (Winter 1989): 11–14.

McLaughlin, Sigrid. "An Interview with Viktoria Tokareva." *Canadian Woman Studies* 10, no. 4 (Winter 1989): 75–76.

———. "Contemporary Soviet Women Writers." *Canadian Woman Studies* 10, no. 4 (Winter 1989): 77–80.

Mercer, Kobena. "Just Looking for Trouble: Robert Mapplethorpe and the Fantasies of Race." In *Sex Exposed: Sexuality and the Pornography Debate*, ed. Lynne Segal and Mary McIntosh. London: Virago Press, 1992, 92–110.

Mercier, Vivian. "Master Percy and/or Lady Chatterley." In Hughes, *Perspectives on Pornography*.

Michie, Helena. *The Flesh Made Word: Female Figures and Women's Bodies*. New York and Oxford: Oxford University Press, 1987.

Modleski, Tania. *Loving With a Vengeance*. 1982. Reprint. New York and London: Methuen, 1984.

Morson, Gary Saul. *Hidden in Plain View: Narrative and Creative Potentials in "War and Peace."* Stanford: Stanford University Press, 1987.

Moscow News, 1988–90.

Mulvey, Laura. "Feminism, Film, and the Avant-Garde." In *Women Writing and Writing about Women*, ed. Mary Jacobus. London: Croom Helm, 1979, 177–95.

Nabokov, Vladimir. "Translator's Foreword." In *A Hero of Our Time*, by Mikhail Lermontov. New York: Doubleday, 1958.

Natali 3–4 (1991).

Nezhdanov, Aleksandr. *Populiarnaia seksologiia*. Riga: 1990.

Nikolayeva, Liliya. "To Love, Care and Cherish." *Moscow News*, 1987, 16.

Palei, Marina. "Kabiriia s Obvodnogo Kanala." *Novyi mir* 3 (1991): 47–81.

———. "Svidanie." *Otdelenie propashchikh*. Moscow: Moskovskii rabochii, 1991.

Pavlychko, Solomea. "A Catfish for Your Thoughts: Ukrainian Literature at the Turning Point." *Agni* 39 (1991): 194.

Petrushevskaia, Liudmila. *Cinzano*. Trans. Stephen Mulrine. London: Nick Herne Books, 1991.

———. "Nam—seks?" *Inostrannaia literatura* 5 (1989): 237–38.
———. *Pesni XX veka.* Moscow: Soiuz teatr. deiatelei. 1988.
———. *Tri devushki v golubom.* Moscow: "Iskusstvo," 1989.
———. *Vremia noch', Novyi mir* 2 (1992): 65–110.
Pornography and Sexual Violence: Evidence of the Links. London: Everywoman Ltd., 1988.
Posadskaya, Anastasia, ed. *Women in Russia.* London: Verso, 1994.
Rabotnitsa 3 (1990).
Radway, Janice. *Reading the Romance.* Chapel Hill: University of North Carolina Press, 1984.
Ransel, David. Review of Tatyana Mamonova's *Russian Women's Studies: Essays on Sexism in Soviet Culture.* In *Women's Studies in Indiana* 15, no. 3 (1990): 1–3.
Rasputin, Valentin. *Farewell to Matyora.* Evanston, Il.: Northwestern University Press, 1991.
Root, Maria P. P., Patricia Fallon, and William N. Friedrich. *Bulemia: A Systems Approach to Treatment.* New York and London: W. W. Norton, 1986.
Rush, Florence. *The Best Kept Secret: Sexual Abuse of Children.* Englewood Cliffs, N.J.: Prentice-Hall, 1980.
Russ, Joanna. *How to Suppress Women's Writing.* Austin: University of Texas Press, 1983.
Sadur, Nina. "Chervivyi synok." *Ne pomniashchaia zla.* Comp. Larisa Vaneeva. Moscow: Moskovskii rabochii, 1990.
Sandler, Stephanie. "Pushkin's Last Love—Natal'ya Nikolaevna in Russian Culture." In *Gender Restructuring in Russian Studies,* ed. M. Liljeström and Arja Rosenholm. Tampere: University of Tampere, 1993, 209–20.
Shcheglova, Evgeniia. "V svoem krugu." *Literaturnoe obozrenie* 3 (1990): 19–26.
Shcherbakova, Galina. "Dochki, materi, ptitsy i ostrova." *Soglasie* 6 (1991): 82–89.
———. "Tri 'liubvi' Mashi Peredreevoi." *Chistye prudy.* Moscow: Moskovskii rabochii, 1990.
———. *Ubikvisty. Soglasie* 2 (1992): 11–88.
Segal, Lynne, and Mary McIntosh, eds. *Sex Exposed: Sexuality and the Pornography Debate.* London: Virago Press, 1992.
Serrill, Michael S. "Defiling the Children." *Time,* 21 June 1993, 53–55.
———. *Sexual Anarchy: Gender and Culture at the Fin de Siècle.* New York: Penguin Books, 1990.
Showalter, Elaine. "Review Essay: Literary Criticism." *Signs: Journal of Women in Culture and Society* 1, no. 2 (Winter 1975): 435–60.
———. "Women's Time, Women's Space." In *Feminist Issues in Literary Scholarship,* ed. Shari Benstock. Bloomington: Indiana University Press, 1987, 30–44.
Sidorov, Dmitry, and Dmitry Demidov. "Pillow Talk." *Moscow News,* 30 September–7 October 1990.
Simons, Margaret A. "Sexism and the Philosophical Canon: On Reading Beau-

voir's *The Second Sex.*" *Journal of the History of Ideas* 51, no. 3 (July–September 1990): 487–504.

Slobin, Greta N. "Remizov's Erotic Tales: Stylisation and Subversion," *The Short Story in Russia: 1900–1917*, ed. Nicholas Luker. Nottingham: Astra Press, 53–72.

Snitow, Ann B. "Mass Market Romance: Pornography for Women Is Different," *Radical History Review* 20 (1979): 141–61.

Sobel, Robert. *The Manipulators: America in the Media Age.* Garden City, N.Y.: 1976.

Soble, Alan. *Pornography: Marxism, Feminism, and the Future of Sexuality.* New Haven and London: Yale University Press, 1986.

Solzhenitsyn, Alexander. "The Relentless Cult of Novelty and How It Wrecked the Century." *New York Times Book Review* 7 (February 1993): 3, 17.

Sontag, Susan. *Aids and Its Metaphors.* 1988. Reprint. New York: Farrar, Straus and Giroux, 1989.

———. *Illness as Metaphor.* 1977. Reprint. New York: Vintage, 1979.

———. "The Pornographic Imagination." In Hughes, *Perspectives on Pornography.*

Sorokin, Vladimir. "Provintsial'nyi 'Roman' Vladimira Sorokina," *Moskovskie novosti* 64 (18–25 December 1994): 19.

Steiner, Wendy. *The Colors of Rhetoric.* Chicago: University of Chicago Press, 1982.

Sukhanova, Natal'ia. "Delos." *Novyi mir* 3 (1988): 69–84.

Tarasova, Elena. "Ne pomniashchaia zla." *Ne pomniashchaia zla.* Comp. Larisa Vaneeva. Moscow, 1990.

Terts, Abram. "Anekdot v anekdote." *Sintaksis* 1 (1978): 77–95.

——— [Andrei Siniavskii]. *Sobranie sochinenii* in 2 vols. Vol. 2. Moscow: SP "Start," 1992.

Tertz, Abram (Andrei Sinyavksy). *A Voice from the Chorus.* Trans. Kyril Fitzlyon and Max Hayward. New York: Farrar, Straus and Giroux, 1976.

Tokareva, Viktoriia. *Lataiushchie kacheli. Nichego osobennogo.* Moscow: Moskovskii pisatel', 1987.

Tolstaia, Tat'iana. "Ogon' i pyl'." *"Na zolotom kryl'tse sideli. . . ."* Moscow: Molodaia gvardiia, 1987.

———. "Samaia liubimia." *Avrora* 10 (1986): 92–110.

Tolstoy, Leo N., *What Is Art?* Indianapolis: Bobbs-Merrill, 1960.

Tolstaya, Tatyana. "In a Land of Conquered Men." *Moscow News,* 24 September–1 October, 1989, 13.

———. "A Little Man Is a Normal Man." *Moscow News,* 1987, 10.

———. *On the Golden Porch.* Trans. Antonina W. Bouis. New York: Alfred A. Knopf, 1989.

———. *Sleepwalker in a Fog.* Trans. Jamey Gambrell. New York: Alfred A. Knopf, 1992.

Tompkins, Jane. "Sentimental Power: *Uncle Tom's Cabin* and the Politics of Literary History." *Feminisms,* Ed. Robyn R. Warhol and Diane Price Herndl. New Brunswick: Rutgers University Press, 1991, 20–39.

Tong, Rosemarie. "Feminism, Pornography, and Censorship." *Social Theory and Practice* 8, no. 1 (Spring 1982): 1–18.

Tytler, Graeme. *Physiognomy in the European Novel.* Princeton: Princeton University Press, 1982.

Ulitskaia, Liudmila. "A Chosen People." Trans. Isabel Heaman. In *Lives in Transit,* ed. Helena Goscilo. Ann Arbor: Ardis, 1995.

———. "Lialin dom." MS.

———. "Narod izbrannyi." In *Piatyi ugol,* ed. Sergei Kaledin. Moscow: Knizhnaia palata, 1991.

van Buren, Jane Silverman. *The Modern Madonna: Semiotics of the Maternal Metaphor.* Bloomington: Indiana University Press, 1989.

Vaneeva, Larisa. *Iz kuba.* Moscow: Sovetskii pisatel', 1990.

———. *Ne pomniashchaia zla.* Moscow: Moskovskii rabochii, 1990.

———. *Skorb' ploti.* Moscow: Sovetskii pisatel', 1990.

Varlamova, Inna. *A Counterfeit Life.* Trans. David A. Lowe. Ann Arbor: Ardis, 1988.

———, ed. *Mnimaia zhizn'.* Ann Arbor: Ardis, 1978.

Vasilenko, Svetlana, ed. *Novye Amazonki.* Moscow: Moskovskii rabochii, 1991.

Vecherniaia Moskva, 25 April 1990, 2.

Velembovskaia, Irina. *Zhenshchiny.* Moscow: Sovetskii pisatel', 1967.

Vicinus, Martha. *Suffer and Be Still.* Bloomington: Indiana University Press, 1972.

Virolainen, M. N., ed. *Legendy i mify o Pushkine.* St. Petersburg: "Akademicheskii proekt," 1994.

Warner, Marina. *Alone of All Her Sex: The Myth and Cult of the Virgin Mary.* 1976. Reprint. New York: Vintage Books, 1983.

Waters, Elizabeth. "Reading between the Novosti Lines." *Canadian Woman Studies* 10, no. 4 (Winter 1989): 31–34.

Williams, Linda. *Hard Core: Power, Pleasure and the Frenzy of the Visible.* Berkeley and Los Angeles: University of California Press, 1989.

Woll, Josephine. "The Minotaur in the Maze: On Lyudmila Petrushevskaya." *World Literature Today* 67, no. 1 (Winter 1993): 125–30.

Women's View (Glas) 3 (1992).

Young-Breuhl, Elisabeth. *Freud on Women: A Reader.* New York and London: W. W. Norton, 1990.

Zenkovsky, Serge A. *Medieval Russia's Epics, Chronicles, and Tales.* New York: E. P. Dutton, 1963.

Zhenskaia logika. Ed. L. V. Stepanenko and A. V. Fomenko. Moscow: Sovremennik, 1989.

Zhenskie dela 11 (1994).

Zhigul'skaia, A. F., ed. *Poemy pobedy.* Voronezh: Tsentr. Chernozemn. kh. izd., 1976.

Ziplow, Stephen. *The Film Maker's Guide to Pornography.* New York: Drake, 1977.

Index

Abuladze, Tengiz, 48
Adventure, 3, 65
Aitmatov, Chingiz, 96
Aksakov, Sergei, 37
Alieva, Svetlana, 71–72
Andreev, Leonid, 96

Bakhtin, Mikhail, 89
Baranskaia, Natal'ia, 6
Basinskii, Pavel, 71–73, 75–79
Beliaeva, Nina, 11
Belyi, Andrei, 96
Binarism, 2, 19, 20, 22, 45, 49, 64, 67, 73, 88, 93, 100, 107–10, 117–18, 151
Bitov, Andrei, 47
Blok, Aleksandr, 96
Body, human, 2, 13, 23, 32, 42, 44, 62–64, 87–110, 136, 147–52
Briusov, Valerii, 45
Bulgakov, Mikhail, 47, 96

Chekhov, Anton, 66
Chukovskii, Kornei, 75
Chuprinin, Sergei, 76
Criticism, 58, 70–80, 89, 96

Dashkova, Ekaterina, 12
Domesticity, 10, 11, 17, 35, 42, 64–66, 119, 129, 131
Dostoevskii, Fedor, 46, 58, 96, 97, 102, 119, 162
Durova, Nadezhda, 12, 88

Erofeev, Venedikt, 92
Erofeyev, Victor (Viktor Erofeev), 43, 153

Feminism, 6, 7, 10, 11, 12, 15, 16, 21, 49, 59, 64, 67, 71, 80, 104, 117, 142–43

Gan, Elena, 88
Gender construction, 1, 7, 10, 15, 22, 25, 106, 156
Gerasimov, Aleksandr, 161
Ginzburg, Evgeniia, 119
Glasnost, 1, 7, 12–15, 17, 18, 21, 24, 25, 35, 36, 37, 42, 132
Gogoberidze, Lana, 59
Gogol, Nikolai, 87, 95
Gorbachev, Mikhail, 35

Gorky, Maksim, 33
Gorlanova, Nina, 60, 67–69, 78, 89, 91, 104
Grekova, I., 121, 122–23, 126

History, Russian, and women, 2, 37–42, 62, 119

Il'ina, Natal'ia, 16, 74
Ivanova, Natal'ia, 16–17, 71–72, 75–77, 79

Karamzin, Nikolai, 66, 145
Katerli, Nina, 66, 80
Kon, Igor', 144
Konstantinova, Mariia, 59
Kretova, Marina, 72, 75
Krishtofovich, Viacheslav, 36–42
Kunin, Vladimir, 43–44, 143–45
Kuraev, Mikhail, 36–37
Kushner, Aleksandr, 46–47

Lakshin, Vladimir, 74, 76
Language, in Russian culture, 19, 21–25, 67, 79–80, 108, 157–58
Latynina, Alla, 71–72, 75–76, 79
Lermontov, Mikhail, 67–69, 87, 90
Leskov, Nikolai, 93, 105
Lipovskaia, Ol'ga, 12

Makarova, Elena, 95, 122, 123
Mamin, Iurii, 48
Mandel'shtam, Osip, 163
Maternity, 2, 8, 10, 18, 20, 32–44, 64, 72, 73, 88, 89, 99, 124–25, 144–45
Matveeva, Bella, 59
Merganbaiba, Razika, 43
Muratova, Kira, 59
Myths, 2, 20, 22, 43, 44, 47, 60–64, 67, 69, 144

Nabatnikova, Tat'iana, 91, 95, 121, 122, 123
Nakhova, Irina, 59
Narbikova, Valeriia, 1, 2, 18, 23–25, 47, 77, 79, 80, 91, 132
Narrative form, 65, 69, 107, 131, 147, 153–56
Nurturing, and Russian women, 9, 20, 23, 32, 42, 73

Odoevskii, Vladimir, 87
Ostrovskii, Nikolai, 74

Palei, Marina, 60, 62–64, 66–67, 69, 80, 89, 91, 95, 106, 107–8, 109, 122, 123, 125, 126
Pasternak, Boris, 47, 96
Pavlova, Karolina, 12
Perestroika, 2, 25, 35, 36, 49, 135
Petrushevskaia, Liudmila, 1, 2, 3, 16–17, 18–21, 24–25, 36–38, 40–42, 75, 76, 80, 91, 95, 97, 104, 105, 107–8, 121, 122, 123, 127–29, 160–61
Physiology, 2, 37, 44, 76–79, 87–110, 128
Polevoi, Boris, 74
Polomova, Raisa, 75
Pornography, 3, 13, 14–15, 49, 135–63
Prigov, Dmitrii, 47
Proskurin, P., 160
Prostitution in Russia, 2, 13, 14, 18, 42–44, 143–45
Pukhova, Zoia, 8
Pushkin, Aleksandr Sergeevich, 44–48

Rasputin, Valentin, 35, 144
Ratushinskaia, Irina, 119
Rostopchina, Evdokiia, 12, 88, 119

Sadur, Nina, 60–62, 67, 69, 79, 80, 89, 94
Shakhverdiev, Tofik, 43
Shalamov, Varlam, 119
Shcheglova, Evgeniia, 71–77

Shcherbakova, Galina, 2, 36–38, 41–42, 43, 105, 106
Shmelev, Nikolai, 43
Sholokhov, Mikhail, 74
Shukshin, Vasilii, 96
Siniavskii, Andrei (Abram Tertz), 48, 127, 158–59
Slapovskii, Aleksei, 96
Sologub, Fedor, 59
Solzhenitsyn, Alexandr, 31, 34, 47, 119, 127
Space, relationship to time, 117–32
Stalin, Iosif, 14, 32, 46, 48, 110, 136, 160–62
Startseva, Natal'ia, 71, 77
Subversiveness, 2, 7, 18–25, 39
Sukhanova, Natal'ia, 122, 123–24

Tarasova, Elena, 64, 78, 79, 96, 97, 99–104
Time, relationship to space, 37–38, 100, 117–32
Todorovskii, Petr, 43
Tokareva, Viktoriia, 16, 76, 122, 123–24, 126
Tolstaya, Tatyana, 1, 3, 9, 16–17, 18, 21–23, 24–25, 47, 57, 60, 64–67, 69, 73, 75, 76, 80, 91, 96, 97, 106, 107–8, 109, 127, 129–31, 144
Tolstoi, Lev, 37, 105, 119, 120, 163
Tsvetaeva, Marina, 45
Turgenev, Ivan, 66, 88
Tvardovskii, Aleksandr, 34

Ulanovskaia, Bella, 132
Ulitskaia, Liudmila, 67, 80, 89, 95, 96, 97–99, 104, 105, 106, 107, 109–10

Vaneeva, Larisa, 80, 89, 91–93, 95, 104, 132
Varlamova, Inna, 120, 122, 123
Vasilenko, Svetlana, 78, 89, 91, 93–94, 95, 104, 105, 106, 132
Velembovskaia, Irina, 120, 122, 123
Vladimov, Georgii, 119
Volkonskaia, Mariia, 119
Voznesenskaia, Iuliia, 122, 123

Zalygin, Sergei, 46
Zamiatin, Evgenii, 47, 105
Zhukova, Mariia, 88